SO-BSH-393

THE BOOK OF BEGINNINGS

A PRACTICAL GUIDE TO UNDERSTAND AND TEACH GENESIS

VOLUME TWO:
NOAH, THE FLOOD, AND THE NEW WORLD

HENRY M. MORRIS III

THE BOOK OF BEGINNINGS

A PRACTICAL GUIDE TO UNDERSTAND AND TEACH GENESIS

VOLUME TWO:
NOAH, THE FLOOD, AND THE NEW WORLD

HENRY M. MORRIS III

INSTITUTE FOR CREATION RESEARCH

Dallas, Texas
www.icr.org

THE BOOK OF BEGINNINGS, VOLUME TWO
Noah, the Flood, and the New World

by Henry M. Morris III, D.Min.

Copyright © 2013 by the Institute for Creation Research. All rights reserved. No portion of this book may be used in any form without written permission of the publisher, with the exception of brief excerpts in articles and reviews. For more information, write to Institute for Creation Research, P. O. Box 59029, Dallas, TX 75229.

All Scripture quotations are from the New King James Version.

ISBN: 978-1-935587-17-0
Library of Congress Catalog Number: 2012955873

Please visit our website for other books and resources: www.icr.org

Printed in the United States of America.

TABLE OF CONTENTS

PREFACE

What is the true significance of the book of Genesis? Is it history? Allegory? A collection of myths? "Spiritual" truth that shouldn't be taken literally?

The answers to these and similar questions depend primarily on the presuppositions one holds prior to evaluating the evidence. If one assumes that God is an ancient psychological and mythological reaction to ignorance about the forces in the universe, then the conclusions drawn from current observations will be naturalistic—i.e., without any supernatural involvement. If, however, one assumes that the God of the Bible does exist, then it would follow that such an omniscient and omnipotent Being would have to reveal Himself truthfully and His actions accurately.

If no God exists, then we can only scrabble about for answers with little assurance about the conclusions that we draw. If the God of Scripture is real, then we have been granted a unique insight about the universe and can be sure of the information that He has provided for us in the creation itself and in the precision of the data that the God of creation has revealed to us through His written Word. These assumptions are foundational to how we view reality. They are presuppositions that shape the way we approach all evidence.

Simply put:

What we *believe* determines how we think.

What we *think* dictates what we do.

What we *do* dominates our life.

This book will approach the words of Genesis as actual history. That history was recorded by eyewitnesses who were supernaturally guided so that their records would be accurate and without embellishment. Since the God of the Bible is a "God of truth" (Deuteronomy 32:4) and a God who "cannot lie" (Titus 1:2), it must follow that His Word will be truthful and accurate. Logic alone dictates that a belief in the reality of the God of Scripture demands an acceptance of His revelation as being without error.

That will be the approach taken throughout this book.

Henry M. Morris III, D.Min.
Dallas, Texas

CHAPTER ONE
THE WORLD OF NOAH

The marvelous story of Noah and the Ark has fascinated people for millennia. Every major culture has a legend about a great flood. Many of these accounts include details that bear a remarkable similarity to the biblical narrative, such as an important man who built a boat and saved his family and a number of animals from a worldwide deluge. The varying differences are intriguing, but the common factors far outweigh them. Where would such a tale come from? Why are the many separated population groups so alike in their accounts? What, indeed, is the truth of the matter?

One Hundred and Twenty Years

> And the LORD said, "My Spirit shall not strive with man forever, for he is indeed flesh; yet his days shall be one hundred and twenty years." (Genesis 6:3)

There are a number of questions generated by this verse, the answers to which make a significant difference to our understanding of the situation prior to the great Flood. Before this, the chronological record is rather easy to follow. By the time the events in Genesis 6 occur, the universe is over 15 centuries old.

The fifth chapter of Genesis provides a listing of the heads of families starting with the birth of Seth 130 years after creation. Each of the successive family heads was identified and recorded for posterity, probably kept in some form of "book" (Genesis 5:1) that was ultimately handed over for safekeeping to the next family leader.

Head of Family	Year of Birth after Creation	Age at Birth of Next Family Head	Year of Death
Adam	1	130	930
Seth	130	105	1042
Enosh	235	90	1140
Cainan	325	70	1235
Mahalalel	395	65	1290
Jared	460	162	1422
Enoch	622	65	987*
Methuselah	687	187	1656
Lamech	874	182	1651
Noah	1056	500	2006

* Enoch did not die, but was taken up into heaven by God when he was 365 years old (Genesis 5:23-24).

These records give us some sense of the key players during the First Age prior to the Flood. Although Noah was born after Adam died, his father, Lamech, would have known both Adam and Seth. These names are listed again in 1 Chronicles 1:1-4 and Luke 3:36-38, verifying that the writers of both the Old and New Testaments accepted the Genesis genealogies as historical fact. Since the listed individuals lived for hundreds of years, why did God say that man's "days shall be one hundred and twenty years"?

Some have suggested that God was reducing the human lifespan to a maximum of 120 years, but that doesn't fit the subsequent biblical record. Noah's children lived several hundred years, as did their children, and their children's children. In fact, it was not until Moses wrote the 90th Psalm that Scripture provides any insight into the average length of a human life.

> The days of our lives are seventy years; And if by reason of strength they are eighty years, Yet their boast is only labor and sorrow; For it is soon cut off, and we fly away. (Psalm 90:10)

Genesis 6:3 does not refer to a reduction in life expectancy, but rather to the fact that God will allow another 120 years to elapse before He brings an end to the world through the judgment of the Flood. The key Hebrew verb *duwn* in this verse is most often translated "judge" or "judgment" in the other 24 passages where it is used. The core meaning of the word and its root (*'adown*) is to administer judgment or justice with the authority of the "master" or "lord." Thus, the simplest translation might be, "My spirit will not eternally judge man. He is flesh. I will allow 120 years." Or perhaps, "My spirit will not delay judgment. Man is flesh. The remaining days will be 120 years."

With this verse, God sets the stage and the time during which Noah will be called, given instruction, and build the Ark.

Judgment Foretold

> Then the LORD saw that the wickedness of man was great in the earth, and that every intent of the thoughts of his heart was only evil continually. And the LORD was sorry that He had made man on the earth, and He was grieved in His heart. So the LORD said, "I will destroy man whom I have created from the face of the earth, both man and beast, creeping thing and birds of the air, for I am sorry that I have made them." (Genesis 6:5-7)

There are several factors that led up to this dreadful summary. The terrible murder of Abel recorded in Genesis 4 and the subsequent banishment of Cain from the nucleus of Adam's family laid the foundation for a wholesale rebellion against the authority and design of the Creator. By the time of Abel's murder (a short time before Seth was born to Adam and Eve), the population of earth could have well grown into the thousands. Just how many were directly descended from Cain and inclined to follow in his rebellion is not indicated. There were enough, however, for Cain to "build a city" as a base for his wanderings (Genesis 4:17). The line of Cain became the focal point for a growing wickedness and sociological mutiny that ultimately resulted in "every heart" of the worldwide population being steeped in evil.

Genesis 4 also provides insight to the family of Lamech, a descendant of Cain in the seventh generation from Adam. Lamech's famous sons were brilliant and led the family of Cain (and perhaps many more) in agriculture, metallurgy, and music. Yet in spite of the commercial success of his family, Lamech was arrogant and openly defiant toward God and toward any who would dare to oppose him. The braggadocios "song" that he composed for his wives gives us insight to the growing rebellion of the day. He said, in essence, "I'm more important than Cain! In fact, I am better able to take care of myself than God did for Cain. God would only avenge Cain's death seven times—I will avenge my wounding 77 times" (Genesis 4:23-24).

Growing Wickedness

The opening text of Genesis 6 describes the awful conditions that existed in the century prior to the judgment of the great Flood.

> Now it came to pass, when men began to multiply on the face of the earth, and daughters were born to them, that the sons of God saw the daughters of men, that they were beautiful; and they took wives for themselves of all whom they chose....There were giants on the earth in those days, and also afterward, when the sons of God came in to the daughters of men and they bore children to them. Those were the mighty men who were of old, men of renown. (Genesis 6:1-4)

Just exactly what these giants and mighty men of old were is not precisely clear in this passage. It is likely that the "angels who did not keep their proper domain" (Jude 1:6) used their power either to control or possess certain men in an effort to raise a "master race" that might subdue the world population. (More about that time is amplified in *The Book of Beginnings, Volume One: Creation, Fall, and the First Age*.)

Whatever may have been the physical appearance of these "men of renown," the result of their spiritual impact on the population of that age was terrible.

> The earth also was corrupt before God, and the earth was filled with violence. So God looked upon the earth, and indeed it was corrupt; for all flesh had corrupted their way on the earth. And God said to Noah, "The end of all flesh has come before Me, for the earth is filled with violence through them; and behold, I will destroy them with the earth." (Genesis 6:11-13)

The world population had reached such a state of evil that the longsuffering and merciful Creator had reached the end of His forbearance. Mankind had become "only evil continually," bringing about a condition throughout the planet that was "corrupt before God, and the earth was filled with violence."

The severity of this condition is difficult for us to grasp, although we can take clues from the post-Flood world. There have been "wars and rumors of wars" throughout recorded history. Nations and empires have risen that were (and are) dominated by evil men and deplorable conditions. The 20th century bled from two world wars and several conflicts around the globe. Human sacrifice has been practiced in various societies, along with cannibalism in several people groups. The histories of Egypt, Assyria, Babylon, Persia, Greece, and Rome are fraught with atrocities. Violence is so common among the "beasts of the earth" that humanity has come to accept carnivorous activity as normal behavior.

Such violence and aberrant behavior was not the way God originally designed the creation.

Growing Violence

Twice in Genesis 6, God notes that the earth was "filled with violence" (vv. 11 and 13). Although the expanded commentary focused on the heart of men, the text records that "all flesh" (v. 12) was involved in filling the planet with the violence that was so abhorrent to the Creator.

Two Hebrew words in these verses—*shachath*, translated "corrupt," and *chamac*, translated "violence"—help us understand the degradation. Both contain the idea of disintegration. The implication of these word choices is that what was happening to the creation was "ruining" the design and purpose of God—hence His anger at the result of man's depraved stewardship of His creation.

During God's summary comments at the end of the creation week, He specifically said that the grass, herbs, and trees created on Day Three were designated as food for the living creatures created on Days Five and Six.

> And God said, "See, I have given you every herb that yields seed which is on the face of all the earth, and every tree whose fruit yields seed; to you it shall be for food. Also, to every beast of the earth, to every bird of the air, and to everything that creeps on the earth, in which there is life, I have given every green herb for food." (Genesis 1:29-30)

After the terrible rebellion of Adam and Eve in the Garden, God sentenced the "ground"—the very elements of creation—to an ever-increasing resistance to man's dominion. Instead of readily available "food" from the herbs and fruits of the earth, thorns and thistles would develop and interfere. Instead of the delight of discovery, there would be the "sweat" of labor to eke out survival. God hates sin and His judgment was severe.

The disintegration of God's original order that began in the Garden continued as Adam and Eve's descendants grew in number. In time, the sin of humanity had become so widespread that the "whole earth" had become "filled" with the awful consequences of that rebellion.

Violent Animals

We are not told what caused some of the animal population to adopt carnivorous behavior, but it is certainly plausible to blame those who were given "dominion" for the corruption that ultimately filled the planet with violence. Mankind was in charge. All living things were under their authority. The initial design was a "very good" relationship. But with the occurrence of the first murder just over a century after the creation, the downhill spiral of violence lurched into its deadly motion.[1]

History is full of so-called "blood sport" activities—everything from the sophisticated British fox hunting to the pagan rituals of various rites of passage. Roman arenas were filled with spectators watching staged carnage for entertainment. Human sacrifice and even cannibalism have been fostered and promoted throughout history. God's own commentary on the condition of humanity during the centuries prior to the great Flood was that "every thought" of man's heart had become so evil that God was sickened by humanity's behavior. It is no stretch to imagine that such thoughts would include "blood sport," both among humans and with animals.

Every recorded age of history has had its hunter heroes. Bold men and a few legendary women have been lauded for killing wild beasts that endangered population centers. Why would we expect any other kind of behavior during the time before the great Flood? The behemoths and the leviathans of Job's day were representative of animals of a prior age. Surely it does not bend logic to presume that the boastful, murdering character represented by Cain's descendant Lamech would not be unique in that society.

---

1. Since Genesis 4:25 indicates that Seth was Abel's "replacement," and Seth was born when Adam was 130 years old, the first human murder would likely have taken place within the previous year, or about 129 years after the Fall.

Today, humans breed and train animals to be vicious. Why would a world population thinking "only evil all the time" be any different? Many modern societies promote animal fighting and cruelty. Why would this not be true in the First Age? When sin entered the human population and "death" by that sin (Romans 5:12), we could anticipate that the "dominion" granted by the Creator to man would be prostituted and distorted among the animal population over which man ruled.

Animals can be made to kill other animals—and that killing breeds a taste for more killing. It should be no surprise that some of the "beasts of the earth" became carnivorous, given the human impetus to instigate evil and to distort, disobey, and denigrate the Creator's design.

Big Teeth

It has become commonly accepted that if an animal has big teeth, it must be carnivorous. This is especially true among paleontologists as they attempt to dig out (pun intended) the lifestyles of the animals whose bones they uncover amid the jumble of fossils buried in the sedimentary layers of geological strata. The *Tyrannosaurus rex*'s six-inch, razor-sharp teeth send shivers down our spines. Surely such a creature must have been a roaring monster, killing and ravening at will in the ages gone by. Yet scientists are beginning to question the ferocity of these animals, given that they had such small forearms and some *T-rex* fossils show signs of having been attacked and badly injured.

The terrifying skull of the seagoing mosasaur, with its double rows of sharp, crocodile-like teeth, appears to be the business end of a marauding dragon predator feared by man and beast alike. Indeed, this creature may have been the leviathan of Job 41. But here's the problem: We do not know this for sure. These creatures are not alive today, and our "evidence" consists mostly of their bones—sometimes scattered widely, and often badly broken and dismembered. But they do have big teeth!

So do fruit bats, who have huge teeth for the size of this little mammal. Yet they only eat the pulp from certain kinds of fruit. Grizzly bears and black bears have more than enough teeth to destroy other animals, but they also use them to eat fruits and vegetables and are quite capable of living off a vegetarian diet. Dogs and cats have the same tooth structure as wild wolves and lions, yet these animals are able to change their behavior and eat cereal that is made mostly from corn meal, soybean meal, and rice.

Remember, God designed all living creatures to eat plants. He did not grant permission to eat animal flesh until after the Flood (more on this later). All living things are capable of functioning solely on a vegetarian diet—even you and I. The animals that we designate as carnivores are actually omnivorous—that is, they can (and do) eat plant material as well. Yes, animal protein is a much more energy-efficient food source and is helpful within certain lifestyles and environments. God's design, however, is still resident in all earthbound creatures.

Noah Found Grace

> But Noah found grace in the eyes of the LORD. (Genesis 6:8)

The word "grace" appears for the first time in the Bible in this verse. Noah lived in the midst of the most heinously evil society the world had known, but because he had found grace, God favored him with personal instruction about the coming catastrophic judgment and details for a new beginning on earth.

The language of Genesis 6:8 gives us insight into Noah's character. "Found" is a simple active perfect verb, not a passive one. Thus, Noah found favor—grace—in God's eyes because he was actively looking for it. Likewise, Adam *found* no helpmate from among the animals that was suitable for him (Genesis 2:20), and Noah's dove did not *find* rest for the sole of her foot (Genesis 8:9). Laban did not *find* his household images that Rachel had stolen and hidden (Genesis 31:35), and Hilkiah the priest *found* a book of the law of the Lord given by Moses (2 Chronicles 34:14-15). God could have used a passive verb in reference to Noah, but He did not.

What can we learn from the life of this great man? Evidently, God intended for us to know this key factor: Noah's life was righteous—in spite of the horrible condition of the world of his day. He was looking for God's direction and for the answers to his heart's cry. Noah wasn't merely hanging around waiting for the inevitable destruction that he sensed must come as a result of the awful rebellion that surrounded him. Noah was anticipating a response from God—and when God finally did give him instruction, Noah "found" the favor that he sought!

Captain of Industry

Many centuries later, God warned Ezekiel of future judgment that would happen to the land of Israel because of its wickedness. God identified three men—Noah, Daniel, and Job—as examples of the best "righteous" men in history (Ezekiel 14:14, 20). If that comparison has any meaning, Noah was much more than a mere chance recipient of God's grace.

Job was "the greatest of all the people of the East" (Job 1:3). His livestock resources (mainly those for caravan duty) were enormous. That certainly meant that he was a successful trade broker and possibly a source for prized stock. He had multiple houses and land—so much so that "bands" from nearby nations were necessary to destroy his wealth.

God had labeled Job "My servant...there is none like him on the earth, a blameless and upright man, one who fears God and shuns evil" (Job 1:8). Job was much more than a "nice guy." He was probably the wealthiest man of his day, and yet he was of such godly character that God used him to teach Satan a lesson!

Daniel was one of the group of king's descendants and nobles from Judah taken captive by Nebuchadnezzar (Daniel 1:3). The account of Daniel and his three godly friends is well known among Christians, but the young adult experiences of Daniel often overshadow the long life that he led as the leader of the "scientists" (learned men) of that day. He was commissioned as a "great man" by Nebuchadnezzar and "sat in the gate of the king" (Daniel 2:48-49). Daniel served in some form of senior political and advisory position for six kings over some 70 years. Not bad for a captive!

God identified Daniel as a "man greatly beloved" (Daniel 10:11). He was privileged to have unusual spiritual insight, which he could have used to his personal advantage. But he always made it clear that he was gifted by God's grace—to whom he always gave credit. Furthermore, God used Daniel to record several of the most remarkable prophecies in all of Scripture. Scholars are still discussing the book of Daniel. He was a significant person indeed!

If the comparisons of the righteous men listed in Ezekiel 14 are to be genuine comparisons, Noah must have been a person of significance in his region—if not well known throughout the world of his day. He clearly possessed or had access to the resources and skills needed to accomplish the monumental task that was assigned to him. Since God's instructions to build the Ark are somewhat general, it is not beyond reason to assume that Noah ran an architectural and contracting business of some kind.

The pre-Flood civilization would certainly have been advanced enough for such an enterprise. The evolutionary cloud has mesmerized most of the world into relegating the "ancient" world into some sort of pre-human existence—living in caves and grass huts with animal skins for clothing. The Bible paints a much different picture! There were cities during Noah's day, as well as developed technology that included metallurgy and the skills to build and market musical instruments (Genesis 4:17-22). Somebody had to construct the habitations for the growing population, and someone had to coordinate the development and distribution of those manufacturing places that produced the products needed by that society.

The world of Noah was very wicked, but it functioned with much the same needs as our current world. When the Lord Jesus wanted to emphasize the suddenness of the destruction in the coming end-times judgment, He did it by drawing a comparison with the "ordinary" life of the populations around Noah.

> And as it was in the days of Noah, so it will be also in the days of the Son of Man: They ate, they drank, they married wives, they were given in marriage, until the day that Noah entered the ark, and the flood came and destroyed them all. (Luke 17:26-27)

Noah was an important man in his day. Whether he was a general contractor, an architect, or a business baron is pretty much an educated guess. But the fact that he found grace is important. Noah was fully dedicated to the work of God during his life.

Walked with God

The Bible lists Noah as one of only two men in all of history who "walked with God" (Genesis 6:9). The other is Enoch, who may be more well known in that capacity since he was taken up into God's presence without dying (Genesis 5:24). Efforts by some to portray Noah as a bumbling, drunken hypocrite are simply not true. God's commentary is that Noah was "just" and "perfect" (upright, without blemish). The Creator entrusted him with a monumental task that is unique in all of history.

Noah was "just." That simply means that he was known for his equitable dealings with others. Even in the wicked world that disgusted the Creator, Noah was "justified" in his dealings. He charged reasonable prices for his work. He gave a good product (whatever it was) to those who employed his services. His honest dealings gave rise to his influence in the community. He was proven to be a man of integrity (Genesis 7:1).

Noah was "perfect." That precious reputation, at least from God's perspective, means that he was a man without condemnation. His "just" dealings resulted in a "blameless" record. Whatever the wicked people of his day may have said behind his back, they *knew* that Noah was above reproach. Just as folks today often resort to rumor-mongering and distortion of facts to cover their own guilt, those around Noah no doubt employed some of the same practices to discredit righteous Noah. He may well have had that kind of treatment, but God saw that he was "perfect."

Preacher of Righteousness

Peter called Noah a "preacher of righteousness" (2 Peter 2:5). Think of what that means in the context of Genesis 6! The whole earth was "filled with violence" and "every heart" only thought of evil. The social milieu must have been a real mess. Yet Noah had the guts to stand up publically for the righteous behavior that just about everyone else openly and loudly rejected.

Perhaps his extended family members—and perhaps even some or most of his employees—were under his influence. But by the time the judgment of God fell, only Noah, his wife, and three of their sons and their wives were willing to follow his leadership into the Ark. Many would consider a ministry with such results a failure today, and yet God insisted that Noah's faith not only "saved" his family but the future world from extinction (Hebrews 11:7)!

We are not told in Scripture what Noah preached about. Enoch (the other man who walked with God) preached about the return of the Lord in judgment (Jude 1:14-15). Noah may well have preached about the coming judgment of the Flood and the desperate need of the world's people to turn back to their Creator for salvation. But whatever he may have preached and however he implemented his heart's desire, Noah was labeled a "preacher of righteousness" by the only Judge who ultimately counts.

World Population

One of the more divisive issues surrounding the biblical record of the great Flood is whether it was a worldwide, planet-covering flood, or more like a regional or local flood that only impacted the Mesopotamian River Valley.

The language of the Genesis text stresses the universal nature of the Flood. But in spite of the textual information, many would insist that such a planet-wide catastrophe cannot be accurate. They claim that science has demonstrated that the appearance of geological ages in earth's strata must be understood as successive eons, not as the combined result of a recent flood event. More discussion of these linguistic and geologic data will follow in later chapters, but a review of the likely population of earth at the time of the Flood is helpful at this point.

The Cultural Mandate

God's earliest command to the first man and woman was that they would assume a stewardship authority over the earth, its living creatures, and all its processes. Such oversight implies the development of science and technology, commerce and education—all honorable human vocations—in order to fulfill this mandate. This command applies to all people, and has never been withdrawn. Basic to this responsibility was the instruction to "be fruitful and multiply" (Genesis 1:28). God further expanded the mandate to Noah after the Flood (Genesis 9:1-7), twice repeating the "be fruitful and multiply" directive.

Obviously, God is looking at His long-range plan that would include the Millennial Kingdom, which is still in the future (Revelation 20:1-2). Subduing and exercising dominion over the entire planet has not yet been accomplished—but it will surely come to pass in the years ahead. That promise is as secure as any of the promises of God. Therefore, the "be fruitful and multiply" command was not just to Adam and Eve, but to all humanity through them. A large human population would be necessary to implement any sort of "dominion" over earth.

Even today, despite all the concern about population growth, vast areas of the earth are still barren and undeveloped, and the earth is far from being filled with people. There are immense deserts and inaccessible mountain ranges, plus the frozen wastes of Antarctica and the extremes of the northern tundra. And even though earth's human population is mainly scrunched into a belt centered on the equator, it continues to grow (some say at an alarming rate).

Population Growth

History has demonstrated that populations can grow very rapidly. For example, the 70 people who came into Egypt with Jacob (Genesis 46:27) developed into a rather large population in only 400 years. Numbers 1:46 gave the census of adult Israelite men (not including the tribe of Levi) who left Egypt with Moses as "six hundred and three thousand five hundred and fifty." Many Bible scholars would suggest that the total population was at least two million (and may well have been larger), since the families of those men would have added a rather significant number.

If we use that model as a basic tool to evaluate either past or projected population groups, most situations would easily multiply into millions over multiple generations. If one assumes that the average family had six children who lived and reproduced (this was less than half the number in Jacob's immediate family), and that just two generations were living at any one time (biblical records and our own experience verify that this assumption is very conservative), a small group of "normal" people would grow rapidly over a short period of time.

The records of population growth rates have varied widely. The most recent peak was in 1962-1963, during which the annual world population growth rate was 2.2 percent. That was an alarming rate and set off a flurry of speculation about a "population explosion" that would have the world strangling itself, with estimates of 50 billion people or more in another 100 years. However, by 2009 the annual growth rate had dropped precipitously to 1.1 percent. The rhetoric has changed just as quickly to worries that nations might rapidly wane as some of them enact "one child per family" policies.

"Replacement" growth (i.e., maintaining a stable population) is based on many studies, but most conclude that merely replacing the existing population would require that the average woman bear 2.1 children in her lifetime. The famous "2.5" children per family assumes a little more than 3/4 of a percent growth (0.0075) over longer periods of time. For instance, the accepted population of the world in

1650 A.D. was around 600 million. In 1800 A.D., the figure stood at 1 billion. Thus, the annual growth rate for that 150-year period was slightly over 1/3 percent (0.0036)—far less than the 1.1 percent average of the recent decade.

But the population has certainly grown since then! If the 1 billion figure for 1800 A.D. is accurate (and most scholars agree that it is), then the current population of 7.2 billion is an enormous increase. The average annual growth rate over the two-plus centuries is around 1.9 percent. That growth rate has sociologists insisting that the world population must be controlled somehow so that we don't use up all the earth's resources and create an epidemic of panic. "Common wisdom" has the world maxing out at around 50 billion.

Pre-Flood Population

The point of all that data is simply this: If the known and measurable population growth rate today demonstrates that human populations expand, then we can expect (both going forward and backward) to project reasonably accurate numbers over time.

Charles Darwin made such assumptions in his evolutionary model. If the human population is somewhere around 1 million years old, then a very conservative growth rate of 0.05 percent would produce a human population that would require a standing-room-only area well beyond the space available in the entire universe!

> The evolution model, on the other hand, with its million-year history of man, has to be strained to the breaking point. It is essentially incredible that there could have been 25,000 generations of men with a resulting population of only 3.5 billion. If the population increased at only 1/2 per cent per year for a million years, or if the average family size were only 2.5 children per family for 25,000 generations, the number of people in the present generation would exceed 10^{2100}, a number which is, of course, utterly impossible (as noted in an earlier chapter, only 10^{130} electrons could be crammed into the entire

known universe).[2]

The evolutionary assumptions are obviously not very helpful. However, assuming that the biblical information is correct, the population at the time of Noah's Flood would have been huge.

The Bible records that Adam and Eve had "sons and daughters" (Genesis 5:4). Pre-Flood humanity lived much longer lives than we experience today, and the genealogical records of the Bible indicate that family size then was significantly more than we see in our current civilized nations. However, if we assume that each family had three children and lived through only one generation, the worldwide population would have exceeded 3 billion in the documented 1,656-year span from creation to the Flood. It may well have been much larger.

All basic models of population growth rates assume that the population increases geometrically—that is, the increase each year is equal to a constant percentage of the population the previous year. Looking toward the past instead of the future, one can use the same model to determine how long it would take to produce a given population at a specific growth per year, starting with two people. An initial population of only two people, increasing at 2 percent per year, would become 3.5 billion people in only 1,075 years.

It is obvious that the early increases would have been much larger. Even if Adam and Eve had only four children ("sons and daughters," Genesis 5:4), with those children marrying as young adults, having an average of four children themselves, etc., etc., over 1,600 years, the geometric progression would have quickly compounded the population. Our current population of 7-plus billion would have developed from six people (Noah's three sons and their wives, Genesis 9:19) starting some 4,500 years ago with an average population growth rate that easily compares to rates from recorded history.

An estimated 3.5 billion-person population at the time of Noah is conservative!

---

2.   Henry M. Morris, 1985, *Scientific Creationism*, Green Forest, AR: Master Books, 169.

The Biblical Setting

God's evaluation was clear. The pre-Flood earth was "filled" with violence. "All flesh" was impacted by that violence and had become "corrupt." Earth's human population had degenerated to the point that their thoughts were "only evil all the time." There were horribly wicked and powerful men leading the earth into a deeper and more open rebellion against God—most likely guided by a group of angelic beings whose heinous mutiny against God later caused them to be imprisoned in "chains of darkness" (2 Peter 2:4).

God had decreed that He would allow only another 120 years before He would destroy the planet and "all flesh" that breathed air. That term is used 13 times in the three chapters describing the great Flood. It is impossible to read those verses without coming to the conclusion that God was going to eliminate air-breathing, land-dwelling life from the surface of the earth. Nothing was to be spared this awful judgment.

Noah was 500 years old when he and his wife began to have the three sons who would later be the great-grandsires of all human population after the Flood. During the 100 years that followed before sudden judgment came (Genesis 7:6), Noah "preached" to all he could—but none listened. "They ate, they drank, they married wives, they were given in marriage, until the day that Noah entered the ark, and the flood came and destroyed them all" (Luke 17:27).

It is likely that the construction of the Ark occupied much of that 100 years.

CHAPTER TWO
BUILDING THE ARK

Any big construction project comes to fruition amid a matrix of complex and interactive factors. There must be a vision or a cause that drives leadership to set their minds on the task. Professional concept designers and engineers are required to codify the vision into specific plans. Resources must be assembled and commitments made by those who are responsible for the capital requirements. Finally, skilled craftsmen and their supervisors must be gathered to build the project. A shopping center, an office park, an apartment complex—or an Ark—does not just "happen."

Since this was to be God's judgment, God Himself provided the vision for the Ark.

> And God said to Noah, "The end of all flesh has come before Me, for the earth is filled with violence through them; and behold, I will destroy them with the earth. Make yourself an ark of gopherwood; make rooms in the ark, and cover it inside and outside with pitch. And this is how you shall make it: The length of the ark shall be three hundred cubits, its width fifty cubits, and its height thirty cubits. You shall make a window for the ark, and you shall finish it to a cubit from above; and set the door of the ark in its side. You shall make it with lower, second, and third decks." (Genesis 6:13-16)

The Box

The Hebrew word translated here as ark, *tebah*, does not mean "boat." The connotation is more that of a box. The word is also used to describe the small "ark" that Moses' mother made to rescue him from Pharaoh's murderous decree (Exodus 1:22–2:3). Size is not the issue: purpose is. An "ark" was any device designed to protect and/or save the occupant(s) from death.

It is worth noting that the little ark that Moses rode to safety was constructed in the same general way as the huge ark designed to "keep the species alive" (Genesis 7:3) during the horrific Flood that destroyed the world. Both were constructed of natural materials. Both were covered with watertight "pitch," and both were designed to float (not navigate) on the water.

A different word, *'arown*, is used to describe the coffin that Joseph was buried in (Genesis 50:26), the Ark of the Covenant (over 100 references), and the chest to hold the gifts of the treasury (2 Kings 12:9-10). The only significant differences are related to the intended use of the container. The "Ark" of Noah and of Moses was to float on water and deliver its occupant(s) alive. The "coffin" of Joseph, the "Ark" of the Covenant, and the "chest" of money had nothing to do with water or survival and were merely receptacles to hold contents for storage or later retrieval.

The New Testament uses the same Greek word, *kibotos*, to describe both the Ark of Noah and the Ark of the Covenant. Obviously, both vessels were some sort of box or chest that was used to house, protect, and preserve valuable contents. There is absolutely no indication anywhere in the Scriptures that would represent the great building project of the Ark of Noah as a "ship" or "boat" in our modern understanding of those words.

The Dimensions

This was one big box! The instructions from the Creator to Noah were to make this Ark 300 cubits long, 50 cubits wide, and 30 cubits high. Without going into a lengthy documentation of all the scholarly research about the appropriate size of the cubit, it is sufficient to note that all but a very few experts agree that the Egyptian, Babylonian, and Hebrew measurements coincided with two basic lengths: a "common" cubit of approximately 18 inches, and a "royal" cubit of some 20 inches—both values based on the length of a man's forearm, from the tips of the fingers to the elbow.

A great deal of analysis has been done on the various buildings of the ancient world, and large tomes have been written on the precise construction of the pyramids. Since our entire modern world measures either in feet or meters, our interpretation of the cubit must of necessity have some room for approximation. The inclination of most biblical scholars is to use the "conservative" length of 18 inches for the cubit. Thus, the Ark would measure approximately:

- 450 feet long
- 75 feet wide
- 45 feet high

The Ark would have a footprint of 33,750 square feet (well over 12 times the footprint of an average house). And since it was constructed with three decks, it would have a total floor space of 101,250 square feet (more than 20 basketball courts). The total storage capacity would have been approximately 1,518,750 cubic feet (more than the storage space of over 300 railroad boxcars). This was a *BIG* box!

Maybe the best way to visualize this is to think of a typical Super Wal-Mart—or perhaps a multi-story office building. Remember, the Ark was designed to house and protect, not to shuttle from one port to another. It was designed to float and be as stable as possible on the surging waters of the Flood, not to plow through the waves to a specific destination. There was no "bridge" from which to steer. There was no engine to drive the Ark, and no rudder to keep the Ark moving along a specified course. God told Noah to build a "chest" that would preserve life on the earth while God was wiping out everything else.

The Building Materials

We are not told how Noah was to construct the Ark, but we are told that he was to use "gopher" wood (Genesis 6:14). This is the only time the Hebrew word *gopher* is used in the entire Old Testament. Pages and pages have been written about what this wood may have been, but the truth is that no one really knows. Evidently even Moses did not recognize the specific type of wood, since he chose just to transfer the term to his writing of Genesis, rather than translating or explaining the term in the language of his day.

Some have suggested that this was a type of cypress or maybe a species of redwood, since those trees are often referred to in ancient history. Perhaps "gopher" was a strong, dense wood like ironwood. Teak has long been used in seagoing vessels. It is both strong and dense, and appears to age slowly (thousands of years). Other, lesser-known woods such as locust, mahogany, and tonquin are each capable of being used to construct a large vessel. Whatever it may have been (or however the term would apply to our knowledge of botany today), the wood would have been well known and plentiful during the century prior to the Flood. Noah obviously knew what material God was referring to.

"Pitch" was to be used to coat both the inside and outside of the Ark. This English translation of the Hebrew word *kopher* is unfortunate. The word is used 17 times in the Old Testament, and is translated "pitch" only in Genesis 6:14. Most of the time, *kopher* is translated with some term that represents money. It is translated once as a "country village" (1 Samuel 6:18), and another time as "camphire" as the name of a perfume or spice (Song of Solomon 4:13).

Since the Hebrew lettering of *kopher* is very similar to *gopher*, some have suggested that the two words in Genesis 6:14 should be the same word, implying that the same construction material (gopher wood) was to be used inside and out. This would simplify the interpretation a bit, except that Noah is told to "pitch" (verb) the Ark inside and out with "pitch" (noun). Whatever material is identified by *kopher*, it is different from *gopher*. The Ark was made of *gopher*. It was coated or sheathed with *kopher*.

Here's the bigger problem, however. The English word "pitch" is a term we normally use for petroleum-based material. Petroleum, as far as we can determine, is made primarily out of animal (biological) material and would have been the result of huge reservoirs of dead and buried creatures. The catastrophic conditions necessary to produce such massive killing and burial wouldn't have existed prior to the Flood, so Noah couldn't have used this kind of material in the Ark's construction. That misunderstanding (that the Hebrew word *kopher* is the same as the English word "pitch") has given rise to all sorts of disclaimers and disagreements.

Since the *purpose* of the Ark was to preserve life during the destruction of the planet's surface by water, and since God Himself issued the order and provided the overall vision for the Ark's construction, it is surely safe to assume that God (who is both omniscient and sovereign) would not have allowed the Ark to be constructed in such a way that it would fall apart or sink during the coming Flood. Whatever skills or experience that Noah may have had, God would have surely insured that Noah did not make foolish choices of either materials or design.

What do we *know*?

The basic construction material was *gopher*. The Hebrew word, however, does not demand that *gopher* is "wood." That noun is supplied by the translators—and since the term is only used this one time in the entire Bible, we are at least assuming that *gopher* is wood. It may have been some sort of manufactured material that was common among the civilizations of Noah's day,

Metallurgy was certainly known and practiced, as was the specialized layers of woods necessary for complex musical instruments (Genesis 4:21-22). We are so used to thinking of ancient peoples as "primitive" that we tend to overlook the clear message of Scripture. These folks were not unsophisticated dullards, but highly intelligent and long-lived. If our modern societies can manufacture composite woods or specialized marine materials, it is certainly no stretch to anticipate that hardened woods and water-safe coatings would have been available at the time of Noah.

Remember, there were *seas* in this first world (Genesis 1:10). It appears that "rain" as we know it was not yet a common factor (Genesis 2:5), but there is absolutely no indication that the huge population at the time of Noah would have been ignorant of navigation across large bodies of water—and, therefore, would have been capable of producing suitable materials for such commerce. *Gopher* may well have been some sort of marine plywood, for all we know.

The *kopher* that sheathed or coated the Ark is not specified. The early translators used the English word "pitch" in Genesis 6:14, but they seemed to have had trouble deciding just how to provide an English equivalent for the word the several other times it appears in the Old Testament. Whatever *kopher* was, it likely was a very valuable product, since the majority of the other usages convey the idea of "importance" or "money."

The idea that *kopher* was liquid is merely assumed. It could just as well have been some sort of overlay (a sheathing). Even if the material was a liquid coating, the development of resins or other non-petroleum coating materials has long been known to man. Any objections to the Flood account stemming from the Ark's construction materials are based on the stubborn idea that Noah and his family were the products of ignorant savagery and had no skills in or access to anything resembling "modern" engineering.

We *know* that *gopher* was the basic construction material of the Ark, and *kopher* was the external and internal protective material. We *know* that the purpose of the Ark was to protect and preserve life during the awful judgment of the Flood. We *know* that the Ark was huge. We can, therefore, safely conclude that God would have instructed Noah to use materials suitable for the task. Speculating about what these materials were may be interesting, but ultimately they are impossible to determine precisely.

Gopher and *kopher* would have been both sufficient and satisfactory to accomplish what God wanted done—a fact confirmed by the comparison of the rescue through the Ark to our salvation through the Lord Jesus (Hebrews 11:7; 2 Peter 2:5).

The Construction Design

Once again, the biblical instructions regarding the Ark's design are not expansive. The external dimensions of the Ark are provided, along with the notation that it was to have three levels and rooms within, and a window above and a door in the side (Genesis 6:14-16). And once again, attempts to describe the Ark have varied from the simplistic to the surreal.

There have been reports of various "sightings" of the Ark since the days of Marco Polo. Many of them seem to coalesce around a plank-constructed object sitting high on Mount Ararat, partially exposed on a ledge. Some highly circumstantial stories have circulated about internal rooms and different entry points, but all of these have lacked demonstrable evidence—or have proved to be nothing more than the repetition of tales heard and rehearsed for decades.

Although there have been repeated claims that the Ark has been "found," no credible evidence has been forthcoming. Older stories and several recent expeditions have been intriguing, but what we *know* is limited to the biblical data.

The Decks

The Hebrew language is interesting. The text simply commands Noah to "make" (fashion or construct) a "lowest," a "second" (or "another"), and a "third." The English word "deck" is supplied to clarify what is implied.

The Ark was a long rectangle (450 feet by 75 feet). It is therefore likely that the Ark would have been constructed with a series of hatchways and passageways that would provide access between and within the levels. Most artistic renderings seem to lean toward making the Ark look as primitive as possible. However, given the potential sophistication of the pre-Flood world, it is more likely that the Ark would have been engineered for maximum use and efficiency.

Any vessel built to survive in deep water for months would have a system of inter-deck and intra-deck mechanisms that would allow for movement and storage of supplies. The care and feeding of the animals—even if only for a short period—would demand a complex design that would enable a few adults (eight people) to move among thousands of creatures. Even the ideas (the architectural and engineering thought) that went into the design would have had to be sophisticated. Such a large and multi-storied project would not be "primitive."

Much has been written about the need for enormous space for the animals. There will be more on this later in the chapter, but it is likely that all of the animals required by God (two of every kind and seven of the "clean" kinds) could have been adequately housed on one deck of the Ark. That would leave the lowest level for storage of supplies and equipment, the second level for the rooms for the animals, and the third for the living and functional quarters of Noah, his wife, and the families of their three sons.

The Rooms

The Hebrew word rendered "room" is *qen*, used 12 additional times in other passages. In every instance except Genesis 6:14, it is translated "nest." The use of this term would favor the idea that the "rooms" in the Ark would be constructed to suit their occupants. Although there are a few large animals, most of the air-breathing, land-dwelling creatures of our planet are rather small. Thus, the "nests" for many of these animals would be like "dens" or "cages" designed to house and protect, not to display the animal. There may have been provision for common activity spaces like an aviary or a required environmental habitat, but the information in Scripture does not suggest it.

It is possible that the height of some of the "nests" would have penetrated into a second level. If the maximum space between decks was one third of the total available, then each level would have had between 10 to 12 feet of headroom for each deck. It is just as likely, however, that the lowest level would have been much like the hold of a modern ship, designed to store the equipment and supplies that would be needed when the Ark was abandoned after the Flood. Each level would have been built around the structural design that suited the purpose for which it was constructed.

Please remember that the purpose of the Ark was to protect and preserve life, not to exhibit it. The large floor areas seen in zoo displays were not needed to house the Ark's occupants. It is likely that all of the animals would have quickly reverted to a settled condition—especially given that the immediate sound and fury of the Flood's storms and explosions would have naturally driven them to their "nests" for protection.

Noah and his family may well have had the entire third level for their own use. Since the footprint of the Ark involved some 33,750 square feet, each of the four families would have had over 8,000 square feet available—assuming they needed that much room to roam around, store their personal belongs, and conduct their private affairs during their year-long confinement to the Ark. They could have, and most likely did, design their "rooms" to be as comfortable and accommodating as they could wish.

The Window Above

Tsohar is the Hebrew word translated as "window" in Genesis 6:16. Of the 24 times it appears in the Old Testament, it is mostly translated "noon" or "noontime." Noah was told to "finish it to a cubit from above," implying that the "noon" was to be approximately 18 inches. But does this mean 18 inches wide, 18 inches square, 18 inches from the top? Obviously, speculation is widespread.

Many have suggested that the "window" could be something like a catwalk on the top of the Ark that could be opened in sections to let in air and light. That is a practical idea and would fit the implication that this "noon" was to be "above" the Ark, though it is certainly not demanded by the text. Whatever this feature was, it was probably not a single porthole in the side or top of the Ark.

Later, after the Ark had grounded on Mount Ararat and Noah "opened the window" to let the raven and dove fly about (Genesis 8:6), the Holy Spirit inspired Moses to use an entirely different word. That word, *challown*, is always translated with the English word "window," and appears to mean just what we would normally envision when we think of a window. Perhaps, this "window" from which Noah sent the raven and the dove was nothing more than a hole that Noah made in a portion of the top level. This "window" does not appear to have anything to do with the "noon" of the Ark's construction.

After the dove had returned with the plucked olive leaf, Noah "removed the covering of the ark" (Genesis 8:13). This "covering" is a very different word, used later to refer to the skins that covered the tabernacle to protect its valuable instruments and construction (see Exodus 26:14; 35:11; Numbers 4:8-25; etc.). Evidently the Ark had a "covering" (roof, sheath, port, door?) in addition to the "window" that Noah used to release the birds—and also in addition to the "noon" that was part of the architectural features of the design itself.

Some have suggested that this covering may have been a shaft to admit ventilation and light throughout the length and height of the Ark—something like a corridor running down the middle of the Ark dividing it into two distinct sides, from which and through which air could circulate and light would flow into every portion of the three levels. This would fit the implication of the descriptive word "noon" and would be "completed" (finished, ended) by an 18-inch protrusion "above" the roof of the third level.

The Door

Not much information is given about the entrance into the Ark, except that it was to be "set" in the "side" (Genesis 6:16). The particular Hebrew word used, *pethach*, strongly suggests a door*way*, an opening without a cover.

Since any entrance into the Ark would have to be large enough to permit the loading of supplies and thousands of animals, this "door" would have had to be rather large. It was definitely in the side of the

Ark as opposed to being in the top deck (as the main entry is in most modern ships). So whatever was ultimately needed to cover the doorway would have had to be very large as well.

That brings up a problem. If Noah and his family were inside the Ark after loading the supplies and animals, how would they shut the door? Perhaps they could have devised some mechanism that would be operated from inside the Ark. Perhaps a scaffold could have been constructed similar to what is used today to support massive rockets that are blasted from launch pads. Perhaps there were some sympathizers who agreed to "help" crazy Noah, but did not believe that the judgment was coming.

The Scripture provides a simple answer: "The LORD shut him in" (Genesis 7:16).

One cannot help but recall that the Lord Jesus described Himself as "the door" (John 10:7). Given the comparisons that Scripture makes between the awful judgment of the Flood and the opportunity of mercy God offered in the Ark, there is little need to exaggerate the terrible consequences of rejecting the grace of salvation. When the "flood came and destroyed them all" (Luke 17:27), there was no second chance. God's gracious "door" to eternal life is closed when death's "door" slams shut on those who have refused to enter in (John 10:9).

Filling the Ark

> "And behold, I Myself am bringing floodwaters on the earth, to destroy from under heaven all flesh in which is the breath of life; everything that is on the earth shall die. But I will establish My covenant with you; and you shall go into the ark—you, your sons, your wife, and your sons' wives with you. And of every living thing of all flesh you shall bring two of every sort into the ark, to keep them alive with you; they shall be male and female. Of the birds after their kind, of animals after their kind, and of every creeping thing of the earth after its kind, two of

every kind will come to you to keep them alive. And you shall take for yourself of all food that is eaten, and you shall gather it to yourself; and it shall be food for you and for them."

Thus Noah did; according to all that God commanded him, so he did....

"You shall take with you seven each of every clean animal, a male and his female; two each of animals that are unclean, a male and his female; also seven each of birds of the air, male and female, to keep the species alive on the face of all the earth." (Genesis 6:17-22; 7:2-3)

To make sure the key elements of the freight carried by the Ark are understood, it may be helpful to list them in tabular form.

Noah, his wife, their three sons and their wives .... 8 people

Two of every *kind* of land creature, male and female....thousands

Seven of each *bird kind*, male and female ....thousands

Seven of every *kind* of *clean* animal, male and female ... hundreds

All kinds of food that is eaten.. tons

Supplies for the new world .... tons

The People

This may seem obvious, since the whole event is built around the obedience of Noah and his family, but God was "selecting" a very defined genetic pool from which to repopulate the planet.

Now the sons of Noah who went out of the ark were Shem, Ham, and Japheth....These three were the sons of Noah, and from these the whole earth was populated. (Genesis 9:18-19)

Noah was a direct descendant of Seth, the replacement son for Abel whom Cain killed. It is the family line of Seth through which the Lord operated during the increasingly rebellious years of the pre-

Flood world (Genesis 5). The more famous descendants were Enoch (who was taken from the earth without dying) and Methuselah (who was the longest-lived of all humanity—969 years).

One might say that God started over with the "best" that the human population had to offer. Adam and Eve were created with DNA containing 100 percent of human genetic information, and that DNA had no taint of sin and death. When they rebelled and God brought judgment on humanity, the death process and the sin process began to proliferate—until the world population was horrifically evil and all except the few remaining righteous people (Noah and his immediate family) were corrupted.

In a recent study reported in the journal *Science*, genetic scientists found proof that the genetic diversity of humanity had essentially exploded around 5,000 years ago.[1] Stated more simply, the "information" in the human DNA population showed very little change for "millions of years" of supposed evolution until some recent catastrophic event caused the human population to diversify. Up until that event, everybody looked alike. There were no "ethnic groups" or easily observable differences in humanity. That is obviously not the case now, and these geneticists discovered the historical benchmark for the sudden changes.

How interesting! The Bible says that except for eight people, all human life was destroyed during the Flood, and that all of present humanity has come from the children of Shem, Ham, and Japheth— which the Bible dates as around 5,000 years ago! Yes, there are "error bars" in these calculations, and the date of the Flood is not precisely identifiable. But the "error" is absolutely miniscule when comparing the biblical explanation against the "millions" of undocumented years in the evolutionary theory.

A later chapter will evaluate the people groups that have descended from the three sons of Noah. The Bible has much to say about the formation of the nations of the world, and a remarkable "table

---

1. Jacob A. Tennessen et al, 2012, Evolution and Functional Impact of Rare Coding Variation from Deep Sequencing of Human Exomes, *Science*, 337 (6090): 64-69.

of nations" is contained in Genesis 10. From God's perspective: "He has made from one blood every nation of men to dwell on all the face of the earth, and has determined their preappointed times and the boundaries of their dwellings" (Acts 17:26).

Our current world population all began on the Ark.

The Animals

Lots of ink has been expended in many, many books and technical papers about the animals that were taken on board the Ark. Those who discount the account of the Flood are quick to point out that no "box" would ever be big enough to house millions of animals. That argument, of course, is based on the assumption that the Ark would have to house two of every species of living organisms that were on the planet.

Taxonomists argue over how to classify "species," and the tabulations run from somewhere just over a million different species, to nearly twice that. Generally, the categories are built around reproductive groupings—mostly related to populations that are isolated in an environmental domain (such as the various finches on the different Galapagos Islands).

Two of Every Kind

The biblical record of classification differs from the technical classifications of today's scientists. When God created living creatures, He used the Hebrew word *miyn* to define the limits of reproductive capability. Evidently, God's view of living categories is much broader than ours. Although a good bit of research is going on in the creationist community, the precise definition of "kind" and the limits within each kind are still open questions. Using the biblical information given in Leviticus, it is more likely that the biblical kind is roughly equivalent to the modern taxonomical family or subfamily—perhaps even to order—than it is to "species." However, to allow a broad path for consideration, one can safely assume that the biblical kind is represented by the taxonomic classification of genus.

Whatever may eventually be uncovered as the biblical structure of "after its kind," it is certainly clear that the miniscule division of "species" does not reflect the descriptions of the animals Noah was instructed to prepare for. Compare God's instructions to Noah with the words used during the creation week.

Creation Week:

> So God created...every winged bird according to its kind. And God saw that it was good. (Genesis 1:21)

> Then God said, "Let the earth bring forth the living creature according to its kind: cattle and creeping thing and beast of the earth, each according to its kind"; and it was so. And God made the beast of the earth according to its kind, cattle according to its kind, and everything that creeps on the earth according to its kind. And God saw that it was good. (Genesis 1:24-25)

Instructions to Noah:

> "And of every living thing of all flesh you shall bring two of every sort into the ark, to keep them alive with you; they shall be male and female. Of the birds after their kind, of animals after their kind, and of every creeping thing of the earth after its kind, two of every kind will come to you to keep them alive." (Genesis 6:19-20)

> ...they and every beast after its kind, all cattle after their kind, every creeping thing that creeps on the earth after its kind, and every bird after its kind, every bird of every sort. And they went into the ark to Noah, two by two, of all flesh in which is the breath of life. (Genesis 7:14-15)

Please note, the terms used by God during the week of creation are exactly the same terms used by God in His instruction to Noah. The *land* and *air* creatures (not the water creatures) "according to their kind" were to be collected in pairs for preservation and protection on board the Ark.

To begin with, this qualification would eliminate the overwhelming majority of taxonomic categories. Of the one million or so species, all but some 22,000 are plant systems or water-based life forms. At maximum, then, the Ark would be required to hold fewer than 50,000 animals. When those numbers are reduced by using genus as the "kind" classification, the required number of land and air animals drops dramatically.

For instance, the dog kind would not have to include pairs of the 175 different breeds of dogs recognized by the American Kennel Club. Nor would Noah have to include the different types of wolves, coyotes, dingoes, and foxes that are all inter-fertile with other "dogs." More than likely, God would have limited the requirement to one pair of "dogs" (probably a pair of wolves) from which the many adaptive (and humanly engineered) species would later come. The same limitation would apply to "cattle," "beast of the earth," "birds of the air," and "creeping things."

The only critical factors were that they have "blood," "life," and "breath," and were a reproducing representative of their "kind."

The Clean Animals

There are not many "clean" animals that would have been included on the Ark. Leviticus 11 provides a list of approved flesh for the Israelites to eat, along with a list of "unclean" creatures that live in the water, air, or on land. Most of the categories are described by the animals' lifestyles (chew the cud, eat carrion), by their feet (cloven-footed or not), or by their covering (scales vs. skin). There are several subcategories, such as "the hare, because it chews the cud but does not have cloven hooves, is unclean to you; and the swine, though it divides the hoof, having cloven hooves, yet does not chew the cud, is unclean to you" (Leviticus 11:6-7).

Even using the "species" filter, the total number of clean land-based animals would not exceed 1,000, since no reptiles at all were included. Attempting to classify the "kind" of clean animals would reduce the number significantly to something fewer than 100. Given that Noah was commanded to take "seven each" of these animals, the total number would certainly be less than 1,000 creatures.

The Birds

Dr. Ernst Mayer, one of America's leading systematic taxonomists, lists 8,600 species of birds.[2] Filtering that number by the genus, we are left with some 700 types. That number could be reduced somewhat by the "unclean" birds. Noah was told to take "seven each" of the birds, requiring approximately 4,600 individual flying creatures on board the Ark.

Woodmorappe's Feasibility Study

The most complete study of the features, capacities, and occupants of the Ark of which this writer is aware is *Noah's Ark: A Feasibility Study* by John Woodmorappe. He has evaluated all of the opposition, possible configurations, assumptive issues, and technical analyses that could likely be done by any human author. Most of those who have written on this subject have studied and quoted from his seminal work.

The book is not bedside reading, but should the reader have particular questions about anything relating to the historicity and feasibility of the Ark, and the information discussed in the Genesis account, there is no more complete analysis available.

According to Woodmorappe, there would be fewer than 16,000 animals on board the Ark:[3]

- All Mammals   7,428
- All Birds   4,600
- All Reptiles   <u>3,724</u>
- TOTAL   15,754

Using very generous calculations, Woodmorappe suggests that

2.   Ernst Mayer, 1969, *Principles of Systematic Zoology*, New York: McGraw-Hill Book Co., 11-12.
3.   John Woodmorappe, 1996, *Noah's Ark: A Feasibility Study*, Dallas, TX: Institute for Creation Research, 10.

for all of the animals—including the few very large creatures like the elephant, the giraffe, the hippopotamus, and the rhino, as well as the fewer-yet animals that are now extinct like the sauropods (four-footed dinosaurs)—the maximum floor space required under the most generous allocations would amount to less than one-half of the space available.[4]

Others have suggested that all of the animals could easily be housed on one deck of the Ark, with the lower deck given over to storage and supplies, and the top deck used for Noah's family. Again, if the reader has serious questions or suspicions—or even curiosity about any possible feature or activity that could be required during the year-long Flood—a study of Woodmorappe's book would be well-advised. (Check online sources for availability.)

Dinosaurs and Kangaroos

There is absolutely no question that "two of every kind" of air-breathing, land-dwelling creature would have been on board the Ark. God ordered it. That means that there would have been at least two of every dinosaur kind, as well as some of the more unusual animals like the marsupials.

Some have claimed that such creatures could not possibly have been included on the Ark, but their objections have either been based on evolutionary assumptions (that dinosaurs lived long before man) or current topography (Australia is separated from Europe). Neither of those conditions would have been valid at the time of the Flood. That world was very different and has long ago been destroyed (2 Peter 3:5-6).

This book is not the place to go into detail about the likely distinctions between our world and the world of the First Age, some of which are covered in the first volume of this series. For readers who want to know more about the subject, below are a few books that provide excellent documentation on conditions of the planet prior to the Flood.

---

4. Ibid, 16.

- *The Book of Beginnings, Volume One: Creation, Fall, and the First Age*, Henry M. Morris III
- *The Genesis Record*, Henry M. Morris
- *The Fossil Record*, John Morris and Frank Sherwin
- *The Global Flood*, John Morris
- *The Young Earth*, John Morris

Although certain details are not specifically stated in Scripture, a number of conditions are implied that provide qualified scenarios that would help explain the gathering of each kind of animal and bird to the area around the Ark.

- Some "division" of waters above the earth would have both reduced the temperature variations on the earth's surface and the harmful radiation from the sun (Genesis 1:6-8; 2 Peter 3:5).

- Reduced temperature variations would have either prevented or remarkably reduced rainfall (Genesis 2:6) and practically eliminated violent storms.

- Such tranquil and stable environmental conditions would have made likely a much larger temperate or subtropical land surface—thus extending the habitable portion of the planet to the edges of all "seas."

- One major reason for the current "continental drift" theories is the tantalizing shapes of the existing continents. Their edges look as though they might fit together, implying that all of the land masses were at one time either contiguous in some way or part of one "mega" continent.

If any or all of these likely conditions were part of the *kosmos* of the First Age, then it is very easy to understand how all forms of life could have lived in nearly every section of the planet. There would be no need for some sort of global "roundup" for Noah to perform. The animals would have been readily accessible in environmental sections near Noah's location.

The idea that Noah would have had difficulty in gathering all the animals is based on naturalistic thinking. It was God who did the gathering. The Bible says that "two of every kind will come to you" (Genesis 6:20). This was God's Flood (not Noah's) and God was the One giving the instructions—and exercising the grace and mercy that would allow a "new world" to start over after the Flood's destruction. It should be no surprise that God would make sure that all the land and air animals necessary to "keep the species alive" (Genesis 7:3) would come to Noah.

Food Supplies

God also instructed Noah to gather "of all food that is eaten, and you shall gather it to yourself; and it shall be food for you and for them" (Genesis 6:21). On the surface that seems rather obvious. If Noah's family members were going to have thousands of animals to care for as well as themselves for some time, there would certainly need to be adequate food.

Mid-way through the pre-Flood era, Genesis 4:20 notes that Jabal, Cain's seventh-generation grandson, was a cattle rancher. Abel, it may be recalled, was a "keeper of sheep," while Cain was a "tiller of the ground" (Genesis 4:2). Every industry requires people who are capable of supplying the needs of that industry. Nothing but a blind bias toward the evolutionary idea of primitive "hunters and gatherers" would prevent us from understanding that these perfectly created and highly intelligent early humans would have quickly "subdued" the earth—with the basic food cultivation, collection, and distribution processes that would "fill" the rapidly expanding needs of a growing population. There would easily have been sufficiently developed food sources and food processing industries within access of the building site of the Ark.

One difficulty on board the Ark might be the huge amount of food that 16,000 animals would need over a year's time. Most animals, even those who often supply their energy from the protein of carnivorous activity, are able to function on a cereal diet. Grain feeds (peas, lentils, corn, etc.) would be easily stored and can last for a long time. Compressed pellets, which were certainly not beyond the agricultural expertise of Noah's day, would have been more efficient than raw grain—and would require less storage. Dried fruits would have served both animals and humans.

There would have been more than adequate food storage for the occupants. The key to estimating the needed storage, however, would be an analysis of the activity level of the animals during transit. All animals are capable of reduced metabolic activity during times of rest, and, indeed, during times of lengthy shelter (due to storms, dark seasons, weather-related isolation, etc.). Some animals enter states of minimal energy requirements during conditions that trigger hibernation or similar behavior. It is certainly likely that such conditions prevailed on the Ark due to the darkness of the 40 days of initial rain, the rocking motion of the Ark caused by the movement of the waves, and the general pall of danger that would have been felt—in spite of the shelter provided.

Most of the animals would have settled down into some sort of hibernation, thus reducing the amount of food needed and the time required to care for them. Once again, Woodmorappe's book has a lengthy section on the detailed calculations for body-mass, necessary exercise, food consumption, manure disposition—everything you might ever want to know about such a monumental undertaking.

Although the situation was remarkable in that it took place within the context of such a huge event, the care of the animals on the Ark was still well within the basic capabilities of "normal" folks.

Other Supplies

Genesis says nothing directly about Noah's preparations for the ultimate landing and disembarking from the Ark. But Noah would surely have known that he would have to survive after the Flood—God told him that the Ark was to be built for that purpose.

There is absolutely no reason, therefore, for us to assume that Noah would not have taken everything that he could think of to assist him and his family in a new world abounding in raw materials but totally devoid of any "civilized" influence.

One of the remarkable evidences of the so-called "early" civilizations (Egypt, China, Babylon) is that they all show a sophisticated knowledge of architecture, construction, engineering, mathematics, astronomy, etc. We are still trying to figure out how the pyramids were built; they appear to have been constructed by peoples who had formed a "nation" not very long after the Flood dissipated.

Surely, Noah would have taken instruction books. Books were known long before Noah's time (Genesis 5:1). Noah would also have taken basic equipment. Since metallurgy was known (Genesis 4:22), he would probably have taken such things as saws, drills, ladders, block-and-tackle, etc. It is also likely that he would have taken some supply of the "gopher" from which the Ark was made to construct his first post-Flood residence.

Given that the early civilizations demonstrate a remarkable knowledge base, it is likely that the Ark was the repository of the best of the techniques, equipment, plant specimens, the most hardy of the "clean" animals, and everything that had been developed by a civilization that had begun with perfect capabilities and had acquired practical experience over lives that lasted centuries.

Please dismiss any depictions of "poor ol' Noah" wrapped in a bedsheet, struggling with his family to pick wild berries in a world devoid of any hope. The planet had indeed been turned upside down by the awful judgment of a holy and angry Creator. But that same Creator had saved Noah's family and animals on the Ark from destruction.

What follows is the result of God's goodness and preservation.

CHAPTER THREE
THE DAY THE WORLD DIED

For this they willfully forget: that by the word of God the heavens were of old, and the earth standing out of water and in the water, by which the world that then existed perished, being flooded with water. But the heavens and the earth which are now preserved by the same word, are reserved for fire until the day of judgment and perdition of ungodly men. (2 Peter 3:5-7)

These three short verses contain absolutely critical information. The "they" of verse 5 refers to those who have laughed at the promises of God and who ignore the obvious teachings of Scripture and the clear principles of science. The principles ignored are these:

- God *created* the universe by His word.

- The first "world" (Greek *kosmos*) was *destroyed* by a flood.

- The existing world is *preserved* (maintained, conserved) by the same word.

The Created Universe

It is not within the scope of this book to revisit the creation week in detail. There is an enormous amount of material available that examines the biblical information as well as the scientific data that demonstrate the clarity of the simple statement "In the beginning God created the heavens and the earth" (Genesis 1:1). The initial book of this series, *The Book of Beginnings, Volume One: Creation, Fall, and the First Age*, explores the biblical and scientific information readily available to all of us.

Creation

The First Law of Thermodynamics states that matter (mass-energy) can neither be created nor destroyed. If there is such a thing as an absolute "law" of science, that principle has been demonstrated, repeated, and verified innumerable times. Essentially, we *know* that the universe could not create itself. There must have been a First Cause that was both omniscient and omnipotent.

Further, we *know* that all systems decrease in order and available energy over time. That is the basics of the Second Law of Thermodynamics. All energy-based systems (everything that we know about) increase in disorder, randomness, and "deadness" over time. Essentially, we *know* that the universe could not be infinitely old—it must have had a beginning. And, of course, that is exactly what the Bible states as the facts of the universe's origin.

God created the heavens and the earth "in the beginning." Prior to the beginning there was nothing but the omnipresent Triune Godhead. He created—from nothing but His own mind and purpose—everything that now exists. That universe was then organized and structured under the eternal plan and counsels of His will during the preparation of Days Two, Three, and Four of the creation week, so that it was ready to sustain the life that God created on Days Five and Six. Finally, when all else was complete, God created His "image"—Adam and Eve—to steward the creation.

Flawless Function

An often overlooked message of the creation account is that God Himself pronounced the results of His work "very good." Scientifically, that would mean that everything functioned flawlessly. The processes of the universe were working as designed, with no aberrant intrusion of "thorns and thistles." Failure of information transfer (e.g., mutations to DNA) would not distort the design in the original creation. No doubt there were structures and processes in place that would have kept the creation "very good" on an ongoing basis.

For instance, Peter's casual mention of "the earth standing out of water and in the water" suggests that the separating of the "waters" on Day Two would have had a major impact on the cosmology of the initial creation. Just what was done or exactly how such a formation would have affected the planet is open for speculation. Fossil evidence indicates that the planet was temperate in the past and that both plants and animals were spread more widely across the globe than is the case now.

Flawless function would mean that nothing was out of order from God's intended purposes. The demands of God's holiness would insure that nothing would distort or counter the message of God's nature in the creation. The demands of God's omniscience would necessarily frame all processes with the most efficient and effective function possible. And the demands of God's omnipotence would insure that every evidence clearly revealed His authority as the source of creation.

The Fallen Universe

Genesis 3 changes everything, and herein lies the problem. Everything that we now have access to (all science, for instance) is under the global judgment rendered by the Creator on His creation. Because of Adam's sin (Romans 5:12), the "ground" (the earth) was "cursed" (Genesis 3:18). The very elements out of which our universe was constructed would no longer function as originally designed, but would produce "thorns and thistles." Just as the first Adam rebelled against the authority of the Creator, so now would the very creation itself resist mankind's management efforts.

As was discussed in chapter 1, the Bible gives us some insight into the spiritual and cultural horrors that spiraled into the awful conditions that existed prior to the great Flood in Noah's day. What may be overlooked, however, is that the physical conditions were growing more "violent" as the judgment on the "ground" increased in intensity. The evil heart of mankind was reaping an ever-growing evil harvest of "toil" and "violence." So much so that Lamech, the earthly father of Noah, chose his son's name to identify with "comfort," believing that his son would experience a radical change in the earth. This hope was "because of the ground which the LORD has cursed" (Genesis 5:29).

Our world today will never experience the full horror and complexity of that "curse." The same Creator-Judge who pronounced the awful curse on the "ground" has also mitigated that curse with His mercy in our world. We surely understand the impact of the curse and we experience the result of the awful judgment that destroyed that world, but the merciful Creator has stabilized the planet and its functions, "not willing that any should perish" (2 Peter 3:9). Our world today "groans and labors with birth pangs" (Romans 8:22), and will ultimately be delivered from the curse (Revelation 22:3) into the "glorious liberty of the children of God" (Romans 8:21).

In the world of the First Age, the Creator-Judge pronounced the death of all creatures: "From under heaven all flesh in which is the breath of life; everything that is on the earth shall die" (Genesis 6:17). That world ended. When the apostle Peter referred to that event, he noted that the *kosmos* (ordered system) was ended by a *kataklustheis*— an overflowing "catastrophe" that destroyed everything. There is much more on that awful catastrophe to come in this book, but please note that the *conditions* of that world no longer exist!

The Preserved Universe

Available to scientists and theologians today are the revealed words of the Creator and the structures and processes of the "heavens and earth which are now." From a scientific perspective, all we can observe and test are the relatively stable and consistent performance of *this* cosmos.

After the animals were unloaded from the Ark and a thanksgiving offering had been given to God for His gracious provision and protection, God made a promise to Noah:

> "While the earth remains, Seedtime and harvest, Cold and heat, Winter and summer, And day and night *Shall not cease*." (Genesis 8:22)

The New Testament expands on this a little when the personal involvement of the Lord Jesus as Creator is amplified. Not only was He the Creator of the universe—and the Judge who gaveled the horrible end to the First Age—but He is also the Sovereign Lord of heaven and earth who keeps the universe that He created from falling apart!

> And He is before all things, and in Him all things *consist*. (Colossians 1:17)

> But the heavens and the earth which are now *preserved* by the same word... (2 Peter 3:7)

Theologically, that comforts us in that we can *know* that He will keep His promises and His covenants with the universe, just as He will with the teachings of the apostles and prophets. Scientifically, that assures us that we can *depend* on the processes and functions that we observe. Both perspectives are necessary. On the one hand, the non-technically trained can be confident that God's protection and guaranteed stability of our planet and its residents are assured on a scale that none of us can truly understand. On the other hand, each scientist can be confident that the processes and worldwide cycles that keep our planet functioning will be stable long enough for us to study, understand, and apply them for ever-increasing efficiency. Humanity depends on that stability for peace and safety. Science depends on that stability for knowledge and progress.

However, our access is only to the *current* processes. Whatever may have been the past structure of the "waters above," we cannot know. However God *created* the original conditions, we cannot know. Whatever was involved in the worldwide synchronized explosion of the "fountains of the great deep" that commenced the Flood, we cannot know. We can't even be sure what the "fountains of the great deep" were! That *kosmos* is gone! The small glimpses into that physical universe are limited to the words of Scripture and the speculations we make about what might have been.

Here's the problem: The current processes are in stasis—they are stable. If we try to project backward with measured processes that are supernaturally kept stable by the promise of the omniscient and omnipotent Creator, we will come to erroneous conclusions. Our time measurements (based on rates measured under stable conditions) will be considerably off—because our scientific access is limited to a *preserved* universe. Our forensic (historical) interpretations of past processes will be based on the current stable processes—processes that are supernaturally preserved. Conclusions about pre-Flood history will simply be wrong if we develop our theories without the Creator and His Word shaping our thinking.

The World That Was

Three things that we can be sure of about the First Age are supplied by information given in the Scriptures.

- The ordered structure of the First Age "perished" (Genesis 6:13; 2 Peter 3:6).

- The destruction was by a "flood of waters" (Genesis 6:17; 2 Peter 2:5).

- The water-based destruction was initiated by the Creator-Judge on a single day (Genesis 7:11; Luke 17:26-27).

Whatever happened to the planet then was global—a worldwide catastrophe. Unless the words of the three Flood chapters in the book of Genesis are absolute nonsense, the language cannot be understood as referring to a "local" event. Yes, there are some biblical commentators who suggest that the "all" of those passages doesn't really mean "all," and that the descriptions of the mountains being covered only refer to the "hills" of the Mesopotamian River Valley. But if such comments are correct, then the words of Scripture are not worth reading. If we can't trust the words to mean what they would normally mean in the context of the events, then they have no more authority than the imaginative "poetic license" of the novelist and playwright.

Universally Destroyed

The three chapters of Genesis that describe the Flood judgment repeat the planet-wide nature of that catastrophe many times, incorporating passages of universal judgment, the reasons for such a universal destruction, and verification that the judgment did indeed destroy "all life" as well as "the world that then existed." Other biblical writers use the same language or quote from the Genesis account, acknowledging their belief that these events were actual history. Here are just a few examples.

> So the LORD said, "I will *destroy* man whom I have created *from the face of the earth*, both man and beast, creeping thing and birds of the air, for I am sorry that I have made them." (Genesis 6:7)

> And God said to Noah, "The *end of all flesh* has come before Me, for the earth is filled with violence through them; and behold, *I will destroy them with the earth.*" (Genesis 6:13)

> "And behold, I Myself am bringing floodwaters on the earth, *to destroy* from under heaven *all flesh in which is the breath of life; everything that is on the earth shall die.*" (Genesis 6:17)

> "I will *destroy* from the face of the earth *all living things* that I have made." (Genesis 7:4)

> And the *waters prevailed exceedingly* on the earth, and *all the high hills under the whole heaven were covered.* The waters prevailed fifteen cubits upward, and the mountains were covered. (Genesis 7:19-20)

> "For as in the days before the flood, they were eating and drinking, marrying and giving in marriage, until the day that Noah entered the ark, and did not know until the flood came and *took them all away*, so also will the coming

of the Son of Man be." (Matthew 24:38-39)

By faith Noah, being divinely warned of things not yet seen, moved with godly fear, prepared an ark for the saving of his household, by *which he condemned the world* and became heir of the righteousness which is according to faith. (Hebrews 11:7)

The world that then existed perished, being flooded with water. (2 Peter 3:6)

The implications of the events described in Genesis will be examined more carefully in the following pages. The result cannot be disputed—unless the words of Scripture are not accepted as accurate and trustworthy. The words tell us that what the great Flood brought on the world by God's judgment was planet-wide destruction that left catastrophe in its wake on and among the structures of the earth, leading to the death of all air-breathing, land-dwelling creatures. The only exceptions were the eight people of Noah's immediate family and the few thousands of biological *kinds* chosen by God to "keep the species alive" on the earth (Genesis 7:3).

One final thought: God promised Noah and the whole of creation never to bring such a flood again (Genesis 9:12-17). If the language of Genesis means anything, the precious rainbow that we often see after a storm is a sign of a covenant that "the waters shall never again become a flood to destroy all flesh" (v. 15). If that statement is not to be taken at face value, then God has broken His promise repeatedly through the many local floods that have occurred since then.

The Flood of Waters

The Scriptures list two main sources for the waters of the Flood: the "fountains of the great deep" and the "rain" that continuously fell for 40 days and 40 nights.

Of these two, the 40-day rain is the best remembered. All of our early stories about this event mention the 40 days. Most of the many flood accounts from other cultures mention rain as the main source for the Flood. Yet, although this is surely an important factor, the rain was not the major contributor of the waters. Whatever was the cause of this unique rainfall, its source must have been the "waters above" that were somehow suspended above the planet. That collapse lasted for nearly six weeks! Nothing like that is possible today. Surely such a deluge would have "flooded" any terrestrial environment upon which it fell.

However, the main source of the floodwaters was the "fountains of the great deep." The trigger for the whole judgment event was the day that God caused the eruption of these "fountains" (Genesis 7:11). That explosion of subterranean waters, along with the 40-day rain, would have surely been enough by itself to "flood" the earth. Yet biblical records insist that the "waters…greatly increased" and "prevailed" for 150 days (Genesis 7:18, 24). Even if these two sources were simultaneously flooding the planet for 40 days, that leaves 110 days that the waters increased. The only source during that three-plus-month period would have been these "fountains."

Taken together—the constant rain for nearly six weeks, along with the continual "prevailing" and "increasing" of the deep reservoirs of water for another nearly four months—the "world that then was" would surely have "perished."

Judgment Day

There are many reasons why a universal, planet-destroying flood is often explained away by theologians, philosophers, and naturalistic scientists. Perhaps the most visceral reason (but often silently ignored) is that the Genesis account gives us one of the few pictures in the Bible of the full wrath of God. Yes, the book of Revelation is pretty scary, but it speaks of things to come in language that is often clearly figurative. The record of Genesis tells us of an event that actually happened. God was really angry!

One of the most obvious reasons that the Genesis record is actual history and not allegory, figurative language, or theatrical melodrama is that this event (the Flood) was launched as planned and assured on a documented day in history. This was *not* an unexplained event of nature (like an unplanned rupture in the earth's mantle). This was *not* a statistical accumulation of stressors (like an earthquake). This *was* truly an "Act of God"—as in, something that we mere mortals can neither expect nor control—but God can!

> Then the LORD said to Noah, "Come into the ark, you and all your household, because I have seen that you are righteous before Me in this generation."
>
> "For after seven more days I will cause it to rain on the earth forty days and forty nights, and I will destroy from the face of the earth all living things that I have made." And Noah did according to all that the LORD commanded him.
>
> Noah was six hundred years old when the floodwaters were on the earth. So Noah, with his sons, his wife, and his sons' wives, went into the ark because of the waters of the flood. Of clean animals, of animals that are unclean, of birds, and of everything that creeps on the earth, two by two they went into the ark to Noah, male and female, as God had commanded Noah.
>
> And it came to pass after seven days that the waters of the flood were on the earth. In the six hundredth year of Noah's life, *in the second month, the seventeenth day of the month, on that day all the fountains of the great deep were broken up, and the windows of heaven were opened.* (Genesis 7:1-11)

This is truly a remarkable passage. The previous chapter had outlined the horrible conditions of violence and evil that dominated the earth. God gave the 120 years of warning and recognized Noah as a "perfect" man who "walks" with Him during those most difficult of days. Noah started the monumental task of building and loading the Ark. Now, the work is completed and Noah enters the Ark with his immediate family and the animals that God has selected. God announces that He will start the Flood in seven days. The Flood explodes as promised: "On the very same day…"—that is, on the 17th day of the second month of the year, when Noah was 600 years old (Genesis 7:13).

Unless God has lied to us, this is recorded precisely as it actually happened.

The Fountains of the Great Deep

Although there is much that is mysterious about this phrase, and it is impossible for present-day scholars to *observe* or *replicate* these conditions, it is possible to gain a reasonable understanding of what God meant by the words "the fountains of the great deep."

The First Mention

The first use of a word or phrase is always instructive. With rare exceptions, the first time a word or phrase is used in any serious piece of literature will provide a context upon which the rest of the writing will both build and amplify how to view the use of the words throughout the book. Bible scholars refer to this phenomenon as "the principle of first mention."

> The earth was without form, and void; and darkness was on the *face of the deep*. And the Spirit of God was hovering over the face of the waters. (Genesis 1:2)

The Hebrew word used here for "deep" (*t'howm*) occurs 36 times in the Old Testament and is always translated as some immeasurable and unknowable place usually connected with liquid (as in oceans, deep rivers, mountain springs, etc.). The word is consistently used as a noun (a place or thing). This is a bit elementary, but some have insisted that the word only applies to the ocean itself, and they pass off its obvious connection to something either within the ocean depths or as the source of springs and other surface manifestations of subterranean reservoirs of water.

There are two clear points from the word used. First, the "deep" almost always contains liquid—usually water. Second, the "deep" is a thing—a place, usually in or under the ocean or in or under the earth. The term is not complex, but it is important for understanding what may have been involved in the horrific explosions on the first day of the Flood.

"Fountain" (singular or plural) translates the Hebrew word *ma'yan*, which always refers to a flow of water from an opening. The word is used 23 times and is translated "spring" or "fountain" unless it is used figuratively (such as "wells of salvation" in Isaiah 12:3). Once again, the first time the word "fountain" is used gives us some insight on how to couple it with the word "deep." Since both words are nouns (places or things), we can expect that the whole phrase is identifying something more specific than either "fountain" or "deep" designates when used by itself.

Ground Misters

> For the LORD God had not caused it to rain on the earth...
> but a mist went up from the earth and watered the whole
> face of the ground. (Genesis 2:5-6)

This short description has been the subject of debate about the first cosmos. Obviously, it is not possible to reconstruct the actual conditions of the centuries prior to the Flood, but some tantalizing pieces of evidence do exist.

- The "waters above the earth" would have likely offered some form of protective environment for the earth's surface, resulting in even temperature distribution, placid air movements, and some form of solar shielding.

- Fossil evidence, such as the vast coal beds all over the earth, strongly suggests that the entire planet had a temperate or subtropical climate in the past.

- A worldwide mild climate would suppress a hydrological cycle as it operates today: evaporation, cooling in the atmosphere, rainfall, evaporation, etc.

- Biblical references suggest that "rain" as we know it was not part of that early cosmos (Genesis 2:5-6).

- Vast underground caverns (Škocjan Caves in Slovenia, Cave of the Ghost in Venezuela, Reed Flute Cave in China, Waitomo Glowworm Caves in New Zealand, Mammoth Cave in Kentucky) are located all over the world—and all of them show clear evidence of having been formed by or having held vast reservoirs of water.

- Geyser and other thermal activity is observable all over the world, suggesting that internal heat from the earth's core is still causing "misting" at various places on the earth's surface.

Given all of that evidence, along with the biblical indications that a different cosmological system was in effect prior to the Flood of Noah's day, it does not seem unwarranted to suggest that the "fountains of the great deep" were part of a vast underground reservoir system that the Creator had designed to water "the whole face of the ground." One might think of them as huge "cisterns" of water storage, hollowed out in the basement rock of the earth, pressurized by the enormous weight of the rock above, and vented by means of conduits to the surface, all controlled by the design and function of an omniscient Engineer.

Whatever they may have been then, some of their emptied remains give us a partial glimpse of their nature when we peek into the mysterious caverns left over from the great Flood.

Worldwide Explosion

In the six hundredth year of Noah's life, in the second month, the seventeenth day of the month, *on that day* all the *fountains of the great deep were broken up,* and the windows of heaven were opened. (Genesis 7:11)

The perception persists that the Flood took some time to develop (like our own experiences today). "Flash floods" are familiar episodes, but they are always localized and usually affect only a few low-lying sections of a countryside or city. What happened on the day God "opened" heaven and "broke up" the fountains of the deep may well be beyond our imagination to grasp.

Suddenly, as though a switch were thrown, "all" the fountains of the deep were blown. Perhaps there was a cascade of eruptions in a horrific sequence of explosions that circled the planet for hours. Possibly all of the "fountains" burst through the surface, all over the earth, all at one time. The language of Scripture does not demand either scenario, but what the text does demand is that the fountains of the deep were broken up "in the second month, the seventeenth day of the month"—all of them on the same day.

Picture in your mind the various local disasters the earth experiences today. Volcanoes, tornadoes, hurricanes, tsunamis, bomb explosions—any or all of these are a tiny fraction of the forces unleashed on the day that the "fountains of the great deep" burst open the surface of the earth. Not only are the sheer energies involved beyond our experience, but the suddenness and total disruption to a worldwide population is horrific beyond anything we currently know!

The human population of the pre-Flood earth would have been extensive. Every population model that can be conservatively evaluated indicates that the population at the time of the Flood would have been at least hundreds of millions, and more likely several billions of people. The cities would have been large and widespread. They would have been built around water sources (as has always been historically documented), and many would have been located close to transportation avenues (seas, inland lakes, rivers, commercial trade routes, etc.). The Bible confirms that all of this was part of that first world (Genesis 4).

There is absolutely no reason to view the pre-Flood peoples as knuckle-dragging, loincloth-wearing, barely sentient beings. Jesus made the observation that "they were eating and drinking, marrying and giving in marriage"—just as though everything was going on as it normally does today. Until "the day that Noah entered the ark," the whole world was functioning just as it always had for centuries. No one was aware of what was going to happen until "the flood came and took them all away" (Matthew 24:38-39).

Hydraulic and Tectonic Upheaval

With torrential rain smothering the atmosphere and soaking the ground, and sub-surface water bursting from its confines, the surface of earth would be quickly torn apart. The explosions from the "fountains of the great deep" would blow enormous rents in the continental plates, allowing magma from the earth's core to erupt. Molten rock gushing into water would generate scalding steam that would add its own energy to the roiling mixture of water and debris.

As the waters of the seas surged to fill the emptying chasms of the fountains of the deep, tsunamis would be generated that would crash against the coastlines, further eroding and dragging continental surface material back into the oceans. Strong rip currents and undertows would rapidly develop, and along with the crashing tsunamis would quickly extinguish any coastal settlement or city within a few hours.

As the Flood continued, the land surface was either being eroded away from the advancing and receding waters, or sucked down into the oceans or the gaping maws of the exploded fountains of the deep. There was nothing "tranquil" about this catastrophe.

Continental Displacement

There is a good bit of speculation about "continental drift"—the theory that all of the continents were joined together at some point in the past and "drifted" apart for eons until they reached the relatively stable positions that they currently occupy. Although there is evidence that at least portions of the continents are still moving, the directions of that drift are often opposing, and the rates are difficult to piece together into any unified way.

The various shapes of the continents do appear to have some relationship to a past configuration, but many of the "pieces" don't fit together as easily as, for instance, Africa and South America. Whatever may have happened in the past, there is no process going on today that could account for the vast energies necessary to "move" continents from one position to another. In fact, the calculated energies necessary to move (or make) a continental crust far exceeds the crushing force of the rock itself. In other words, whatever energies were involved in "moving" the continents would have first reduced the continents to powder before anything could be moved!

Could the biblical description of the Flood be right? Could a worldwide explosion of subterranean and pressurized reservoirs blow the continental land masses apart? Such an explosion would have certainly provided enough energy. The release of force on that massive scale would have surely destroyed the existing crustal plates, and may have thoroughly mixed the material into slurry that was later deposited as "new" continents.

The crust that covers the earth varies from some three to six miles thick on the ocean bottoms to an average of 18 to 30 miles thick on the land masses. That's a lot of dirt and rock to "drift" from one spot to another. Geological mapping has given scientists and engineers a pretty good picture of the structure of the earth's crust. Much of it is sedimentary rock, originally deposited as sediments by water flows. That rock, identified in "layers" on the earth's crust, has been solidified through pressure, heat, and various cementing agents. The igneous rock (granite, basalt, lava, etc.) appears to have been "spewed out" in huge batholiths from rents in the mantle, or "squeezed" into the softer sedimentary rock as dykes and sills running across or along the layers of sedimentary rock.

The enormity of these formations is the puzzle. Nothing that is happening today can account for the vast sedimentary layers or the huge plains of lavas and granites that are known to exist. The geologic and hydraulic events of today do not have enough energies (or material) to deposit the hundreds of feet-thick and hundreds of miles-long and wide sedimentary layers that make up the earth's crust. Nor do any of the modern tectonic forces that can be identified provide the necessary energies to explain what exists. Yes, there are theories and scenarios aplenty, but they are just that—theories! Making up a theory is relatively easy. Testing and verifying that theory is another matter altogether.

If the biblical record of the worldwide Flood is true, those events would provide both the energies and the activities necessary to destroy the existing topography of that day, and would have rearranged the planet surface so completely that "the world that then existed perished, being flooded with water" (2 Peter 3:6).

Forty Days of Rain

Since an event such as the global Flood has not been observed in modern times, there is a tendency to ignore the implications of the biblical record. If, however, that biblical record is true, then the continual rain onslaught of "forty days and forty nights" (Genesis 7:12) would have been catastrophic! Certain portions of the world experience months of rainy days—months where rain descends day after day. But those periods of daily rain are *not* continuous rain. There are strong storms that bring torrential rain that quickly exceeds the ability of the ground to absorb it. But those storms do *not* last for weeks. These unusual events cause havoc in the areas where they happen, but they do *not* cover the entire globe!

The rain of God's judgment recorded in Genesis would have *added* to the catastrophe of the worldwide explosions of the fountains of the deep. That rain would have further mixed the ground-up slurry from those explosions and would likely have provided the extra-fine debris around which the "waters above" would have coalesced into rain droplets. Catapulted into the atmosphere and stratosphere of the planet, the wreckage of the continents would have intensified the rain deluge and added the stinging impact of a "dirty" rain to the forces already released on the ground.

Waters Prevailing

The waters prevailed and greatly increased on the earth,

and the ark moved about on the surface of the waters. And the waters prevailed exceedingly on the earth, and all the high hills under the whole heaven were covered. (Genesis 7:18-19)

Twice in these verses an emphasis is made that the waters (both from the rain and from the fountains of the deep) "prevailed" on the earth. The translators of most Bible versions do a fairly good job recognizing the intensity of the references. The waters "greatly increased" and "prevailed exceedingly." However one wants to view this flood, it is obvious that the record itself insists that it was both global and deep.

The Ark was quickly launched onto the watery surface and "moved about" the earth. It is likely that the first day of the Flood was the most destructive, but as the water got deeper and deeper, with the rain pouring down and the sub-surface water continuing to gush from its source, the damage below would intensify as the counter-currents scraped and scoured, stirred and sorted the widely varied debris, marine life, and dead land animals that had been so horribly killed in the first few hours of God's judgment.

And the waters prevailed on the earth one hundred and fifty days. (Genesis 7:24)

This is an important part of the record. The depth of the Flood did not come primarily from the 40 days of rain (although that surely was a significant part), but from the constantly erupting "fountains of the great deep" that continued for an additional 110 days. This Flood—this awful obliteration of an entire world order—totally inundated the earth with a constant deluge of water that increased in depth for nearly five months! Nothing like that has happened before or since. This event was and is unique in all of world history.

The Length of the Flood

The precision with which the major events of the Flood are noted gives us assurance that the Flood was recorded by the participants themselves. Noah, his sons, and their wives were the only humans to come through the Flood alive, and it is their precise record that gives us the accurate duration of the Flood event.

Start of the Flood: 2nd month, 17th day; Noah was 600 years old (Genesis 7:6-11)	
Continuous rain from above (Genesis 7:12)	40
Continuous "prevailing" of the waters after the rain had stopped: 150 days minus the 40 days of rain (Genesis 7:24)	110
Waters "decreased continually" until the 10th month, 1st day: 2-plus months from 17th day of 7th month (Genesis 8:4-5)	74
Forty days before Noah sent out the raven (Genesis 8:6-7)	40
Dove sent out for the first time (Genesis 8:8)*	7
Dove sent out for the second time (Genesis 8:10)	7
Dove sent out the third time (Genesis 8:12)	7
Waters dried up: 1st month, 1st day; Noah was 601 years old (Genesis 8:13)	29
Noah removes the covering of the Ark and the end of the episode is recorded as the 27th day of the 2nd month (Genesis 8:14)	57
Total days elapsed	371

* The fact that the raven and dove were not sent at the same time is indicated by the phrase that it was "yet another seven days" before the dove was sent out for the second time.

The month and day calculations were made on the basis of a 30-day month, not a 365-day year. There are "hints" throughout the Bible that a year of 360 days was used in the various prophetic events. If the earth's sidereal year was actually 365 days, then the days between each event would have added as much as five extra days to the otherwise 371 days of the Flood.

Some have suggested that the planet formerly circled the sun in a regular orbit of 360 days, and that the axis of the earth was not tilted as it is now at about 23.5 degrees from perpendicular. There is no direct evidence either in current scientific data or the biblical record to verify such a change. If it was indeed the case, the only energies large enough to impact the rotational circuit of the earth around the sun and, perhaps, tilt the axis of the planet to its present position would have been the gigantic forces unleashed during the initial day of the Flood.

Biblical Flood Language

There has been a constant stream of criticism of the biblical account from those who insist that the Flood of Noah's day could not have been global. Science, they all say, has proven that the earth is billions of years old, and therefore such an event as "seems" to be described in Genesis could not have taken place. Such scholars (both scientists and theologians) would insist that the biblical record must be "interpreted" as a local event covering only the Mesopotamian River Valley, or some sort of "tranquil" event that rose and receded without leaving any geological damage behind.

It may be worth noting that everyone who holds to an ancient earth (ostensibly to accommodate evolutionary ideas) must and does espouse some form of a local flood. If the Flood of Noah's day took place as described in the Genesis record, then the so-called "ages" represented by the massive layers of sedimentary rock all over the earth would have been deposited during or shortly after that event.

The language used in Genesis leaves no doubt that the Flood in question was sudden, cataclysmic, and global in extent.

Sudden Onslaught of the Flood

- In the six hundredth year of Noah's life, in the second month, the seventeenth day of the month, on that day all the fountains of the great deep were broken up, and the windows of heaven were opened. (Genesis 7:11)

- On the very same day Noah and Noah's sons, Shem, Ham, and Japheth, and Noah's wife and the three wives of his sons with them, entered the ark. (Genesis 7:13)

- But as the days of Noah were, so also will the coming of the Son of Man be. For as in the days before the flood, they were eating and drinking, marrying and giving in marriage, until the day that Noah entered the ark, and did not know until the flood came and took them all away. (Matthew 24:37-39)

Death of All Air-breathing, Land-dwelling Life

- So the LORD said, "I will destroy man whom I have created from the face of the earth, both man and beast, creeping thing and birds of the air, for I am sorry that I have made them." (Genesis 6:7)

- "And behold, I Myself am bringing floodwaters on the earth, to destroy from under heaven all flesh in which is the breath of life; everything that is on the earth shall die." (Genesis 6:17)

- "For after seven more days I will cause it to rain on the earth forty days and forty nights, and I will destroy from the face of the earth all living things that I have made." (Genesis 7:4)

- All in whose nostrils was the breath of the spirit of life, all that was on the dry land, died. (Genesis 7:22)

Global Extent of the Flood

- Now the flood was on the earth forty days. The waters increased and lifted up the ark, and it rose high above the earth. (Genesis 7:17)

- The waters prevailed and increased greatly on the earth, and the ark moved about on the surface of the waters. (Genesis 7:18)

- And the waters prevailed exceedingly on the earth, and all the high hills under the whole heaven were covered. (Genesis 7:19)

- The waters prevailed fifteen cubits upward, and the mountains were covered. (Genesis 7:20)

- And the waters prevailed on the earth one hundred and fifty days. (Genesis 7:24)

Although this short chapter has covered much concerning the record of this great water judgment, several books have been written that more extensively examine the enormous geological and hydrological evidence for this planet-wide cataclysm. *The Genesis Flood*, written by my father, Dr. Henry M. Morris, and Dr. John C. Whitcomb, has been in continuous print since 1961. Recently, it was reprinted in a 50th anniversary edition. *Earth's Catastrophic Past: Geology, Creation & the Flood*, written by Dr. Andrew A. Snelling, is a two-volume set that covers the biblical information and offers a thorough technical analysis of the geological evidence. Dr. John D. Morris has just released a new book titled *The Global Flood: Unlocking Earth's Geologic History* that is both technically sound and eminently readable, with full-color pictures, charts, and graphs that provide a clear understanding of the vast evidence for this critical event in earth history.

The Flood of Noah's day is amply identified in Scripture. If it took place when and as described, it would have radically altered the earth's surface and, subsequently, would be vital to our understanding of the history of the planet. If the information and implications contained in the biblical record were studiously applied, current forensic geology and paleontology would be transformed from an understanding of earth's past based on slow-and-gradual processes suitable to an evolutionary model, to a catastrophic model involving sudden, cataclysmic change. This in turn would lead to a more accurate understanding that the majority of the vast sedimentary layers and fossil deposits seen in the geologic record were formed during the year of the Flood—with some residual geological and ecological trauma unfolding during the following centuries.

More details on the Flood's aftermath will be covered in a later chapter.

CHAPTER FOUR
THE NEW BEGINNING

And in the second month, on the twenty-seventh day of the month, the earth was dried. Then God spoke to Noah, saying, "Go out of the ark, you and your wife, and your sons and your sons' wives with you. Bring out with you every living thing of all flesh that is with you: birds and cattle and every creeping thing that creeps on the earth, so that they may abound on the earth, and be fruitful and multiply on the earth." (Genesis 8:14-17)

The enormity of the empty planet must have hit Noah and his family within moments after they disembarked. For a year they had been enclosed in the confines of the Ark, and had seen nothing but the animals and themselves. No doubt they had spent long hours remembering the world from which they had come, and had most likely discussed what and how they would survive for the remainder of their lives. Now the reality began to sink in.

The Genesis record identifies the area of the Ark's grounding as "the mountains of Ararat" (Genesis 8:4). Today, we would place that area in northeastern Turkey. There is a mountain there bearing that name, and tribesmen in the area still claim to be guardians of the Ark. Although there have been many searches for the remains of the Ark, no one has as yet found sufficient evidence to definitively identify its location. But whatever may have been the precise location of the grounding of the Ark, it is without question that Noah would have found the land empty and the prospects for survival a bit frightening.

The First Worship

As was discussed at some length in volume one of *The Book of Beginnings*, animal sacrifice was established by God Himself in the Garden that had been prepared for Adam and Eve "east of Eden." That initial sacrifice set the stage for a formal ceremony that appears to have continued throughout the centuries of the first world.

Surely this was the case at the time of Cain and Abel's recorded offerings to the Lord.

> And in the process of time it came to pass that Cain brought an offering of the fruit of the ground to the LORD. Abel also brought of the firstborn of his flock and of their fat. (Genesis 4:3-4)

The phrase "in the process of time" would be better translated "at the end of the days," indicating that the ceremony had been practiced regularly—probably as an annual memorial of the day that the Creator had provided covering for Adam and Eve. Later, after Seth's son Enosh was born, the line of Seth began to "call upon the name of the LORD" (Genesis 4:26), which implies a formalized practice of sacrifice, worship, and prayer. Noah and his family were direct descendants of the line of Seth (Genesis 5:6-32). They would have been aware of this practice, and would have followed the family commitment to the Creator.

It is clear from the records in Genesis that Noah lived during the same time period as all of the direct descendants of Seth (see the genealogical chart in chapter 1). The only exception was Enoch, who was taken directly into heaven when he was 365 years old. Family gatherings during those centuries would have insured that the family history and traditions were carefully preserved. Indeed, it is likely that Lamech, Noah's father, would have personally known Adam, since their lives overlapped by 56 years. Obviously, Noah would have known the spiritual relationship that his family had with the Creator, and would have been keenly conscious of his responsibility to worship the One who had made all things.

The Altar

After unloading the animals and some of the equipment from the Ark, Noah gave his attention to the formal worship that he had no doubt practiced with his father's family prior to the Flood. The phrase "to the LORD" is used over 600 times in the Old Testament, and always has the meaning of dedicating something or submitting oneself to the authority of God. (Contrast that practice with the later effort of Nimrod and his followers at Babel to build a tower "to heaven." That focus was not on the God of creation.)

When Noah "built an altar to the LORD" (Genesis 8:20), he must have either gathered stone from the area or used material from the Ark to erect a platform of some size, since the offerings included some larger animals. Later instructions given to Moses about the tabernacle and to David about the temple provided rather specific details about the size and function of the formal altar of sacrifice, so it is not without precedent that the altar that Noah built would have had some historical significance behind its construction.

The line of Seth contained major prophets and a "preacher of righteousness" like Noah (2 Peter 2:5). Abel and Enoch were both cited for their close personal walk with God. Is it any surprise, therefore, that Noah would have had a clear idea of what God's altar should look like? Since God had directly communicated with Noah about the building of the Ark, it was very likely that Noah had long practiced a sacrificial recognition of his submission to the Lord and need for atonement. Whatever may have been Noah's awareness of the construction details, he took the time, early in the new world, to honor the Lord with this altar.

The Animals

The sacrifice of "every clean animal and of every clean bird" was a major gift of resources to God. Although God had insisted that Noah bring "seven each of every clean animal...also seven each of birds of the air" into the Ark (Genesis 7:2-3), this offering would represent more than a tithe of the total means available to the entire family. This represented their livelihood and future security. They were alone. There was nothing else to draw from—except the promise that God had preserved them and the animals to "keep the species alive on the face of all the earth."

Moses was the inspired editor of the book of Genesis. Many centuries after the Flood, God met with Moses on Mount Sinai and gave him specific instructions for the nation of Israel. A good portion of those laws dealt with dietary restrictions, including descriptions of the "clean" animals God's people were permitted to eat (Leviticus 11). The instructions God gave to Noah in Genesis 7:2-3 appear to assume that Noah would know which animals were "clean." The details of the initial post-Flood sacrifice do not specify the kinds of animals Noah offered, but it is certain that the offering would have included the cattle (bulls, goats, lambs, etc.) and the fowl (doves, pigeons, etc.) that were the centerpieces of the sacrificial system of future Israel.

Again, this worship offering was an enormous sacrifice for Noah and his family. The "clean" animals would be the source for domesticated animals used in future agricultural work. And since God would now give humans permission to eat animal flesh, these animals would represent the major food and energy source in the new (and far more hostile) environment into which humanity was thrust. Sacrificing over 14 percent of their initial resources was a major declaration of trust.

The Attitude

Since God does not change (Malachi 3:6; Hebrews 13:8), it is clear that the physical act of sacrificing animals is not at the core of God's desire for human worship (Hebrews 10:5-6). These offerings were indeed the required practice for the nation of Israel—and evidently for the pre-Flood line of Seth, as well. However, as Samuel clearly announced to a disobedient King Saul, "to obey is better than sacrifice" (1 Samuel 15:22). God is always pleased with a heart attitude that joyfully follows His will (Mark 12:33)—even if it appears to cost us more than we would consider humanly prudent.

Noah had already proven himself to God through his lifelong behavior of righteousness. Please note the recognition given to Noah's character in several biblical references.

- Thus Noah did; according to all that God commanded him, so he did. (Genesis 6:22)

- Then the LORD said to Noah, "Come into the ark, you and all your household, because I have seen that you are righteous before Me in this generation." (Genesis 7:1)

- And Noah did according to all that the LORD commanded him. (Genesis 7:5)

- By faith Noah, being divinely warned of things not yet seen, moved with godly fear, prepared an ark for the saving of his household, by which he condemned the world and became heir of the righteousness which is according to faith. (Hebrews 11:7)

- Noah, one of eight people, a preacher of righteousness... (2 Peter 2:5)

Once the ordeal of the Flood was over, Noah responded in the way that he had always responded—he worshiped his Creator. Later, it would become clear that at least one of his sons had some serious reservations about worshiping God. But now, as the head and leader of his family, Noah built an altar and sacrificed from each of the clean animal kinds, as he had been taught to do. Everything was different now. The world they knew before the Flood was gone, and they faced a future filled with unknown challenges. Noah wanted to begin this new world with the proper recognition of the Creator and Judge.

God's New Promises

After Noah completed the sacrifices, God "smelled a soothing aroma" (Genesis 8:21). This should definitely not be taken in the sense that God loves the smell of roasting beef and mutton. The "soothing aroma" often spoken of in Scripture when sacrifices are made is the heart attitude and cry that brought the person to the altar in the first place. As the psalmist pleads, "Let my prayer be set before You as incense, The lifting up of my hands as the evening sacrifice" (Psalm 141:2). The "sacrifice of praise" is continually offered in the same manner—the "fruit of our lips" bringing our petitions and thanksgiving to our Lord (Hebrews 13:15). Even in the courts of heaven, the prayers of the saints are blended in an eternal "incense" before the throne (Revelation 8:4).

Right after accepting the worship and sacrifice of Noah and his family, God responded with a promise that would impact all His future dealings with mankind.

> Then the LORD said in His heart, "I will never again curse the ground for man's sake, although the imagination of man's heart is evil from his youth; nor will I again destroy every living thing as I have done. (Genesis 8:21)

No New Curse

Although the anger of God had been awful in the Garden when He cursed the very elements of creation (Genesis 3:17), the total destruction caused by the Flood moved God's "heart" to promise that He would never again pronounce such an awful sentence. Perhaps this was in sympathy with humanity for their long road ahead. Nonetheless, "the whole creation groans and labors with birth pangs together until now" (Romans 8:22).

It was suggested earlier that the curse of Genesis 3 was more vigorous prior to the Flood of Noah's day. The reader may remember that Noah's father chose his son's name because he anticipated that God would mitigate the curse in some way in Noah's lifetime (Genesis 5:29). But since we cannot access those days now, our only source of information is the current cosmos and the record of God's relationship with His creation given to us in His Word. That Word tells us that the curse is still in effect, even if God's mercy is temporarily retarding the impact of that judgment today. God's judgment, once rendered, remains.

No Utter Destruction of Life

There will one day be an absolute meltdown of the entire universe (2 Peter 3:10-13). Everything on earth will be destroyed and all life that remains will be terminated in that awful conflagration. At first glance, this might seem like a contradiction of God's statement in Genesis 8:21. How could God make the promise not to "destroy every living thing" at the time of Noah's sacrifice, and then later destroy everything just before He makes "a new heavens and a new earth"?

The answer to this seeming paradox lies in the other promises given throughout the New Testament that God will rescue His redeemed saints from the earth. God has promised to raise the justified dead and change the living saints "in the twinkling of an eye, at the last trumpet" (1 Corinthians 15:52). "Then sudden destruction comes" (1 Thessalonians 5:3), when God pours out His wrath on those who "did not receive the love of the truth, that they might be saved" (2 Thessalonians 2:10). Thus, our Creator harvests the earth with His angels before the horrible end of the planet, and fulfills both His extended mercy and grace, and His unwavering holiness by not killing all living things, having brought His redeemed to His side.

No Rapid End

The last part of God's declaration in Genesis 8:21-22 almost seems like an afterthought. Tagged on at the end of the other two promises, God makes another vow:

> "While the earth remains, Seedtime and harvest, Cold and heat, Winter and summer, And day and night Shall not cease." (Genesis 8:22)

The earth and its people have benefited from that promise for so many centuries that it almost seems irrelevant. However, set in juxtaposition with the horror of the First Age and the catastrophe of the Flood, this promise has stunning applications. No longer will the earth and its resident life spin rapidly downward into chaos and destruction, but they will be maintained with the supernatural intervention of the Creator Himself. No longer will there be the threat of agonizing resistance of the very "ground" itself, but the gracious Creator will stay His hand.

The New Testament has some significant testimony to the power of this promise. Speaking of the Lord Jesus, the apostle Paul makes a strong statement about the ongoing work of God through the supernatural intervention of the Lord Jesus.

> For by Him all things were created that are in heaven and that are on earth, visible and invisible, whether thrones or dominions or principalities or powers. All things were created through Him and for Him. And He is before all things, and in Him *all things consist*. (Colossians 1:16-17)

Here, it is clear that Jesus Christ is not only our Savior, but also "the" Creator of everything that exists. That same Creator-Jesus, incarnate in human flesh, offered Himself as the complete sacrifice in substitution for our sin, took our eternal punishment on Himself, and rose from the dead that we might have proof and assurance of the eternal sufficiency of His sacrifice. That same Creator-Jesus is now "holding things together."

Peter states it more succinctly.

> For this they willfully forget: that by the word of God the heavens were of old, and the earth standing out of water and in the water, by which the world that then existed perished, being flooded with water. But the heavens and the earth which *are now preserved by the same word,* are reserved for fire until the day of judgment and perdition of ungodly men. (2 Peter 3:5-7)

The word that spoke the heavens and earth into existence (Psalm 33:8-9; Psalm 148:1-5) is the same word that now keeps the "seedtime and harvest, cold and heat, winter and summer, and day and night" working in constant and preserved function. We may never know the full reason why the God of the Flood judgment was moved in His heart to "hold together" and "preserve" the earth for the past many centuries. But we can know the main reason—He is "not willing that any should perish but that all should come to repentance" (2 Peter 3:9).

Long before the world was created, the Triune Godhead determined that the Second Person of the Trinity would make "Himself of no reputation, taking the form of a bondservant, and coming in the likeness of men. And being found in appearance as a man, He humbled Himself and became obedient to the point of death, even the death of the cross" (Philippians 2:7-8). Having accomplished that work in eternity past (1 Peter 1:20; Revelation 13:8), our Creator-Savior who "loved the world" promised to "preserve" that world.

This is a profound assurance for those of us who have lived since Noah's time. But the impact of God's promise to "hold together" and "preserve" the functions of our planet also has an enormous effect on the studies and disciplines of science. The knowledge of how our world works depends on the stability of the processes of that world. Accumulation of that knowledge requires that the facts determined in previous research do not change. That "preservation" of the earth's functional processes is absolutely vital to the development of our world.

If any experiment is to be devised that can uncover how "things" work, a theorist must assume that the basic laws of physics, chemistry, biology, etc., will not change. An engineer or a medical doctor must then depend on the stability of the knowledge uncovered by the theorist if bridges are to be built and surgery is to be successful. All of science functions under these assumptions. No information could be depended on if the laws of physics were fluctuating or deteriorating so rapidly that the measurements of today would be worthless the following week.

When man seeks to understand his origins, he often takes the stable processes of today (which are indeed deteriorating very slowly) and extrapolates the rate of those decaying processes into the distant past to "find" their beginning point. But if those processes are "preserved" and supernaturally "held together" by the Creator, the extrapolated answer will be off by huge factors. If God did create the heavens and the earth and is now holding everything together for the merciful purposes of salvation, then the only way humanity will ever know the correct dates of our beginnings is by God's own revelation.

The Expanded Mandate

When the Creator brought Adam and Eve into existence in the magnificent Garden estate that He had especially made for them, He issued what biblical teachers have come to call the dominion mandate. Essentially, that command was the authorization for humanity to be the "managers" of the planet—to be "fruitful and multiply; fill the earth and subdue it; have dominion over the fish of the sea, over the birds of the air, and over every living thing that moves on the earth" (Genesis 1:28). This initial mandate is much more closely examined in chapter 7 of *The Book of Beginnings, Volume One*.

After the Flood, God repeated that instruction to Noah and his family. It can be assumed that they would have been familiar with the core of that responsibility from their forefathers, yet God's restatement of the mandate was a reminder to them that nothing had been abrogated even though the planet had undergone such horrible judgment. Humanity was still responsible to "be fruitful and multiply, and fill the earth" (Genesis 9:1). But there were some very important additions that must be clarified because of the demands of this new world.

Fear and Dread

And the fear of you and the dread of you shall be on every beast of the earth, on every bird of the air, on all that move on the earth, and on all the fish of the sea. They are given into your hand. (Genesis 9:2)

As the First Age drew to a close, the Lord's comment was that "the earth was filled with violence" and that "all flesh had corrupted their way on the earth" (Genesis 6:11-12). That surely was not the way God created the earth to be. Not only had God pronounced His creation "very good," but He designed all of the animals to feed only on plants. Much later, after the fall of man and the horrible Flood that destroyed the world, God promised a future time when "the wolf and the lamb shall feed together, The lion shall eat straw like the ox, And dust shall be the serpent's food. They shall not hurt nor destroy in all My holy mountain" (Isaiah 65:25).

The time between, however, would be marked by a "fear" and a "dread" of humanity on the part of the earth's animals. Although these two terms are closely related, they capture a broad spectrum of the "terror" and the "dismay" that creatures might feel when they come into contact with humans, especially in the context of hunting or slaughter. They now have an instinctive mistrust and an awareness that humans can cause them harm or death. The last decades of the First Age had turned the animals' natural tendency from "good" to "violent"—an aggressive behavior that was not part of their original character. Now, however, all of the animal kind would naturally be afraid of man.

Authorizing New Food

Every moving thing that lives shall be food for you. I have given you all things, even as the green herbs. (Genesis 9:3)

The animals now had very good reason to fear people. In the expanded mandate, God authorized humanity to use animal flesh for food. Perhaps this does not seem like such an important distinction, since humanity has been eating animal flesh for millennia. At the time of the giving of this permission, however, Noah and his family would not have expected this liberty—especially since God had given them instructions to care for the animals on the Ark. They had spent a year tending to these creatures, following God's orders to preserve animal life. Now they were being given permission to take that life at their own discretion.

It was not that killing animals was unknown to Noah. He had just accomplished that in his sacrificial worship. Noah surely knew that the Creator gave managerial authority to humanity on the sixth day of creation, and he had just heard the same instructions reiterated. However, *eating* animal flesh was a new idea, and it is unlikely that Noah would have immediately understood why God would offer such liberties to mankind.

Noah would no doubt have been unable to foresee the hostile environment he would face as the earth convulsed after the Flood. All he had known before was a stable environment designed to last forever. Yes, the curse would have made itself felt, and Noah would have known something of the awful anger of God because of the Flood. But it is unlikely that he could have understood the need for more rapid protein assimilation to provide the extra energies necessary for coping with the rigors of the new world. It is also unlikely that he or his family would have anticipated the radical shift in climate changes, shortened growing seasons, and the encroaching advances of the polar ice.

God, of course, knew all of this and made sure that humanity would feel no guilt as it became necessary to consume the flesh of animals that shared certain life qualities with humanity. Veggies were still to be eaten, since they were designed for basic food sustenance, but stronger and more efficient sources of energy had now become necessary.

Prohibiting Blood Foods

> But you shall not eat flesh with its life, that is, its blood.
> (Genesis 9:4)

The mystery of life stumps scientists. It obviously exists, but what exactly defines it? No one understands where it came from or how it got here—unless one believes the Bible. It is absolutely clear from

Scripture that "the life of the flesh is in the blood" (Leviticus 17:11), a fact that science and modern medicine have affirmed. This unique quality of living creatures is not disclosed in the record of the creation week. Now, however, God makes sure that Noah understands the priceless value of blood, as God demands that humanity avoid its consumption.

Much of the world today ignores that prohibition. Blood sausage, or black pudding, is common throughout Asia, Europe, Mexico, and South America. Blood pancakes are favorites in Scandinavia and the Baltic. Many soups, stews, and sauces use blood as part of the broth. Famous dishes like Peking and pressed duck include the animal's blood as part of the recipe. It is interesting to note that the only religions that forbid the use of animal blood in food are Christianity, Judaism, and Islam.

But God's prohibition is not "religious." The Creator designed blood to be the source for life. Blood is the major distinction between the plants that were designed as food and the living creatures. It is this vast difference that lies at the heart of God's ban on eating blood from any living thing. Later, when Moses was given the laws for Israel to follow, the command to Noah was repeated and codified into specific instructions.

> "Therefore I said to the children of Israel, 'No one among you shall eat blood, nor shall any stranger who dwells among you eat blood.' Whatever man of the children of Israel, or of the strangers who dwell among you, who hunts and catches any animal or bird that may be eaten, he shall pour out its blood and cover it with dust; for it is the life of all flesh. Its blood sustains its life. Therefore I said to the children of Israel, 'You shall not eat the blood of any flesh, for the life of all flesh is its blood. Whoever eats it shall be cut off.'" (Leviticus 17:12-14)

In a summary sermon to the nation of Israel toward the end of his life, Moses again reiterated the somber warning.

> Only be sure that you do not eat the blood, for the blood is the life; you may not eat the life with the meat. You shall not eat it; you shall pour it on the earth like water. You shall not eat it, that it may go well with you and your children after you, when you do what is right in the sight of the LORD. (Deuteronomy 12:23-25)

Demanding Capital Punishment

But as distinctive as the blood of animals is, the blood of humans is far more precious. Mankind alone bears the image of the Creator, and alone has been delegated the responsibility for the care of the planet. Individual men have been given authority over the lives of all things—except for the liberty of taking the life of another human. So serious is the killing of another person that God demanded the execution of any animal or human who would dare to do so.

> Surely for your lifeblood I will demand a reckoning; from the hand of every beast I will require it, and from the hand of man. From the hand of every man's brother I will require the life of man. Whoever sheds man's blood, By man his blood shall be shed; For in the image of God He made man. (Genesis 9:5-6)

There were to be no exceptions. When an individual man's life was taken, those in authority were to administer judgment. Whether beast or human, the one who killed a human being would forfeit his life.

Much has been written about this concept. Political debates over the millennia have been intense in many countries. If all that was available for our understanding were these few words in Genesis, it might be more difficult to grasp the reason for corporate authority to execute capital punishment. However, when the God of creation rescued the children of Israel from Egypt under the leadership of Moses, He made sure that His judgment concerning capital punishment was clearly expressed.

"He who strikes a man so that he dies shall surely be put

to death. However, if he did not lie in wait, but God delivered him into his hand, then I will appoint for you a place where he may flee. But if a man acts with premeditation against his neighbor, to kill him by treachery, you shall take him from My altar, that he may die." (Exodus 21:12-14)

"If an ox gores a man or a woman to death, then the ox shall surely be stoned, and its flesh shall not be eaten; but the owner of the ox shall be acquitted. But if the ox tended to thrust with its horn in times past, and it has been made known to his owner, and he has not kept it confined, so that it has killed a man or a woman, the ox shall be stoned and its owner also shall be put to death." (Exodus 21:28-29)

These and other crimes are dealt with in the Law given to Israel, which is recorded in the books of Exodus and Leviticus for any who would read them. Western countries have made a bad mistake by abrogating the need for severe punishment for serious crimes—even something as severe as capital punishment for those who take another life.

Some have suggested that the sixth of the Ten Commandments—"you shall not kill"—is at cross purposes with the instructions God gave to Noah, and that it may even demand a hypocritical violation by the other laws that require capital punishment. However, anyone who reads these laws knows that God is forbidding the *willful murder* by one person of another, not the just forfeiture of the murderer's life in punishment for the murder. And this stern demand for capital punishment has not been abrogated in the New Covenant era, as God makes perfectly clear in Romans 13.

For rulers are not a terror to good works, but to evil. Do you want to be unafraid of the authority? Do what is good, and you will have praise from the same. For he is God's minister to you for good. But if you do evil, be afraid; for he does not bear the sword in vain; for he is

God's minister, an avenger to execute wrath on him who practices evil. (Romans 13:3-4)

God has made this requirement clear in many places in His Word that deal with major cultures and diverse circumstances—the murder of another human being is to be punished by death. That punishment is to be carried out by corporate man in the form of civil authority. That authority is ordained by God to bear His "sword" for the punishment of evil. When that authority delays or abrogates its role to punish evildoers, society suffers.

Because the sentence against an evil work is not executed speedily, therefore the heart of the sons of men is fully set in them to do evil. (Ecclesiastes 8:11)

The Promise to Noah

There are several covenants made by God with individuals in Scripture. Some of them were personal with national implications. Some of them were broad with global implications. God's promise (or covenant) to Noah is far-reaching, even including the life of all animals on the earth.

Then God spoke to Noah and to his sons with him, saying: "And as for Me, behold, I establish My covenant with you and with your descendants after you, and with every living creature that is with you: the birds, the cattle, and every beast of the earth with you, of all that go out of the ark, every beast of the earth. Thus I establish My covenant with you: Never again shall all flesh be cut off by the waters of the flood; never again shall there be a flood to destroy the earth." (Genesis 9:8-11)

No Worldwide Flood Again

The words "never again" are used twice! It would seem impossible to interpret this passage in any other way than that God is making this most solemn of promises to never again destroy the earth by water. Please note the intensity of the words. God promises to Noah and his descendants, along with "every living creature" that came with Noah on the Ark, that He, the God of creation and of judgment, is establishing a covenant. That covenant, given by the personal word of the thrice-holy God, could not contain a hint of untruth or confusion (Titus 1:2). There would *never again* be a flood of waters that would destroy the earth.

That seems simple enough. Yet some would insist that the Flood during the days of Noah was a local or regional flood—a flood that only impacted the "known" world of the Mesopotamian River Valley. Those who espouse such teachings are usually strong supporters of an "old" universe that allows for long ages for natural evolution to take place. Such scholars and some theologians embrace the idea that God used evolutionary processes of natural development to "create" by evolution. Others would suggest that God used His omnipotence and omniscience to direct certain events or control natural processes in such a way that His design was ultimately carried out "naturally" over long eons.

All of these variations on the theme of naturalistic evolution must do two things to make their teachings sound plausible. First, they must interpret the language of Scripture in such a way that a "day" of the creation week is understood as an age of indeterminate length, and they must also manipulate the text describing the Flood to try to make it fit some form of local or regional event. Secondly, such teachers must take the observable data that support a recent creation and a global flood and work them to match the dogmas of evolutionary science.

When it comes to this particular promise by God that He would "never again" bring a flood as was done in Noah's day, these local flood proponents must totally ignore the words of God and either make Him out to be a liar hundreds and thousands of times over, or such an ignorant and powerless God that He could not fulfill His promise. In either case, those who propose such teachings come dangerously close to blasphemy.

Tweaking the biblical account to accommodate evolutionary dogma is not some form of "blended" theology. Denying the precise words of Scripture in order to appease or embrace the so-called science of evolutionary ages is not godly. The language contained in the account of the worldwide Flood recorded in Genesis is not vague or unclear. There really is no excuse for reading those chapters and then insisting that the Flood spoken of is only "local" or "regional"—or, even more preposterous, a "tranquil" flood.

May God have mercy on those who teach "as doctrines the commandments of men" (Matthew 15:9) and embrace the atheistic philosophies "of what is falsely called knowledge" (1 Timothy 6:20). Once someone has decided that the teachings of men can override the words of Scripture, there is nothing that would inhibit them from disregarding the biblical doctrines of "resurrection" or "salvation" or "hell"—or anything else.

> Every word of God is pure; He is a shield to those who put their trust in Him. Do not add to His words, Lest He rebuke you, and you be found a liar. (Proverbs 30:5-6)

The Rainbow in the Cloud

In fact, this promise of God to never again destroy the world with water was so important that He caused a rainbow to appear in the clouds after a rain to remind *God Himself* of the promise made to Noah, his descendants, and to the animals of the earth.

> And God said: "This is the sign of the covenant which I make between Me and you, and every living creature that is with you, for perpetual generations: I set My rainbow in the cloud, and it shall be for the sign of the covenant between Me and the earth. It shall be, when I bring a cloud over the earth, that the rainbow shall be seen in the cloud; and I will remember My covenant which is between Me and you and every living creature of all flesh; the waters shall never again become a flood to destroy all flesh. The rainbow shall be in the cloud, and I will look

on it to remember the everlasting covenant between God and every living creature of all flesh that is on the earth."

And God said to Noah, "This is the sign of the covenant which I have established between Me and all flesh that is on the earth." (Genesis 9:12-17)

Although we can enjoy the beauty of the marvelous refraction of light that is filtered through the moisture in the clouds and the surrounding atmosphere, the rainbow is not for our benefit—it is to remind the Creator of the promise that He made to Noah and the life on the earth. We can see some of those that appear nearby, but the rainbow coalesces all over the planet, whether or not any people or animals are there to see it. No doubt, that wonderful, beautiful "sign" is appearing every day of every year in a constant "reminder" of this gracious covenant. God will "never again" judge the entire world by a life-destroying flood.

But there is also this: Around the throne of God in the heavens is a "rainbow" (Revelation 4:2-3; Ezekiel 1:28). Perhaps that rainbow is there to mimic the rainbow that God set in the clouds, but more likely the rainbow in the clouds is patterned after the rainbow that is around the throne. It is also likely that the rainbow tells us something about the nature of God.

What could that be? It is clear that God intends for us to "clearly see" something of His power and divine nature by the things that He has made (Romans 1:20). No doubt the heavens "declare" and provide "knowledge" through which we are able to sense something of God's "glory" (Psalm 19:1-3). Even the earth itself "speaks" and the animals "tell" us of the marvelous care of our Creator for what He has made (Job 12:7-8). When God answered Job's agonizing questions, He posed rhetorical demands about the observable function of the stars, the sunrise, the winds, and the wild animals. Surely there is something about the rainbow that can give us insight and encouragement beyond mere assurance that there will never be another global flood.

Perhaps it is this—God uses the rainbow to remind Himself of His faithful promises. May we not be encouraged by the same understanding?

- O Lord, You are my God. I will exalt You, I will praise Your name, For You have done wonderful things; Your counsels of old are faithfulness and truth. (Isaiah 25:1)

- If we are faithless, He remains faithful; He cannot deny Himself. (2 Timothy 2:13)

- For what if some did not believe? Will their unbelief make the faithfulness of God without effect? (Romans 3:3)

- He who calls you is faithful, who also will do it. (1 Thessalonians 5:24)

- But the Lord is faithful, who will establish you and guard you from the evil one. (2 Thessalonians 3:3)

God will remember His promise to us when He sees the rainbow. Each of us would do well to remember His faithfulness each time we see one.

The Fundamental Warrant for Humanity

The core of the delegation of God's authority as Creator-Owner to those who bear His image is stewardship. Humanity is to manage the creation for the glory of the One who owns it. And with the responsibility of management comes great liberty to exercise that authority.

The "job description" given to Adam and Eve in the Garden and again to Noah and his children after the Flood was not very detailed. A comparison could be made between those who are first entering the workforce and those who have wide spheres of responsibility. The young entry-level employee has a very detailed description of his or her tasks, since they must be directed carefully. The seasoned manager may well only be governed by the bylaws of the company and its board of directors.

So it is with the dominion mandate. It is given as a fundamental warrant for all disciplines that are required for the efficient function of the planet. Humanity is given "dominion" and is requested to "subdue," while "multiplying" and "filling" the earth. These are broad responsibilities indeed!

Perhaps these orders can be understood more easily by looking at them through the lens of modern terminology.

Science

Science uncovers *how* things work. Theoretical science and the scientists who are trained to research are required to obey the "subdue" (bring under control) part of the mandate. That is, scientists are granted the particular intellectual curiosity and tenacity to carefully observe, test, and codify the processes of earth so that the rest of humanity may be empowered to fulfill their roles.

Scientists usually don't care much what is done with their knowledge as long as they are given liberty to continue their research. They are driven by an insatiable desire to find out how things work. Sometimes their questions are driven by *why* something works a certain way, but at the bottom line scientists love to find the secrets of the earth.

Technology

Those who are driven to *make* things that are useful are drawn into careers like engineers, contractors, inventors, and medical practitioners. These folks are required to obey the *rule* side of the mandate. That is, they have the talents and seek the skills that would take the information uncovered by the scientists and apply it to develop new devices that would aid humanity in having *dominion* over the earth.

Without the science, the engineers would not understand how to build safe bridges. Without the knowledge of biological functions, doctors would not know how to treat illness or surgically correct serious malfunctions. But without the engineers, doctors, contractors, and inventors, the science would be little more than interesting tidbits in academic environments, having little impact on the world.

Commerce

This field involves the people who have business instincts and skills. They take the useful things that are developed by the engineers and inventors and distribute them to everyone. Business is responsible to obey the "fill the earth" mandate. Without the distribution and logistical systems of the business world, very little would be accomplished. The "multiplying" required does not just apply to increasing the population, but also (if not primarily) to building and distributing (not redistributing) the wealth of the population so that all may live better.

Thus, the world of manufacturing, banking, wholesale, retail, and a host of supply and information systems would be included in this part of the dominion mandate. Without these processes and the people with the inclination and skills to implement them, the world would be throttled. After science finds how things function and technology experts apply the information by inventing ways to use that data, business (commerce) must distribute the resulting devices to the world.

Education

And of course, once information has been developed, a system of transmitting that information must be maintained or the information dies. Education is responsible to teach the various specialties (science, technology, commerce) to everyone. The bigger the population, the more demand there will be for this transmission process. The more complex that science, technology, and commerce become, the more difficult and challenging the education.

In the broadest sense, teachers obey the commandment of the Lord Jesus when He required His disciples to "observe all things that I have commanded you" (Matthew 28:20). Jesus is the Creator. He is the one who spoke the words to Adam and Eve in the Garden and re-iterated them to Noah centuries later. It should be no surprise that the gift of "teaching" is addressed in the New Testament more than any other gift. Without the accurate transmission of truth (all truth belongs to God), the world would quickly fall into disrepair and chaos.

Humanities

Of all the requirements for human stewardship, this is the most subjective and demanding. Assumed in the creation week instructions, but amplified many times throughout the rest of Scripture, the chief end of man is to glorify the Creator with praise and beauty. This involves the disciplines of the arts. Music and drama were widely used by the Lord during the exercise of worship in the Old Testament. Craftsmanship skills were granted to many and praised by God Himself as the tabernacle and the temple were built. How barren indeed would worship be without the arts!

Once again, this is not directly stated in the initial mandate, but it is widely applied and commanded in the rest of Scripture. This sweeping responsibility is summarized by the apostle Paul: "Therefore, whether you eat or drink, or whatever you do, do all to the glory of God (1 Corinthians 10:31).

Government

After the Flood, God granted the authority to corporate humanity to take human life in certain circumstances. This authority grows as the population of earth grows. Implied in this authority over human life is the authority to protect human life. Thus, while the government (corporate man) has the authority of capital punishment, it also has the responsibility to organize and legislate structures that protect against and prevent evil.

The first major ruler identified in Scripture after the Flood is Nimrod. He is an evil man, and God intervenes to prevent his political influence from bringing the wrath of God down on humanity—again! As the Scripture unfolds, good and bad kings are recorded with their associated influences on society. "Wars and rumors of wars" (Mark 13:7) are the normative problem of a sin-cursed society, and governments are not to be "a terror to good works, but to evil" (Romans 13:3). Political skills and responsibilities are required by the Lord, and we are all told to "submit yourselves to every ordinance of man for the Lord's sake, whether to the king as supreme, or to governors, as to those who are sent by him for the punishment of evildoers and for the praise of those who do good. For this is the will of God" (1 Peter 2:13-15).

Responsibility in the New World

From the Creator's perspective, He is keeping the current world stable, "not willing that any should perish but that all should come to repentance" (2 Peter 3:9). Humanity is still under the sweeping commands of the Genesis mandate, and all mankind *should* be operating as a manager on behalf of the Owner.

Obviously, the majority of the population is not thinking like a steward of someone else's property, but are instead striving to "gain the whole world" for themselves (Matthew 16:26). Tragically, even the Christian family is throttled by "the cares of this world, the deceitfulness of riches, and the desires for other things [that] choke the word, and it becomes unfruitful" (Mark 4:19). Such behavior, of course, is not what our Lord intended. His plan was "that they may have life, and that they may have it more abundantly" (John 10:10). Every legitimate job is sanctioned by the great fundamental warrant granted to humanity by the Creator. Submission to God's authority brings both peace and prosperity to a nation. Disobedience only brings frustration and emptiness.

Unfortunately, even though the grace and mercy of God gave humanity another opportunity to excel, their early efforts were not encouraging.

CHAPTER FIVE
THE SONS OF NOAH

The early chapters of Genesis are very selective. God has chosen a few major foundational elements that give us a structure upon which to build and to relate the subsequent books of the Bible. In the first nine chapters out of the 50 that Genesis contains, some 17 or 18 centuries are covered. Not much information is provided for such a long period of history. Evidently, the incidents covered are important.

After providing a significant amount of detail on the year of the Flood, God has Moses record a series of cameos in the life of Noah, and a rather lengthy table of the descendants of the sons of Noah, interspersed with short bursts of insight about Nimrod and the confusion of languages at Babel. Noah lived another 350 years after the Flood. Why were these specific instances in his life chosen? Why give such a detailed record of the lines of Shem, Ham, and Japheth? What is the significance of Nimrod? What are the implications for the Tower of Babel and the confounding of human language? The answers are important.

The Gene Pool

Now the sons of Noah who went out of the ark were Shem, Ham, and Japheth. And Ham was the father of Canaan. These three were the sons of Noah, and from these the whole earth was populated. (Genesis 9:18-19)

The little one-liner in Genesis 9:19 regarding the earth's post-Flood population has enormous implications for modern science. According to the Bible, all of today's human population has descended from the three sons of Noah and their wives. There are approximately 7 billion people alive today with many variations within some 200 nations, and over 6,000 languages and dialects that parse the recognized nations into much smaller functional tribes with their own social structures and practices.

How did all that come about from three families less than 5,000 years ago?

Evolutionary thinking rejects this out of hand, of course, insisting that modern man is much older than a few thousand years and more likely developed from the early hominids over two million years in the past. Obviously, the two teachings cannot both be right. One or the other is simply wrong.

Reproductive Basics

Every birth of a human child represents a recombination of the information stored within the chromosome banks of the parents' DNA. Humans have 46 chromosomes. There are approximately 20,000 genes in the human DNA, which is made up of some 3 billion base pairs. The total number of base pairs is called a genome. As a new human zygote is formed at conception, the information stored in 23 chromosomes from each parent is transmitted to the new person. This person now has a complete set of chromosomes, but the information in the DNA that will provide the instructions to make that new person is unique, since the recombination of the base pairs is always unique.

It would be reasonable to assume that the DNA of the first human couple, Adam and Eve, had the ability to diversify. Each of their children, however, would have some subset of that information recombining within the new child, diversifying the total genetic potential across the population. As the population grew, the gene pool would become more widely distributed. By the time Noah was born, his DNA would have contained a unique combination of the line of Seth. Although each of us have some of Adam's and Eve's characteristics in us, our most direct genetic lineage is from the six data sets of the three sons of Noah and their wives.

Genetic Diversity

Obviously, each new human person will have very similar DNA sequences (the sequence of the base pairs that make up the genome) because all humanity shares the same physiological design (two arms, two legs, etc.). However, with each birth the recombination of the information presents itself in a diversity of characteristics as well. Some are born with information that expresses itself with a longer torso. Facial features vary, with oval, heart, and rectangular facial shapes. Skin tones are darker or lighter depending on the amount of melanin present. Eyes and hair come in a variety of shades. Those differences are brought about genetically by a change in the "spelling" of the chemical information within the DNA. The changes occur through the recombination process or by mutations.

As each birth of a new person takes place, the unique combination of information produces a trail of genetic diversity. That is, the positions of the base pairs (AT–CG) shift (AT–GC) into measurable changes that can be tracked. For instance, the G chemical (guanine) would appear in one position with the C chemical (cytosine) in one family, but switch places in another family—even though there might be thousands of bases up or down the rest of the genetic information stream that are exactly the same.

Not long ago, a core of highly qualified secular geneticists analyzed the placement of four DNA chemical bases within thousands of genes in over 2,000 people, looking for the differences in the genes that code for proteins. Those genes have the most reliable record of past DNA changes. The results were quite startling for the researchers. They were expecting a long history of diversity (hundreds of thousands of years), but instead found that the maximum possible time for the present genetic diversity to develop in the human gene pool could not exceed 5,115 years.[1]

That timeline fits the biblical information very well, but is an enormous difficulty for those who believe that modern humans have been on earth approximately 200,000 years. If that were so, the plotted curve of the diversity would be rather linear (slow and gradual over time). Instead, the plot takes a sharp curve upward at around 5,100 years ago and skyrockets upward. Essentially, that confirms what one would expect to find if the population now in existence came from a very small group of people not very long ago.

World Population

World population at the time of this writing is slightly over 7 billion people. Many would argue that this huge number could not have developed since the time of the biblical Flood recorded in Genesis. Even the biblical date of the Flood is difficult to ascertain. If one simply adds up the years identified from event to event, the date for the arrival of Noah and his family in the new world would have been approximately 2350 B.C. Some have suggested that the known gaps in the genealogies (a grandson listed instead of a son) could add another 1,000 years or so. Perhaps, but there is certainly no possibility of 200,000 years—let alone the two-plus million years ago that early man is supposed to have evolved on our planet.

Growth Rates

Back in the mid-1900s, the world population growth rate was a bit more than 2 percent per year. That rapid growth set off alarm bells in the academic and political spheres, since it was thought that such a rate would result in standing-room-only on the earth's surface in little more than a century. Many conferences and think-tank efforts were spent to determine how to reduce population growth. In fact, the very formula that was employed to reach these alarming conclusions indi-

---

1. Jacob A. Tennessen et al, 2012, Evolution and Functional Impact of Rare Coding Variation from Deep Sequencing of Human Exomes, *Science*, 337 (6090): 64-69.

cated that the then-population of around 3.5 billion would have been reached in a little less than 1,100 years, starting with just two people!

It is certainly obvious that the population growth rate would have had to be less than 2 percent per year over time. By the end of the first decade in the 21st century, the worldwide population growth rate had come down to approximately 1.1 percent. But even that slower rate was much too fast to apply to population estimates going forward, so the political authorities of several countries, notably China, tried their best to limit the reproductive rates to less than replacement levels (such as dictating one child per family).

Six People

The obvious implication of these current statistics is that the human population cannot be very old. If we employ the same formula that statisticians used to alarm the world about a "population explosion" to calculate how long it would take the present world population to arise from just three child-bearing couples (Noah's three sons and their wives), the results would indicate that a population growth of somewhat less than 1/3 percent is all that would be necessary to reach 7 billion in about 4,000 years.

All the known data confirm the biblical record. The genetic diversity studies insist that the human population did not start to diversity before 5,100 years ago. The population models all indicate that the current worldwide population would have been reached within the 5,000 years of recorded history—even starting with two people instead of six. Conversely, if *Homo sapiens* has been actively populating this planet for some 200,000 years, the current population would far exceed all the available space on earth—including the oceans!

And of course, that is precisely what the Bible demonstrates. "Now the sons of Noah who went out of the ark were Shem, Ham, and Japheth....These three were the sons of Noah, and from these the whole earth was populated" (Genesis 9:18-19).

Noah's Fall

> And Noah began to be a farmer, and he planted a vine-yard. Then he drank of the wine and was drunk, and became uncovered in his tent. (Genesis 9:20-21)

It should be observed that the lapse of Noah can be compared to the fall of Adam. Both men were commanded to fill the earth and exercise managerial authority over it. Both men were the federal head of the human race of their world. Both men fell into sin through involvement with a fruit. Both men were naked and needed someone else to cover them. Small decisions can lead to terrible consequences.

It can take from two to three years for a grapevine to mature and produce grapes suitable for making wine. Even though Noah had been instructed to take "of all food that is eaten" on board the Ark, it is likely that there were several years of basic survival preparation before a "luxury" food was planted and harvested. Whatever the time involved, this incident took place after the family had been settled on the lower slopes of "the mountains of Ararat" for some time.

Noah's Drunkenness

No doubt Noah had dealt with the awful consequences of drunken debauchery during the several hundred years of his life before the Flood. The world of the First Age was exceedingly sinful, and no doubt Noah and his family had been vexed and impacted by that horrible environment. Perhaps, with the pressure and tension of the year on board the Ark and the early years of setting up a new home now abated somewhat, Noah let down his guard to enjoy a few hours of relaxation with "wine that makes glad the heart of man" (Psalm 104:15).

But the great Enemy never sleeps, and "the devil walks about like a roaring lion, seeking whom he may devour" (1 Peter 5:8). Noah still had the sin nature inherited from Adam, and was as susceptible to fall as any other man—even in spite of holding steadfast for so long in the face of a terrible society. Whatever may have been the circumstances or the mental state that caused Noah to lapse, the Scripture simply notes that he "was drunk, and became uncovered in his tent." If nothing else, this should serve as a warning to every believer. Even the most spiritually sincere can fall into sin in an unguarded moment.

As the wine began to take control, Noah became more and more insensitive to his condition. The stimulant of the fermentation increases the heart rate and blood pressure, making the drinker feel hot and flushed. Emotions begin to swing from happy to near depression. Motor coordination begins to fail, and normal inhibitions and character safeguards slip away. Sooner or later, the mind starts to lose concentration and may black out for short periods. Ultimately, the alcohol overcomes the system and a comatose condition ensues.

Sometime in the later stages of his drunkenness, Noah took off his clothing—probably in an effort to feel some relief from the growing heat in his body. He may have reasoned that he was in his own tent, and no one would normally disturb him without first asking permission. Should he be interrupted, he would surely be able to grab his robe and regain his dignity. With his reason and inhibitions failing him, Noah essentially drank himself into unconsciousness and lay down or fell down naked, foolishly and shamefully exposed.

Noah's Sons

> And Ham, the father of Canaan, saw the nakedness of his father, and told his two brothers outside. But Shem and Japheth took a garment, laid it on both their shoulders, and went backward and covered the nakedness of their father. Their faces were turned away, and they did not see their father's nakedness. (Genesis 9:22-23)

No doubt all of Noah's sons would have had a relationship with God. There is no indication up until this moment that Ham was rebellious or discordant within the family. However, there must have been lurking some form of envy or jealous distance between Ham and Noah, for when he chanced to enter Noah's tent and saw him naked, Ham reacted badly.

Some have suggested that Ham "did" something personal to Noah based on the comment in Genesis 9:24 that Noah woke up and "knew what his younger son had done to him." There is no implication in that short verse of any overt erotic activity, however, and commentators of the past who have suggested that possibility have usually done so to justify their blatant prejudice against blacks. This will be discussed in more detail shortly.

What did take place, however, was at least a voyeuristic titillation upon seeing his father so helplessly exposed. No doubt, Ham felt a flush of self-righteous satisfaction at seeing this "preacher of righteousness" so pathetically sprawled in nakedness. And, rather than feeling embarrassed for his father and doing whatever he could to prevent others from seeing Noah like that, Ham quickly told his two brothers—evidently thinking that they would join him in mocking their father.

Shem and Japheth, however, reacted very differently. Rather than smirking or assuming a false sense of superiority over their father, their immediate response was to cover him and prevent any further embarrassment. Taking as much precaution as possible to avoid inadvertently seeing their father in that state, they spread a garment of some sort across their shoulders (probably the same robe that Noah had discarded) and shuffled backward together until they could lay it over Noah, an action that demonstrated Peter's later injunction to "above all things have fervent love for one another, for 'love will cover a multitude of sins'" (1 Peter 4:8).

Noah's Prophecy

> So Noah awoke from his wine, and knew what his younger son had done to him. Then he said: "Cursed be Canaan; A servant of servants He shall be to his brethren."
>
> And he said: "Blessed be the Lord, The God of Shem, And may Canaan be his servant. May God enlarge Japheth, And may he dwell in the tents of Shem; And may Canaan be his servant." (Genesis 9:24-27)

As Noah regained his composure and the full character of his sons was revealed to him, the future of their descendants became clear in his mind. Noah had had ample time to observe his sons under the pressure of building the Ark and living so closely with them during the year on board. All that Noah had sensed during those times, as well as having watched them develop further in the new world, co-alesced in a moment of prophetic declaration. No doubt the Holy Spirit was guiding Noah as he spoke, since "God, who made the world and everything in it....has made from one blood every nation of men to dwell on all the face of the earth, and has determined their preappointed times and the boundaries of their dwellings" (Acts 17:24, 26).

The Curse on Canaan

> Then he said: "Cursed be Canaan; A servant of servants
> He shall be to his brethren." (Genesis 9:25)

This short sentence has been the source for a long-standing prejudice against the descendants of Ham, with blacks receiving the bulk of the denigration. It was used to justify slavery for centuries in Europe and America, and is often referred to as "the Curse of Ham" since Ham was the disrespectful son. Some have also suggested that the name Ham means "dusky" or "dark," thereby implying that those who have darker skins are to be considered inferior and are condemned to be slaves for the rest of humanity. Neither of those ideas is correct.

To begin with, the name Ham has an uncertain derivation. The Hebrew *cham* is also translated "hot" or "warm," but never as "dark" or "dusky." The future nations that would descend from Ham have mixed skin tones from dark to light, as do various Jewish and Arabic groups that are descended from Shem. While it is certain that the genetic ability to develop different skin tone expressions was present in all of Noah's sons, the outward physical appearance of these men was not the reason for the Noahic prophetic declaration.

It is not clear in the context why Noah spoke of his grandson Canaan and not Ham. Perhaps, since the sovereign foreknowledge of the Lord would have known of the trouble that the future Canaanites would cause the nation of Israel, the Holy Spirit inspired Noah to mention Canaan's name. Perhaps Noah could not bring himself to name his son in the only harsh part of the prophecy. But whatever may have been the reason, the curse does not just apply to Canaan or his direct descendants.

Noah's three declarations concerning his sons were obviously meant to be symmetrical and worldwide, covering all of the coming populations of the new world. Indeed, if the curse were only to apply to the direct descendants of Canaan, then it was only partially and selectively fulfilled. Several of the Canaanite nations (the Phoenicians and Hittites, for instance) were large and successful realms that dominated the growing world population for a long time. And of course, since it was Ham and not Canaan who committed the sin that precipitated the pronouncement in the first place, it would have been bizarre if Noah had singled out only one of Ham's sons for the object of his judgment.

Servant of Servants

The phrase "a servant of servants" is, of course, the core of the burden laid on the descendants of Ham. Although the term for "servant" appears many times in the Old Testament, this is the only time the unusual superlative "servant of servants" appears. Those who have favored justifying slavery have insisted that the phrase should mean "slave of slaves." There is absolutely no linguistic justification for that, nor is there any such fulfillment in history among any of Ham's four sons. The Sumerians, the Egyptians, and the Ethiopians, as well as the Canaanites, were great nations of antiquity who, if anything, enslaved others rather than becoming slaves themselves.

Later, as European nations began to expand, some industrialists and theologians propagated the idea that the Negro peoples were the main group that came under the "curse." Added to those voices was the idea that the black tribes were primary examples of subhuman "races," an evolutionary concept used by Charles Darwin, Thomas Huxley, and Ernst Haeckel, among others, to rationalize their view of white supremacy. This was never the teaching of Scripture. "Have we not all one Father? Has not one God created us?" (Malachi 2:10). "He has made from one blood every nation of men to dwell on all the face of the earth" (Acts 17:26).

If, then, the phrase did not apply just to Canaan's descendants, how should this unusual prophecy be understood? Both Shem and Japheth were to be served by Ham's descendants. Does that mean the coming Semitic and Japhetic nations would enslave Egypt and Phoenicia? If anything, the reverse was the case among ancient peoples. If not physical slavery, then, what does "servant of servants" mean?

Stewards for Mankind

More often than not, the word "servant" is not used in the sense of "slave" in the Scriptures, but rather as a "steward" or "manager" on behalf of someone else. The classic examples would be Joseph and Daniel, both of whom became the political leaders of world powers, but saw themselves as the "servants" of their respective kings (Genesis 41:40; Daniel 1:12-15). And the fullest extent is demonstrated by the Lord Jesus Christ Himself, who became a "servant" so that He might sacrifice Himself on behalf of all humanity (Philippians 2:6-8). Great men of faith in both eras of the Bible saw themselves as servants of God. The idea that Noah is condemning the descendants of one of his sons to base slavery is not warranted in this passage.

The immediate purpose of the prediction is obvious. The lineage of Ham would serve the future nations that would come from Shem and Japheth. Their "service" would be to assist the nations of the world to fulfill the great mandate given to all of humanity by God in the Garden to Adam and Eve and repeated to Noah's family as they came off the Ark. That vast responsibility would have still been fresh in all of their minds, and the role that each of them was to play in the future would no doubt have been the subject of many a family gathering. Hearing their father declare what he sensed God intended for them to do would have been understood as an immediate and obvious application.

Needs of World Stewardship

If the descendants of Ham were to serve the other nations, how best might it be recognized in the history that was later recorded? A quick review of the dominion mandate might help. Essentially, man would have to develop and utilize the "ground" to sustain life—a predominantly physical pursuit. Man was also responsible to exercise "dominion" over the earth and all animal life, which would demand an understanding of those spheres—a predominantly intellectual pursuit. Finally, man was to serve the Creator and "fill the earth" not only with descendants, but ultimately "with the knowledge of the LORD" (Isaiah 11:9)—a predominantly spiritual pursuit.

It is no coincidence that these responsibilities correspond to the tri-partite nature of man. The "spirit, soul, and body" will one day be restored to the holy perfection that God has designed for His twice-born (1 Thessalonians 5:23). And although each person has all the properties of human nature, one characteristic usually dominates that is then transferred by genetic recombination and modeled by parental influence to future generations. It should be no surprise, then, to find that these generalizations would be noted historically among the nations of the world. That is, some would be recognized by physical considerations, others by intellectual excellence, and still others by religious zeal.

Shem's Blessing

> And he said: "Blessed be the LORD, The God of Shem,
> And may Canaan be his servant." (Genesis 9:26)

If all we had from the Scriptures was this short declaration, it might be difficult to understand why Noah singled out Shem to receive the blessing "of Jehovah, the God of Shem." Later, of course, it becomes clear that the Messianic line would be through the descendants of Shem. The records of Genesis 10 and 11 give us the genealogical details through Abraham, then the rest of the Old Testament verifies the magnificent line of Isaac, Jacob, Judah, and David, and the records of the New Testament confirm the careful attention of the

Creator to the One "slain from the foundation of the world" (Revelation 13:8).

Even at this early stage in the new world, Noah would have recognized Shem's interest in spiritual issues, and no doubt saw in Shem a love for Jehovah, the Creator and Lord of Adam, Seth, Enoch, Methuselah, and others of his famous forebears, including his own father. Now, in stark contrast to the physical dominance of the character of Ham, Noah was moved to pronounce that Shem would inherit God's blessing and, as a result, lead the nations toward the Creator's love and bounty.

It must be noted, however, that among every nation there will be both good and evil expressions of the dominant characteristics. Although the line of Shem was to come to fruition in the incarnation of the Messiah, the nations that descended from Ishmael, Abraham's son by Hagar, have been followers of a false god and still stir up religious violence and mayhem. And through the centuries, descendants of Ham have helped the people of God, just as Egypt became the land that succored the budding nation of Israel (Genesis 46) and King Ahasuerus of Persia issued the order to save the Jewish nation from the genocidal plot of Haman (Esther 9).

Even though God's sovereign choice was to use the descendants of Shem to fulfill the promise of redemption given to Adam and Eve (Genesis 3:15), God also always has a "remnant" among all nations and will use even "the wrath of man" to praise Him (Psalm 76:10).

Japheth's Enlargement

"May God enlarge Japheth, And may he dwell in the tents of Shem; And may Canaan be his servant." (Genesis 9:27)

The Hebrew word translated "enlarge" in this passage has a negative connotation in the majority of its 27 appearances in the rest of the Old Testament. Most of the time, it is used in passages that suggest "seduction" and is translated by English words like "entice" or "persuade" or "flatter," or even "deceive." Even though the various lexicons insist that its basic meaning is "to be open, spacious, wide," the only time that it is translated "enlarge" is here in Genesis 9.

Part of Noah's prophecy was that the descendants of Japheth would "dwell in the tents" of Shem. Again, the word choices are significant, especially in the contrasting of the long-term "settling" of Japheth in the short-term "tents" of Shem. The words appear to support the idea that peoples of Japheth would "seduce" the descendants of Shem out of their land and possessions, and "occupy" much of what the Semites had developed.

History confirms that the majority of Japheth's progeny are the Caucasian ethnic groups that settled in Europe. History also demonstrates that the European nations have ultimately absorbed, conquered, or otherwise appropriated the lands and blessing of Shem. Much of the turmoil of the millennia after Christ is connected to the expansion of the Japhetic descendants at the expense of the Jewish and Islamic peoples (both descendants of Shem).

The Service of Ham

As was discussed earlier in this chapter, the judgment passed onto the descendants of Ham was for them to "serve" the rest of the world's population. Since the initial dominion mandate given to Adam and repeated to Noah would be implemented by the physical pursuits of subduing the ground, the intellectual pursuits of ruling the earth, and the spiritual pursuits of worship and honoring the Creator, it appears to follow that the basic tri-partite design of man's body, soul, and spirit would manifest itself in dominant people groups throughout history.

Every human being has a physical aspect to their nature, an intellectual component, and a spiritual element as well. In most people, one side dominates the other two. Even though some seem to have equal expressions of all three, one characteristic will express itself more often. Since all personality traits are transferred by genetic recombination and by parental modeling that shapes the behavior of those traits, most people groups (families, tribes, nations) will display a propensity to favor one of those three major attributes.

Hence the significance of the prophetic declaration of Noah. God was signaling through Noah how the populations of the world would carry out His dominion mandate over the millennia to come. And if future generations were to be able to observe God's will being carried out, the subsequent nations would have to display that fulfillment. Some nations would be remembered for their physical achievements—athletics, military prowess, mechanical inventions, etc. Others would be recognized for intellectual interests—science, academics, finances, etc. Still others would be dominated by religious pursuits—with pious leaders like rabbis, imams, priests, and teachers, along with zealous movements of various kinds.

Although the Bible is focused on the Semites and the nation of Israel, history provides us with a sufficient record to follow the development of nations and the part they have played in the implementation of God's plan.

Noted earlier was the biblical emphasis on "stewardship" for this concept of service, rather than "slavery." History has certainly demonstrated that the Hamitic nations were not enslaved by other nations, but rather prospered for at least centuries, and some of them still exist today as significant powers in the world. What, then, would be their "stewardship" to the world?

The dominant Hamitic nations have been Egypt and Sumer, certainly two of the greatest nations of antiquity. Spreading out over the Near East were the Phoenicians, the Hittites, and the Canaanites, who ruled and conquered many of the budding Semitic groups of that time. The African tribes began to settle and develop the African continent, and the Mongols, Chinese, and Japanese peopled the Far East. How can their contributions to the world demonstrate their "management" of physical necessities for the rest of the world?

Dr. Henry Morris' classic book *The Genesis Record* lists several noteworthy means by which these nations were "servants" of mankind.[2]

- They were the original explorers and settlers of practically all parts of the world, following the dispersion at Babel.

- They were the first cultivators of most of the basic food staples of the world, such as potatoes, corn, beans, cereals, and others, as well as the first ones to domesticate most animals.

- They developed most of the basic types of structural forms and building tools and materials.

- They were the first to develop most of the usual fabrics for clothing and the various sewing and weaving devices.

- They discovered and invented a wide variety of medicines and surgical practices and instruments.

- They invented most of the concepts of basic practical mathematics, as well as surveying and navigation.

- The machinery of commerce and trade—money, banks, postal systems, and so forth—was developed by them.

- They developed paper, ink, block printing, movable type, and other accouterments of writing and communication.

Yes, there was (and is) the obverse side to their distinctions. Over time, the Japhetic and Semitic nations have appropriated these inventions, and used them to excel and overcome the Hamitic groups. But when traced back far enough, it is the descendants of Ham who originated nearly every device or system that has been needed for physical provisions or personal convenience. These nations have indeed been the "servant of servants" to the world.

The Death of Noah

And Noah lived after the flood three hundred and fifty years. So all the days of Noah were nine hundred and fifty

---

2. Henry M. Morris, 1976, *The Genesis Record*, Grand Rapids, MI: Baker Book House, 241.

years; and he died. (Genesis 9:28-29)

Noah was the last of the men who exhibited the physical strength and longevity of humanity before the Flood. Although his sons were born within the final century of the First Age, they came under the more hostile environment of the Second Age after the Flood, and their lifespans were reduced by a third. If there are not gaps in the genealogies recorded in Genesis 10 and 11, Noah would have lived through the dispersion of the nations at Babel, and during his "senior" years could have known both Abraham and Job.

Genesis 11 provides the fathers' ages at the birth of nine generations after Shem. The total number of years that passed after the Flood until the birth of Abram (later Abraham) was only 292 years. Although the Bible does not record the ages at birth for the sons of Ham or Japheth, it is clear that the famous cities of Babel and Nineveh "in the land of Shinar" were built under the leadership of Nimrod, Ham's grandson (Genesis 10:6-11). Noah was certainly alive during these important days. Understanding the time scope will often help clarify the placement of events throughout the early centuries.

The Significance of the Nations

The particular relationship of the various genealogies in Genesis 10 and 11 will be covered in some detail in the next chapter. At this juncture, however, it will be helpful to examine the broader perspective and purpose for God's direction and implementation of the great Noahic prophecy about the coming role of his three sons.

Japheth is recorded as having seven sons and seven grandsons (Genesis 10:2-5). Since the several genealogies of Scripture rarely list daughters unless they played a significant part in the fulfillment of prophecy, it must be assumed that Japheth (as well as Ham and Shem) had multiple daughters and granddaughters as well. It is also at least possible that Japheth (and Ham and Shem) had other sons and grandsons who are not recorded, since the obvious purpose of these two chapters is to help identify the nations that would later be recognized in the world.

111

It is also obvious from the ages of the fathers at their sons' births recorded in the genealogy of Shem in Genesis 11 that the start of new generations came much more rapidly after the Flood than is recorded in the ages before the Flood. Shem's first son was born two years after the Flood, and his son Arphaxad was 35 when his son was born. Arphaxad's son Salah was only 30 when his wife gave birth to Eber. And so it went until the birth of Abram, when his father Terah was 70 years old. Even if there were any "missing" sons in this genealogy of Shem, the total dates are still accurate; the addition of the birth records still adds up to 292 years—whichever way it is evaluated.

As was the case right after creation, early marriages after the Flood would have included brothers and sisters, cousins, or nephews and nieces. Genetic mutations had not yet accumulated enough in the gene pool to warrant any kind of social prohibition of such close marriages. Indeed, such laws did not come into effect until the time of Moses, well over a thousand years after the Flood. And of course, it was absolutely necessary for close marriages to occur if the human population was to grow, not to mention to insure obedience to the twice-repeated command of the Creator to "be fruitful and multiply, and fill the earth."

For the sons and daughters of the Japhetic progeny, the Lord gives this simple summary.

> From these the coastland peoples of the Gentiles were separated into their lands, everyone according to his language, according to their families, into their nations. (Genesis 10:5)

The names given for descendants of Ham and Shem are an interesting counterpart to the names listed for Japheth. The children of Japheth are identified only through the third generation, with only two sons cited providing grandsons. Ham has the names of the children from three of his sons and one grandson, and Shem has some of his descendants listed to the fifth generation. Just why this selection was determined is not clear. Perhaps those listed are the main "fathers" of the nations that would ultimately form after the confusion of tongues at Babel. Perhaps, since Shem is apparently the author of these early lists (Genesis 11:10), it may well reflect the loss of contact that was inevitable after the disbursement of the people when "the LORD confused the language of all the earth; and from there the LORD scattered them abroad over the face of all the earth" (Genesis 11:9).

Another genealogy in 1 Chronicles 1 essentially parallels the tables in Genesis 10 and 11. The two genealogies given in the New Testament are also an important help in verifying the accuracy of the recorded history of Genesis. Matthew 1 provides the list of the human forefathers of the Lord Jesus starting with Abraham, emphasizing the lineage of Mary's husband, Joseph. Luke 3 gives a listing of the lineage of Mary, all the way back to Adam.

Luke inserts the name of Cainan between Arphaxad and Salah (listed as Shelah in Luke 3:35). Some have suggested that this proves that the Old Testament genealogies are wrong—or at least that we should add another generation between all the names. Those who make such assertions are usually the same people who would like for the Flood to be a local event and the age of the earth to be very old. However, even if it is granted that another generation must be inserted between each name (a totally unwarranted demand), the forced "age" could never add up to tens of thousands of years, let alone hundreds of thousands or millions of years.

But, as pointed out above, the specific record of the age of each father at the birth of the son recorded in the Genesis list forbids the addition of additional years—no matter how many sons were left out of the table. All of the evidence in the rest of the genealogical lists, including the copies by the Masorites and the Samaritan Pentateuch, verify the completion of the list of names. Even if it is assumed that the lists are merely to identify the primary forefather from which the nations came, the dates remain the same. The addition of Cainan in Luke's account only tells us of another son whose name was not included in Genesis.

All of that information, according to God's own analysis, was to record for future generations how the nations were divided on earth after the Flood.

> These were the families of the sons of Noah, according to their generations, in their nations; and from these the nations were divided on the earth after the flood. (Genesis 10:32)

CHAPTER SIX
THE DAYS OF PELEG

Genesis chapters 10 and 11 provide a wealth of information about the progression of the new world after the Flood. But, just like the six chapters that deal with creation, the Fall, and the First Age, and the three that cover the specifics of the great Flood, the information in chapters 10 and 11 is quite selective. God gives His perspective of the history He considers necessary for us to understand the continuity of humanity and the singular event that caused division among the family groups.

Two comments are made in Genesis 10 that identify a major event.

> From these the coastland peoples of the Gentiles were separated into their lands, everyone according to his language, according to their families, into their nations. (Genesis 10:5)

> To Eber were born two sons: the name of one was Peleg, for in his days the earth was divided; and his brother's name was Joktan. (Genesis 10:25)

The first reference follows a list of the sons and grandsons of Japheth. The second occurs in the list of the descendants of Shem. In between these two verses are listed the sons and grandsons of Ham.

It is helpful to summarize these records in an attempt to understand why God listed these specific men.

Genealogy of Japheth

Japheth, the oldest son of Noah (Genesis 10:21), had at least seven sons: Gomer, Magog, Madai, Javan, Tubal, Meshech, and Tiras. Gomer had at least three sons: Ashkenaz, Riphath, and Togarmah. Javan had at least four sons: Elishah, Tarshish, Kittim, and Dodanim. It is obvious that daughters were born to the first three families, or none of the second generation could have been born.[1] Of note in this first genealogy is that only the major sons of two of Japheth's sons are listed—those of Gomer and Javan.

Genealogy of Ham

Ham, by implication of the reference to Japheth and Shem in Genesis 10:21, was probably the youngest son of Noah. Twice in Genesis 9 (vv. 18 and 22), Ham is noted as "the father of Canaan." Although nothing is said directly, it appears that this unusual emphasis relates to the enmity that later grew between the young nation of Israel and the "Canaanites" who occupied the land that God promised to Abraham.

Ham has at least four sons: Cush, Mizraim, Put, and Canaan. The major sons of three of Ham's children are listed. Cush has at least six sons: Seba, Havilah, Sabtah, Raamah, Sabtechah, and Nimrod. Mizraim has at least seven sons: Ludim, Anamim, Lehabim, Naphtuhim, Pathrusim, Casluhim, and Caphtorim. Canaan has, apparently, eleven sons, two of whom are named—Sidon and Heth—and nine others from whom come the nations of the Jebusites, Amorites, Girgashites, Hivites, Arkites, Sinites, Arvadites, Zemarites, and Hamathites. Ham's grandson Raamah has two sons: Sheba and Dedan. Only the major sons to the fourth generation are listed, with the additional no-

---

1. Many conventional treatments start the post-Flood generational count with Noah, in which he is the first generation and the subsequent generations are numbered sequentially after that. For the purposes of this chapter, however, the numbering is started with the family head first mentioned in each genealogical list. Thus, Japheth is considered the first generation, Gomer et al the second, and so forth.

tation that the nations of the Philistines later came through Mizraim's son Casluhim.

As with Japheth, these early families were prolific and would have had many daughters who became wives of the multiplying family heads. Please recall that there were no indications of difficulties with genetic defects this early in the human race, thus making close marriages safe from potential physical harm. As was discussed in the last chapter, close marriages did not become prohibited until God gave the Law to Moses over a thousand years after the end of the Flood. The two lists of Japheth and Ham give no indication of how quickly the births occurred. However, as was noted in the previous chapter, the genealogy of Shem provides a careful record of the timing of the births of the listed sons of each generation, giving us an accurate picture of how rapidly the population was developing.

Genealogy of Shem

The lineage of Shem is given in two separate places: Genesis 10:21-31 and Genesis 11:10-26. The first list in chapter 10 gives the sons and grandsons to the fifth generation. The second list names the heads of nine generations through the birth of Abram, who was later named Abraham.

Five sons are listed for Shem: Elam, Asshur, Arphaxad, Lud, and Aram. His son Arphaxad was born two years after the Flood (Genesis 11:10), and Shem lived another 500 years after that and "begot sons and daughters." Arphaxad is said to have lived 438 years and to have had "sons and daughters," but only his son Salah is listed. Likewise, Salah is recorded has having lived 433 years, producing "sons and daughters," but only his son Eber is named. Two sons are listed for Eber: Peleg and Joktan. Eber lived another 430 years after Peleg was born and also had "sons and daughters." Joktan, Peleg's brother, has thirteen notable sons: Almodad, Sheleph, Hazarmaveth, Jerah, Hadoram, Uzal, Diklah, Obal, Abimael, Sheba, Ophir, Havilah, and Jobab.

Several of Joktan's sons are remembered throughout the Old Testament in the formal names of nations, and it is certainly interesting to see the comment that follows this list.

> And their dwelling place was from Mesha as you go toward Sephar, the mountain of the east. These were the sons of Shem, according to their families, according to their languages, in their lands, according to their nations. These were the families of the sons of Noah, according to their generations, in their nations; and from these the nations were divided on the earth after the flood. (Genesis 10:30-32)

The Days of Peleg

Something significant must have happened during the fifth generation after the Flood. All three sons of Noah have their descendants listed up until the third generation. Although some of the names of Ham's and Japheth's lineage are recognized in nations and peoples beyond the third generation, only Shem's family line is carried out beyond the "days" of Peleg. Obviously, the Bible makes note of a major event.

> To Eber were born two sons: the name of one was Peleg, for in his days the earth was divided; and his brother's name was Joktan. (Genesis 10:25)

The short phrase "the earth was divided" has caused no end of "division" among scholars over the years. Most Bible students attribute it to the dividing of the people groups by the supernatural intervention of God during the construction of the tower at Babel. That division was both linguistic and geographical, since the people groups that could no longer communicate would be forced to relocate and start their own "nations."

Some, however, suggest that this is a reference to the dividing of the continents in some sort of cataclysmic event that ripped apart the earth's structure, thus physically separating the populations of men and animals by force. Others reason that such an enormous "earth-split" would not be noted by a mere three-word phrase in the biblical record. Surely an event that was almost the equivalent of the world-wide Flood would have a greater record than just a few words—or at least there would be comparable stories (or legends) among other nations, as there is for the Flood. There are none.

The Earth Divided

Before attempting to determine what the division really was, the actual language of Scripture must be examined. First, and most obvious, the division of the nations is mentioned twice in Genesis 10. In both references, the division seems to be broken along the lines of families, or lands, or languages—or a combination of all of those factors.

> From these the coastland peoples of the Gentiles were *separated* into their *lands*, everyone according to his *language*, according to their *families*, into their *nations*. (Genesis 10:5)

> These were the *families* of the sons of Noah, according to their *generations*, in their *nations*; and from these the *nations were divided* on the earth after the flood. (Genesis 10:32)

It is also worth noting that the two genealogical records in Genesis 10 and 11 contain precisely 70 families. A prophetic declaration by Moses insists that this is no coincidence.

> When the Most High divided their inheritance to the nations, When He separated the sons of Adam, He set the boundaries of the peoples According to the number of the children of Israel. (Deuteronomy 32:8)

That statement, of course, is a reference to the number of "souls" that came into Egypt with Jacob to be protected and preserved under the initial patronage of Joseph (Exodus 1:1-5). It would appear that the biblical data emphasize a "division" because of a sovereign intervention in the affairs of men rather than a catastrophic geological event.

A simple reading of the text would lead one to believe that the event being referred to was the radical change to the human population specifically cited in chapter 11. That event was the supernatural division of the language of humanity by the direct intervention of the Creator (Genesis 11:1-9).

Linguistic Issues

However, there is an interesting play on words in these key verses. The proper name of Eber's son was Peleg (a direct transliteration of the Hebrew word). The verb translated "divided" is the Hebrew *palag*. 1 Chronicles 1:19 cites the same genealogy and uses exactly the same textual construction. But in Genesis 10:5 and 10:32, a different verb is used to tell of the "division." That Hebrew verb is *parad*. Some have suggested that this would indicate that two different types of division occurred. Does this make a difference?

The verb *parad* is used 26 times throughout the Old Testament and is always translated by an English word that means "separated." The verb *palag* is used only four times, but is always translated "divided," except for "cleft" in Job 38:25 in some of the more recent versions. On the surface, it appears that these two verbs are merely synonyms describing the same action—dividing.

The more interesting issue is the name Peleg. Seven times that Hebrew noun is used to reference the person Peleg, and an additional 10 times it is translated as "river" (often in the plural form). Here are some of the more familiar passages.

> He shall be like a tree Planted by the rivers of water, That brings forth its fruit in its season, Whose leaf also shall not wither; And whatever he does shall prosper. (Psalm 1:3)

> There is a river whose streams shall make glad the city of God, The holy place of the tabernacle of the Most High.

(Psalm 46:4)

You visit the earth and water it, You greatly enrich it; The river of God is full of water; You provide their grain, For so You have prepared it. (Psalm 65:9)

Rivers of water run down from my eyes, Because men do not keep Your law. (Psalm 119:136)

Since these other references obviously refer to some sort of watercourse, it has been suggested that the name Peleg should be understood as "River," thereby referencing a geological-ecological event that occurred in the life of Eber (Peleg's father) and caused him to name his son in commemoration of that monumental occasion. Perhaps, but such a linguistic connection seems a bit thin to this author.

Assuming that such a connection is to be made, however, what kind of geological or ecological episode would have caused a water-based phenomenon of the magnitude that would "divide" the earth?

The Ice Age

It is certain that an "age" occurred in the past in which massive amounts of water were frozen into enormous glacial ice sheets that covered much of the northern and southern hemispheres. Glacial moraines (soil and rock debris) were pushed southward by the advancing ice, then deposited in huge beds along large fronts left as the ice melted away. Some rock formations show long striations (scouring and scratching), and there are isolated deposits of huge boulders that did not originate in the terrain in which they are found. Geologists have spent careers studying the many and varied evidences for the Ice Age(s).

There is no question that such phenomena occurred in the past. There is no question that these advancing glaciers melted back and away in both hemispheres, with the more obvious trails left throughout northern lands. Questions remain, however, on when these episodes occurred and what caused the massive ice formations to retreat from their forward positions.

The naturalistic (uniformitarian) interpretations of the evidence attempt to apply the knowledge gained from present processes to explain these past events. What can be studied today are the remains of former glaciers and the recent records for current glaciers, many of which are slowly melting back and disappearing. Those interpretations lead to a "slow and gradual" explanation, suggesting that the glacial periods impacted the earth as long as 2 billion years ago, with the more recent ice sheets retreating between 100,000 to 40,000 years ago. The majority of geologists would embrace those theories.

Obviously, those naturalistic theories do not take into account the record of the global Flood so carefully documented in the Bible. Such an event would be so catastrophic that all geological evidence would have to be understood as being recent—certainly less than 10,000 years ago, if the biblical data are to be taken as accurate history.

Among creationist geologists and climatologists, therefore, the Ice Age is considered to be a result of the enormous tectonic and climatic changes that occurred after the Flood. Simply put, the earth's oceans would be abnormally warm from the huge volumes of superheated water coming from the "fountains of the deep" and the exposure of mantle liquid rock erupting out of the rents in the earth's surface. The warm oceans would then cause vast evaporation to occur all over the planet, resulting in frequent storms from intense weather patterns that would deposit huge snowfalls in the polar and sub-polar regions. Those continuing snowfalls would pack and freeze rapidly, developing advancing glaciation over the early centuries after the Flood.

The basic differences between these interpretations are scale and time. That is, if the naturalistic interpretation is correct, the glaciation occurred by the same basic causes as it does today, but slowly over tens of thousands of years. The later melt-back would also cover multiple thousands of years. Most naturalistic models further postulate multiple "ages" in which ice advanced and retreated cyclically over eons. If the creationist catastrophic models are right, there was only one Ice

Age that occurred within the early centuries after the biblical Flood and in which the glaciation happened much more rapidly, with the melt-back also taking place within a comparatively short period.

Does either model have anything to do with the "dividing" of the earth cited in Genesis?

Rising Sea Levels

Essentially, the question boils down to "What happened to all the water?" It is obvious that the present coastlines are much farther inland from the continental shelf than they were in the past. Evidence of former land bridges is relatively easy to see; common examples are the Bering Strait and the Malaysian Strait. Other former bridges are suggested that stretched from the West Indies to North Africa, from Brazil to South Africa, from Central America through Hawaii to Northeast Asia, and from South America to Antarctica.

Submerged Greek city ruins lie in the sea off the Nile Delta in Egypt. Ruins under the Black Sea are well known. Recent discoveries indicate likely ruins in the Caribbean and the Yucatan peninsula. The legend of Atlantis was not fabricated from wishful thinking.

Something happened to raise the ocean water levels in the past.

The naturalist would insist that this increase was slow and gradual over millennia. Some creationists suggest, however, that a rapid melting of the glacial ice after the biblical Flood eroded the earth's mostly intact land mass of the past and shaped much of the present continents as the sea level rose by some 600 feet. This event could not have been a sudden and catastrophic melting of the worldwide glacial ice, however. Such an event would produce tsunamis and convulsions on a scale nearly as great as the Flood itself. Modern "calving" of glacial ice today is fearful and destructive to local environments—yet its destructive potential could hardly compare to a worldwide meltdown of an Ice Age. It is hard to imagine that God would have ignored that scale of destruction by merely noting a "dividing" during the days of Peleg.

Catastrophic River Systems

Knowing that the glacial sheets did melt, the main question is whether that melting occurred slowly or rapidly. There is ample evidence that hydraulic forces can and do cause major environmental damage. Storms like Hurricanes Katrina and Sandy have left thousands homeless, caused significant migration of families, and inflicted billions of dollars in property destruction. Tornadoes, cyclones, and large thunderstorms all generate water damage far beyond the destruction caused by the wind that accompanies them.

The well-documented eruptions of Mount St. Helens in 1980 and 1982 provided a "lab" that demonstrated the enormous power of water erosion, displacing vast deposits and carving canyons through many layers of volcanic ash and mud buildup. In southern Brazil, a 1974 rainstorm took barely five minutes to carve out a 1,600-foot-long, 16-foot-deep scar by following a small gully in a gently sloping valley. Similar stories of horrific devastation are documented from locations as widespread as New Zealand and the U.S. state of Georgia.[2]

The earth bears witness to similar, even more cataclysmic events in the past. Early in the 20th century, a dry lake bed was discovered in Missoula, Montana, confirmed geologically by extensive glacial lake deposits, which was roughly the size of Lake Michigan. Somehow that old lake had drained, carving wide-ranging canyons and gorges now called the Channelled Scablands. Dr. John Morris, an ICR geologist, reviewed the work of the early secular catastrophic geologist Dr. J. Harlen Bretz.

> Bretz proposed that an enclosing dam of ice or glacial moraine had catastrophically failed, releasing torrents of water that flooded across Idaho and eastern Washington. It eroded the hard rock in its path and left deep canyons reminiscent of Grand Canyon, along with immense gravel ripples and boulder fields strewn across the landscape. When the waters were forced to temporarily pond behind ridges, they deposited extensive sedimentary layers of re-

---

2. Steven A. Austin, 1984, Rapid Erosion at Mount St. Helens, *Origins*, 11 (2): 90-98.

cently eroded material and then made their way quickly to the Pacific Ocean. Now the water is gone, with meager streams and "dry falls" entering the canyons—or "coulees," as they are known—testifying to greater water volumes in the past.[3]

These evidences, along with the observed effects of cavitation and other hydraulic phenomena, are used to support the theory that Peleg was named in memory of a "riverization" event that took place after glacial melt resulted in flooding that carved out deep channels and gorges in the earth. That flooding, it is proposed, rapidly "divided" the surface of the earth and forced people and animal groups to migrate to safer environs.

Continental Drift

It is often noted that the continents are still drifting today. At first glance, the world map surely looks as though there was once a single land mass that broke into pieces that then moved to their current positions. There is some similarity to the "puzzle pieces" (the west coast of Africa and east coast of South America are the most obvious examples), yet many of these continents do not fit. There are several favored theories, of course, all of which assume some sort of "Pangaea" super-continent that was set in motion through an unknown radical event that caused the single continent to break apart and "wander" across the globe. Although this idea stubbornly persists, it has yet to be proven by any demonstrable scientific evaluation.

The current rate of "drift" is between 4 and 5 centimeters per year (less than 2 inches). Obviously, wandering around the planet at that rate, the continents would take far more than the supposed 4.5 billion years of the earth's existence to relocate! Even those geologists who study the science of plate tectonics recognize that whatever or however the continental plates were set in motion, the forces and conditions are *not* what we see happening now. So, the proponents of continental drift postulate that today's drift measures only the "slowing down" of

---

3.   John D. Morris, 2011, The Channeled Scablands, *Acts & Facts*, 40 (10): 15.

the early movements.

The sheer force necessary to move a continent would far exceed the crushing force of the rock itself! Even if such energy could overcome the inertia of a seated continent without pulverizing the rock (though the thought staggers the mind), the continuous energies necessary to force the continent to "wander" are beyond imagining—unless there was a water or liquid sheet (perhaps the upper films of the mantle) upon which the continents could "slide."

Something like that is proposed by naturalists and some creationists to account for the "division" of earth in the ancient past. Although the process points of the various theories are similar, the major difference lies in both the scale and the time involved. The creationists would suggest that the melting glacial packs "riverized" the super-continent by their strong melt currents, carving the earth into segments and unbridgeable gaps as the "rivers" increased in intensity. This supposition is based primarily on the use of the Hebrew word *peleg* in Genesis 10.

The thought is that the phenomenon of "riverization," known to leave similar geological evidence in the past, could account for the dividing of the land mass. Sea floors would also be altered by similar currents as the cold meltwater sank to the bottom in vast "rivers," thereby deepening the ocean basins and preventing catastrophic overflow onto the land surfaces. Those same hydraulic features could (plausibly) move the land masses themselves by providing a "slide" of water under the continents, thereby inducing "drift" onto the surface.

These ideas are all speculative, of course, each of them trying to provide some feasible (and naturalistic) idea of how the earth was "divided" during the days of Peleg. And that, in the opinion of this author, is the problem. Rather than allowing the obvious reading of the biblical passage, an effort is made to come up with an explanation for how such an event could have occurred naturally. Here is a good maxim to follow: The simplest explanation is usually the best. The more sophisticated and technical an explanation is required to be, the more chance there is to introduce error. The more convoluted an argument, the more likely it hides an effort to confuse and persuade the reader.

This is especially true with biblical information.

The Fifth Generation

Most Bible students and scholars recognize that Genesis chapters 10 and 11 are a historical unit, with chapter 10 covering the genealogy of Noah's three sons up to at least the third generation and chapter 11 continuing that history through the birth of Abraham. It is important, therefore, to be aware of the contemporary relationship of Nimrod and Peleg. As Ham's grandson, Nimrod would most likely have been born within the first 50 years of the new world. Peleg was born around 100 years after the Flood, so given the relative lifespans at that time, the two men would have been contemporaries.

Peleg's date of birth is verified by the specific chronology of the birth of Shem's descendants recorded in chapter 11. Shem's son Arphaxad was born two years after the Flood. Arphaxad's son Salah was born when Arphaxad was 35. Salah was 30 when his son Eber arrived. Eber had Peleg when he was 34 years old. Adding them up (2 + 35 + 30 + 34) allows only 101 years passage before the birth of Peleg. (This could include plus or minus 4 years for development in the womb after the "begetting" of each son.) The ages of the descendants of Ham are not given, but it is certainly plausible to suggest that Nimrod and Peleg lived at approximately the same time.

It is also important to note that although chapter 10 covers the descendants of Shem for multiple generations, the descendants of Japheth and Ham are listed only through the third or fourth generation. The event of "division" connected to the "days" of Peleg would have taken place during his lifetime. Since he was born 101 (± 4) years after the Flood and lived 239 years (Genesis 11:18-19), that gives a range of around 100 to around 390 years after the Flood during which the division could have taken place.

Of further significance is the radical drop in lifespans in the fifth generation after the Flood (counting from Shem). Noah lived for 350 years after the Flood (Genesis 9:28), making him 950 years old when he died (v. 29). His lifespan was very similar to that of the pre-Flood people (912 years on average). The three sons of Noah were born after Noah was 500 years old (Genesis 5:32), making Shem—who lived for 502 years after the Flood (Genesis 11:11)—around 600 years old when he died. There is no reason to assume that Ham and Japheth died significantly before Shem, indicating that the first generation after the Flood had a life expectancy about 33 percent *less* than pre-Flood humanity.

Arphaxad lived 438 years, nearly 200 years less than his father, Shem. Salah, in the next generation, lived about the same length of time, 433 years. Eber lived 464 years. But then there is a sudden drop of almost 50 percent in the fifth generation with Peleg, who lived only 239 years! The rest of the descendants survived about the same number of years. Reu (sixth generation) was also 239 when he died. His son Serug (seventh generation) was 230, Nahor (eighth generation) was only 148, but Terah (ninth generation) lived to 205.

Something radical obviously happened in in the days of Peleg.

Nimrod

> Cush begot Nimrod; he began to be a mighty one on the earth. He was a mighty hunter before the LORD; therefore it is said, "Like Nimrod the mighty hunter before the LORD." And the beginning of his kingdom was Babel, Erech, Accad, and Calneh, in the land of Shinar. From that land he went to Assyria and built Nineveh, Rehoboth Ir, Calah, and Resen between Nineveh and Calah (that is the principal city). (Genesis 10:8-12)

Nimrod was the grandson of Ham through Cush. Nimrod's significance is that he is cited as "the mighty hunter before the LORD" and as the founder of the city of Babel. Babel, of course, is significant because it was there that humanity rebelled against God and built the famous tower to worship the host of heaven.

Historical writings are full of references to this ancient king. Often the name is easily recognized, but it is sometimes connected with Sargon, with the god Marduk, and with other variations that are etymologically related. The common denominator between all of these wide and varied accounts is that this "mighty" person is recognized as the founder and first king of Babel, later known as Babylon.

Nimrod is mentioned in the parallel genealogy in 1 Chronicles 1:10 and in Micah 5:6, where his name is connected with Assyria as "the land of Nimrod." The Greek Septuagint translates the word rendered "mighty" in Genesis 10:8-9 with *gigas,* "giant." Perhaps this is to recognize the strength of earlier legends. One such legend tells that Nimrod had clothing worn by Adam and Eve, stolen by Cush from the Ark, which gave Nimrod magical powers. That story insists that when Nimrod wore these clothes, the animals would lie down and remain docile as he killed them, thus earning Nimrod the saying "Like Nimrod the mighty hunter before the LORD."

Some Bible commentators even go so far as to suggest that the passage in Isaiah 14:4-23 refers to Nimrod, because the passage starts with "take up this proverb against the king of Babylon." With the likely exception of the section that specifically names Lucifer (vv. 12-14), the information could well be applied to Nimrod as the founder of Babylon. The passage, however, appears to be a prophecy about the current city, and could fit the future prophecies in Revelation 17 and 18, as well. If that is so, as it seems to be, the Isaiah foresight would not apply to Nimrod himself, but—as do many of the Old Testament prophetic declarations—instead includes a second statement referencing another event. This section appears to be about the Chief Enemy, Lucifer, as the one empowering the King of Babylon.

The Mighty Hunter Before the Lord

The most interesting fact about this Hebrew phrase is that the English word "before" is the translators' choice for the Hebrew noun *paniym,* which is almost always translated "face" in the many other passages where it appears. That noun always appears in the plural form, perhaps alluding to the multiple features that make up the whole face. The use of *paniym* is the reason most commentators consider the saying about Nimrod to be a negative statement, concluding that Nimrod is a mighty hunter "in the face of" or perhaps a mighty hunter "facing" the Lord.

That rendering certainly agrees with the later information given in Genesis 11. In that account, Babel (Nimrod's city) is the place where the Lord comes down in a preemptive strike and enforces a dispersion of all the people by confounding their languages.

The descriptive epithet "mighty hunter" is probably meant to be taken literally. A figurative application would be hard to define, with no other biblical record to provide additional information. All of the historical records cite such prowess as the reason that Nimrod became a leader and ultimately the founder of several cities. It is not difficult to picture the need for protection among the growing population by the second century after the Flood. The environment would be more hostile, driving the larger animals toward cultivated fields for food, requiring some skilled hunter to ward off or kill the more threatening creatures.

God had also allowed the consumption of animal flesh for humanity, suggesting that those with extra bravery and tracking acumen might be quickly recognized and honored above the "ordinary" folks. Stories abound throughout history of such heroes who saved villages from being ravaged by a savage beast. Those legends have survived into this period in such characters as Conan the Barbarian, Saint George and the dragon, and the many tales of "gods" and demi-gods who rescued major cities and did exploits for various kings.

The difference with Nimrod was that he showed off his powers "in the face of" the Lord of creation, thus defying both the authority of the Creator and God's delegated responsibility of stewardship over the earth. While this may have gained Nimrod popularity and notoriety among the growing population of earth, his direct rebellion against God reflected the pre-Flood *nephilim* (Genesis 6:4) who led that world into a rebellion that ultimately caused its destruction.

The Population

> Now the whole earth had one language and one speech.
> And it came to pass, as they journeyed from the east, that
> they found a plain in the land of Shinar, and they dwelt
> there. Then they said to one another, "Come, let us make
> bricks and bake them thoroughly." They had brick for
> stone, and they had asphalt for mortar. And they said,
> "Come, let us build ourselves a city, and a tower whose
> top is in the heavens; let us make a name for ourselves,
> lest we be scattered abroad over the face of the whole
> earth." (Genesis 11:1-4)

Many Bible commentators have dated this event at around 100 years after the Flood, based on the birth date of Peleg clearly documented in Genesis 11:10-16. However, given that Nimrod was most likely born near the same time as Peleg, it seems a bit premature to assume that he could have established himself as a "mighty hunter" and developed enough leadership to found cities so soon after his birth.

Furthermore, these people (the descendants of Noah) had time to migrate from the regions around western Turkey (Ararat) to the "east" around "the land of Shinar." Shinar is most likely equivalent to ancient Sumer, the general area of land commonly referred to as Mesopotamia. Some history books refer to this area as the "fertile crescent." That equates to most of Iraq and some of Syria today. Shinar is referenced eight times in the Old Testament, most of which clearly refer to the lands of Assyria or Babylon. Obviously, some time must be involved for the growing population to migrate from Turkey to Iraq, start a city, and unite in an effort to build a colossal tower.

Peleg lived 239 years. It is likely that Nimrod lived to a similar age; there is certainly no reference to the contrary. Given the strong inference in Genesis 10 that something major happened during the "days" of Peleg, it would therefore seem likely that the migration of the "whole earth" and the events that led to the tower construction under the implied leadership of Nimrod would have taken a considerable amount of time. Thus, dating the events of Babel at around 100 years after the Flood (the birth date of Peleg) appears to be too soon. The more likely date would be within a century or so after that.

One Language

This is a significant issue. Moses notes it editorially and God Himself insists that this is a major facilitator of the rebellion. No one is sure what that language may have been. However, since the Assyrian lands seem to be the central point from which the earth was populated after the supernatural change in the common language, it may be that the core language was related to the early Old Akkadian preserved for us in cuneiform writings. Recall that Accad was one of the cities established by Nimrod (Genesis 10:10). The Akkadian language is usually clustered together with others as part of the Semitic language group. The more well-known Semitic languages spoken today are Arabic, Hebrew, and Aramaic.

Functionally, language is the stabilizing force behind national identity. Neither political nor geographical boundaries keep people from easily migrating from one area to another. Language is still the main inhibitor for any kind of unity, and is a main force behind the inability of any nation to unite in common causes. Hence the observation by God: "Now nothing that they propose to do will be withheld from them" (Genesis 11:6). The common language kept that population together as nothing else could have done.

Also noted should be the double emphasis in the phrase "the whole earth had one language and one speech." The Hebrew terms do not focus on "common" but on the numeral "one." That is a specific emphasis that there was no other dialect or regional difference in the spoken tongue, but the entire population had only a single way of communicating with each other. The Hebrew term *dabar* translated here as "speech" is more often translated "word." In many passages, *dabar* emphasizes the "sound" or the "idea" of the thing spoken. Thus, the emphatic declaration is that there was no other means of communication known to the entire population.

One City

Although the summary comments on the life of Nimrod list several cities that he later had influence in founding, this section of Genesis 11 seems to indicate that the entire population was located in a single area, with an intention to build a city for them to live in and around. Since this was taking place some 200 to 400 years after the Flood, the population would probably be in the thousands.

After the murder of Abel, Cain was banished from the family center and sent into "Nod" (Genesis 4:16). The term "nod" is not necessarily the name of a land, but a condition of "wandering." In defiance of the judgment of God, Cain built a city that he named after his son, Enoch. Earlier studies of the Adamic world indicated that there would have been nearly 10,000 people alive at the time Abel was murdered—and that number developed from only two people in a little over 100 years. The calculated population growth rate from the list in Genesis 10 at the time of the fifth generation would be over 500 percent! There is no reason to suggest that the population, apparently under the leadership of Nimrod, would not have been more than large enough to establish a city.

Archaeological digs in the region of ancient Babylon verify the use of natural resources as the source of the building products. Nothing is stated in Scripture about the habitations of the pre-Babel population. The likely living area prior to the migration "from the east" would have been western Turkey around the plateaus and valley floors of "the mountains of Ararat." There is no question that Noah and his sons would have brought the sophisticated knowledge of the pre-Flood world with them on the Ark—and quite probably some basic construction equipment as well. However, whatever may have been the method of shelter (whether something as simple as tents made from skins or more permanent buildings from wood), the population found the area too hostile to remain and migrated to the Mesopotamian area.

Having arrived, a permanent location was desirable. There were ample natural resources—clay to fire into brick and bitumen to use as a cementing agent. The skills were already there among the population, the leadership had at least begun to coalesce around Nimrod, and the people were motivated to build.

One Tower

During the process of building the city structure and the various centers of population needs, the idea of building a "tower" took root among them. The Hebrew word *migdal* is used 50 times in the Old Testament to describe everything from a castle for royalty to a guardhouse in the middle of a vineyard. Often it signifies some sort of military construction that was designed for defensive protection of a city. Such construction survived into the Middle Ages in the form of watchtowers and defensive guard towers at the corners of city walls.

The tower at Babel was probably some form of stacked pyramid. That is, each layer is built on top of the previous layer, with the size of the base determining the overall size of the monument. Early archaeological sites in the area of ancient Babylon have uncovered remains of such efforts. Those early towers are usually referred to as ziggurats. More sophisticated versions of that form are well known from the pyramids of Egypt (including some stacked pyramids) and the Aztec worship centers in Mexico.

The purpose of the tower in Babel is expressed by the statement "whose top is in the heavens" (Genesis 11:4). The Lord's reaction to this event makes it abundantly clear that this was much more than a mere architectural triumph.

> But the LORD came down to see the city and the tower which the sons of men had built. And the LORD said, "Indeed the people are one and they all have one language, and this is what they begin to do; now nothing that they propose to do will be withheld from them. (Genesis 11:5-6)

Whatever God saw was far more than a mere tower. Something must have triggered His righteous judgment. Nothing in the subsequent annals of history indicates that the mind of God is angered by building projects alone. God has intervened in the affairs of men often enough after the Flood, but never anything of this scale, where the entire population of earth was affected in one moment.

There are two later passages in the Bible that may give us a clue to the focus of the people of Babel that incurred the anger and judgment of God. After Israel had been rescued from Egypt and had endured 40 years in the wilderness as punishment for not trusting their Rescuer to take care of them in the land of promise, Moses warned them about reverting to the worship of "the host of heaven" as had their fathers.

> And take heed, lest you lift your eyes to heaven, and when you see the sun, the moon, and the stars, all the host of heaven, you feel driven to worship them and serve them, which the LORD your God has given to all the peoples under the whole heaven as a heritage. (Deuteronomy 4:19)

Much later during the reign of King Hoshea of Israel, the Lord severely punished the nation for returning to the worship practices of the early nations that had been their enemies for centuries—the very nations that were the descendants of Ham, Cush, and Nimrod.

> So they left all the commandments of the LORD their God, made for themselves a molded image and two calves, made a wooden image and worshiped all the host of heaven, and served Baal. (2 Kings 17:16)

Baal was one of the names repeatedly attributed to Nimrod himself among the various tablets uncovered in ancient Assyria. The "host of heaven" is obviously the demonic powers behind the prostituted message of the stars that modern scholarship calls astrology. Later under the reign of Manasseh, the nation of Judah fell away from the revival that had taken place under King Hezekiah and returned to the awful worship of the demonic practice of astrology.

> For he rebuilt the high places which Hezekiah his father had destroyed; he raised up altars for Baal, and made a wooden image, as Ahab king of Israel had done; and

he worshiped all the host of heaven and served them. (2 Kings 21:3)

Given the startling reaction of God against the building of the tower in Babel, and the subsequent practice of astrology worship by Israel and Judah, it is certainly not a wild extrapolation to suggest that the purpose of the tower was to build a center of worship against "the face of" the Creator by personifying, praising, and serving the demonic powers thought to be represented by the "sun, moon, and stars."

The apostle Paul made clear to the Corinthian church what such worship really was.

> Rather, that the things which the Gentiles sacrifice they sacrifice to demons and not to God, and I do not want you to have fellowship with demons. (1 Corinthians 10:20)

The Division of Earth

> So the LORD scattered them abroad from there over the face of all the earth, and they ceased building the city. Therefore its name is called Babel, because there the LORD confused the language of all the earth; and from there the LORD scattered them abroad over the face of all the earth. (Genesis 11:8-9)

This is the event that caused the entire population of earth to be split up and forced to migrate across the globe. Not a continental drift. Not a "riverization" of the land masses. During the lifespans of Peleg and Nimrod, God "came down" in judgment on the rebellious population and prevented them from ever uniting in worldwide rebellion again. There will be an attempt in the last days by the Satan-empowered Antichrist to re-unite the world's populations into a total warfare and rebellion against the Creator. But he will be horribly defeated and finally cast into the eternal judgment of the "lake of fire."

The Scripture is clear and not ambiguous at all. The Sovereign Creator and Triune God forced the earth to be divided in the "days" of Peleg, just like is recorded.

CHAPTER SEVEN
THE DEVELOPING NATIONS

There can be no question that God had a reason for confounding the language of the growing population of the planet—He must prohibit a second worldwide rebellion, one that was focused this time against His repeated command to "fill the earth" (Genesis 9:1). The entire population was again coming under evil leadership. Nimrod had become so powerful that the people were openly turning against God. Something must be done that would permanently divide the people and cause them to disperse over the earth. Different languages would be the tool to accomplish that.

> "Come, let Us go down and there confuse their language, that they may not understand one another's speech." So the LORD scattered them abroad from there over the face of all the earth, and they ceased building the city. (Genesis 11:7-8)

God then inspired Moses to add an editorial comment in the very next verse.

> Therefore its name is called Babel, because there the LORD confused the language of all the earth; and from there the LORD scattered them abroad over the face of all the earth. (Genesis 11:9)

Moses wrote Genesis much later, probably during the 40 years Israel spent wandering around the Sinai Peninsula. Toward the end of Moses' life, he delivered a series of sermons that are recorded in the book of Deuteronomy. By that time, all of the rebellious Israelites who had been afraid to go into the Promised Land were dead. Moses was now preaching to the Israel that would begin the difficult task under Joshua of claiming the land that been promised to Abraham over 400 years before. Something about that setting reminded Moses of the people and events recorded in Genesis 10 and 11.

> When the Most High divided their inheritance to the nations, When He separated the sons of Adam, He set the boundaries of the peoples According to the number of the children of Israel. (Deuteronomy 32:8)

The "number of the children of Israel" is a specific reference to the census recorded immediately after Jacob and his family migrated to Egypt with the permission of the Pharaoh to live under the protection of Joseph.

> And the sons of Joseph who were born to him in Egypt were two persons. All the persons of the house of Jacob who went to Egypt were seventy. (Genesis 46:27)

If these words of Scripture are to mean anything at all, they must give us an overview of the original genetic groups that were assembled at Babel. These 70 groups of people constituted the beginning of the disbursed nations of earth as they migrated away from the city-center in Shinar (Mesopotamia). Genesis 10 identifies 14 "nations" coming from Japheth, 30 from Ham, and 26 from Shem.

God's Sovereign Plan

God is not whimsical or capricious. If we are to gain an insight into the bigger picture over the millennia as the nations grew and fulfilled their destinies, we must grasp something of how God's hand guides the affairs of men during all the ages. God does have a plan for the nations. Human efforts can be powerful and they are often aided by Lucifer and his host. But the foundational decrees of the Creator will not be thwarted.

> "Declaring the end from the beginning, And from ancient times things that are not yet done, Saying, 'My counsel shall stand, And I will do all My pleasure'....Indeed I have spoken it; I will also bring it to pass. I have purposed it; I will also do it." (Isaiah 46:10-11)

Part of this counsel includes the sequence in which the nations rose to power and then died out or were absorbed into other nations. God even has specific territories defined which the nations will occupy.

> And He has made from one blood every nation of men to dwell on all the face of the earth, and has determined their preappointed times and the boundaries of their dwellings. (Acts 17:26)

God has predetermined political details for one major purpose— to make sure that every nation would be able, over the "times appointed," to have an opportunity to find its personal (and national) part in the timeless expression of the love of God, the gospel.

> ...so that they should seek the Lord, in the hope that they might grope for Him and find Him, though He is not far from each one of us. (Acts 17:27)

Therefore, God has decreed that He will not close history until the gospel has been openly declared among all nations on earth.

> And this gospel of the kingdom will be preached in all the world as a witness to all the nations, and then the end will come. (Matthew 24:14)

In fact, to insure that every nation will have heard the gospel, God will commission a great angel in heaven to circle the planet with an announcement of the "everlasting gospel" before the end of all things is brought to pass.

> Then I saw another angel flying in the midst of heav-

en, having the everlasting gospel to preach to those who dwell on the earth—to every nation, tribe, tongue, and people—saying with a loud voice, "Fear God and give glory to Him, for the hour of His judgment has come; and worship Him who made heaven and earth, the sea and springs of water." (Revelation 14:6-7)

While the presentation of these verses in this format may seem a little choppy, it does provide a quick overview of how important the development and placement of the nations are to the Creator—and how careful He has been to insure that the clarity of His presence and His purposes have been made available to every nation in all times.

God's Creation Message

Yes, there have been times "in bygone generations [when God has] allowed all nations to walk in their own ways" (Acts 14:16). However, since the completion of the creation week, the information contained in the "things that are made" has so clearly demonstrated the "invisible attributes" of God that those who ultimately reject God's love "are without excuse" (Romans 1:20). Even the stunted wisdom of Job's friends knew that anyone could "ask the beasts" or "speak to the earth" and the animals would "tell" and the earth would "teach" the wonders of the creation (Job 12:7-8). The psalmist knew that every day has "speech" and every night provides "knowledge" (Psalm 19:2). God has designed the universe with a clear message written throughout it.

Although it is not quite as clear, it is certainly within reason that God would have designed the stars of heaven to carry an unbreakable message of His long-term plan of creation and redemption. It is clear that the stellar host (including the sun and moon) were created "for signs and seasons, and for days and years" (Genesis 1:14). Their more obvious function was for timekeeping, but there are also passages in Scripture that indicate that God uses them to teach mankind about Himself and about His purposes. Ancient Job knew of "the Bear, Orion, and the Pleiades, and the chambers of the south" (Job 9:9). His friends knew that the Spirit of God "adorned the heavens; His hand pierced the fleeing serpent" (Job 26:13). God Himself asked Job if he could control "Mazzaroth in its season? Or can you guide the Great Bear with its cubs?" (Job 38:32).

Those "signs" in the stellar configurations look absolutely nothing like a "bear" or a "lion" or a "virgin" or the other names of the constellations. Someone must have given them a significant meaning and purpose, and then transmitted that information from generation to generation. Whatever that original meaning would have been, it is absolutely clear that it could not be the astrology of pagan worship. That awful prostitution of the original message is strongly condemned in Scripture

> And take heed, lest you lift your eyes to heaven, and when you see the sun, the moon, and the stars, all the host of heaven, you feel driven to worship them and serve them, which the LORD your God has given to all the peoples under the whole heaven as a heritage. (Deuteronomy 4:19)

> ...who has gone and served other gods and worshiped them, either the sun or moon or any of the host of heaven, which I have not commanded. (Deuteronomy 17:3)

God gave this stellar host "to all the peoples under the whole heaven as a heritage." What, then, was that heritage? What would the Creator have "written" in the heavens? It is certainly probable that this heritage would have been some indelible message of "signs" and "seasons" that could not be physically altered. Some "story" in the heavens that could, with the proper designation, explain the plan and purpose of God for the redemption and restoration of humanity. A "gospel" written in the stars that would tell of the coming Savior and His redemption of and reconciliation with the lost, and His ultimate victory over all who would dare to defy Him.

Several scholars have written extensively on this possibility. E. W. Maunder was a great English astronomer of the late 19th and early 20th century who was widely heralded for his discoveries of sunspots and the solar magnetic cycle. Maunder wrote *The Astronomy of the Bible*, a book that is still used today. Noted theologians Joseph Seiss and E.W. Bullinger have also provided excellent treatments of this subject. Jewish historian Josephus, writing at the time of Christ, tells that this stellar gospel was first written down by Seth, Adam's son. That document, it is suggested, was in the material carried by Noah on the Ark and subsequently transmitted by the patriarchs to Jacob, then preserved in Egypt under Joseph and ultimately obtained by Moses, who was inspired to record Genesis.

That, of course, is not specified in the Bible. There are implicit statements of purpose in the Scripture, as well as circumstantial evidence in history. The combination of these resources strongly suggests that an original gospel message was intended to be passed on to the nations by means of the stars. One must be careful not to force acceptance of the extra-biblical data as being equal to the statements of Scripture. However, it is intriguing that many have sensed a doctrinal purpose for the heavens, as well as a magnificent statement of the Creator's design and power.

Satan's Distorted Message

But that message was distorted. The Lord Jesus names Satan "a liar and the father of it" (John 8:44) Since the Devil is not capable of changing the physical position of the stars, it appears that he has misled many by redefining the configurations to mean something other than what God intended. Thus, the fallen and spiritually dead mind of sinful man has been led by a false message into a corrupted worship of the "light holders" rather than the Light-Giver. It is entirely likely that Satan himself corrupted the message by some personal communication to Nimrod, and through Nimrod to the population at Babel. The top of the tower became a sacrificial altar to the "host of heaven," thereby bringing the judgment of God as He confounded the language of the 70 original nations.

Once again, this is not specified directly in the language of the biblical text, but it is significant to note that the apostate message has been so widely used in the world. That distortion must have begun somewhere, and must have begun early in the history of the nations. Given that Babylon is later called "the mother of harlots" (Revelation 17:5), it is certainly not a far stretch to surmise that this false teaching began at Babel.

But as Job and the psalmist note, both the "beasts" and the "earth" are full of knowledge about their Creator. If the great Enemy is to confront the message that is written all throughout the creation, he must invent some philosophy that would countermand the obvious "speech" and "knowledge" available every day and night. Satan must devise some scheme of origins that would satisfy the sinful mind. Lucifer was himself created (Ezekiel 28:15). He, whom the Lord Jesus told us "fathered" the lie, must have deceived himself into believing that he "just happened" and could successfully wage war against the only other Being who appeared to be superior to himself.

It is no accident that the ancient creation legend of Babylon speaks of two equal "gods" who arose out of the watery chaos and battled for supremacy. It is no accident that all of the eastern religions speak of a "duality" of nature—that "good" and "bad" are merely two sides of the same reality. It is no accident that the Egyptians worshiped the sun as the chief god Ra, who worked with his vast host of servants against the underworld. It is no accident that the Greeks and Romans taught that the Titans waged age-long war in the chaos of the "early days" of the universe and were ultimately conquered by Zeus, who with his consorts battled Hades for supremacy over man.

Nor is it an accident that modern man teaches his gospel of naturalistic evolution, with "natural selection" operating in place of the divine hand over billions of years—where the concepts of "good" and "bad" have no place in rational thinking. Nor is it surprising that the *Star Wars* saga of recent memory is based on the co-equality of a good and bad "Force" that is operating through each and every living thing in the universe, although one must be specially trained to "sense" it. The message distortion continues unabated.

God's Dominion Mandate

Nowhere has God's message been more rigorously fought than at the level of the initial command for all humanity (Genesis 1:28 and 9:1-7). Since this topic was covered at some length in chapter 7 of the first book of this series, *The Book of Beginnings, Volume One: Creation, Fall, and the Frist Age*, it is not necessary to repeat much of that information here. However, for purposes of understanding God's development of the nations on earth, it may be helpful to review the main directives of the mandate.

- **Be Fruitful and Multiply**. The concept of choice and selection is obviously involved in this command, but it also entails a desire to "multiply" so that the future is impacted. God intended for mankind to take the responsibility of "multiplying" far more seriously than merely having lots of children. The pressure to protect and direct the next generation is a God-placed propensity. An instinct to be fruitful and multiply is the fountainhead from which the rest of the Genesis mandate flows.

- **Fill the Earth**. God Himself is involved in "filling" the earth with the nations under His sovereign plan; it seems that this initial mandate to "fill" may imply more than merely biological reproduction. The capacity to "fill" would involve informational capacity (DNA) within each "kind" to adapt to new environments, intellectual capacity to plan for and carry out successful "filling," and geometric growth patterns that stabilize generations and communities.

- **Subdue the Earth**. God asks Adam (and through him all of us) to "conquer" the earth. Mankind would have to learn about the earth's systems and processes, organize and utilize that knowledge in productive ways to benefit others and honor the Creator, disseminate the information gained and the resulting products to everyone, and receive and detail the divine evaluation ("very good").

- **Have Dominion**. The authority to rule comes from the Owner. Sin has distorted the implementation of this authority. But disobedience and unfaithfulness do not abrogate the intent with which the initial authority was given. Man does indeed have authority over the resources of the planet, including its life forms. Proper stewardship is to be exercised on behalf of and within the purposes of the Owner.

- **Man as Steward**. God (the Creator) owns everything. Either one accepts the ownership of the Creator, or it is rejected. The message is not ambiguous. If God is the Creator, then He is the Owner, and mankind must one day answer to Him.

- **Man as Governor**. This final application is added after the Flood, giving all of humanity the authority to take human life when human life has been murderously taken. Obviously, this authority is not applicable to individuals, but to corporate man in exercise of God's authority to punish evil (Romans 13:3-4).

These foundational mandates are the principles by which God judges the nations and exercises His authority upon and among them. Each individual person is responsible to respond to these commands, of course, but individuals are not capable of impacting the whole of the planet or of carrying out the long-term plan of the Creator. That must involve the actions of the nations of men implemented over time.

God's Control over Nations

It should be no surprise, then, to find that the Bible is replete with examples of God directly intervening in the affairs of men. It is clear that God is sovereign. It is clear that God will work His will through to the completion of that will, and that even the "wrath of man shall praise" the One who created the world (Psalm 76:10).

> Why do the nations rage, And the people plot a vain thing? The kings of the earth set themselves, And the rulers take counsel together, Against the LORD and against His Anointed, saying, "Let us break their bonds in pieces And cast away their cords from us." He who sits in the heavens shall laugh; The Lord shall hold them in derision. (Psalm 2:1-4)

> Behold, the nations are as a drop in a bucket, And are counted as the small dust on the scales; Look, He lifts up the isles as a very little thing. (Isaiah 40:15)

Satan has been behind the plots of the nations to derail God's plan or to destroy His people. That began, of course, in the Garden of Eden with the temptation and subsequent fall of Adam and Eve. It was consummated in the First Age with the rise of the "giants on the earth," the horrible *nephilim* who attempted to raise a "master race" to defy the Creator (Genesis 6:4). Even the angelic world was involved in that rebellion. Yet not only did God destroy the plot and imprison the angels, casting "them down to hell and deliver[ing] them into chains of darkness" (2 Peter 2:4), but He destroyed the entire wicked human population except for Noah and his family.

Time and again, the great Enemy has attempted to raise a world empire to challenge the Creator. Only a few generations after the Flood, Satan empowered Nimrod to persuade the population to follow his rebellion at Babel. That ended when God confounded the languages of man and caused his disbursement all over the earth. Nor did it end there. Again and again, the foibles of men were exploited by the Devil to turn away from God's care and provision. Again and again, the empires of the earth were ridden by the "great harlot" astride the seven-headed beast (Revelation 17:1-3). The battle still rages.

One of the greatest nations on earth was Babylon under the rule of Nebuchadnezzar. The nation of Judah had been taken captive to Babylon (by God's will and under His judgment), and young prince Daniel had been taken into the king's entourage to serve at his pleasure. God had great plans for Daniel—and for Babylon. On two occasions, Daniel was asked to interpret dreams God had sent to King Nebuchadnezzar. One of those dreams was a prophecy for the rest of the age. Another was to teach Nebuchadnezzar a lesson on authority.

When Daniel first learned of God's message to Nebuchadnezzar foretelling the sequence of nations over the remaining age, he fell on his face and understood, perhaps for the first time, how much God was really in control.

> Daniel answered and said: "Blessed be the name of God forever and ever, For wisdom and might are His. And He changes the times and the seasons; He removes kings and raises up kings; He gives wisdom to the wise And knowledge to those who have understanding. He reveals deep and secret things; He knows what is in the darkness, And light dwells with Him." (Daniel 2:20-22)

God sent Nebuchadnezzar another dream that foretold an awful judgment: Unless he gave appropriate honor to the One who had granted him the power to rule, Nebuchadnezzar would be reduced to madness and live like an animal for years. Daniel was awestruck, and pleaded with Nebuchadnezzar to "break off your sins by being righteous" (Daniel 4:27). Nevertheless, Nebuchadnezzar refused to listen. He later reveled in his own majesty and the wonders of his success in building the nation and its magnificent cities, and was "that very hour" sent into exile. When he returned, he had this to say:

> I blessed the Most High and praised and honored Him who lives forever: For His dominion is an everlasting dominion, And His kingdom is from generation to generation. All the inhabitants of the earth are reputed as nothing; He does according to His will in the army of heaven And among the inhabitants of the earth. No one can restrain His hand Or say to Him, "What have You done?" (Daniel 4:34-35)

The Beginning of the Nations

All of this background may provide a strong enough perspective to encourage the reader to see the nations in a much different light. Nothing that happens is outside of God's purview. All nations are functioning under His oversight and will bring about the consummation of His plan. We who are on the closing end of God's plan should be all the more interested in what He has been doing and how these events are developing over time to bring to fruition the return of Christ and the reconciliation of the universe to God's purposes.

Several of the nations mentioned in Genesis 10 are recognized throughout Scripture and play major roles in the waxing and waning of the Kingdom's progress. Dr. Henry M. Morris notes in his excellent book *God and the Nations* the importance of watching the implementation of God's plan through the nations.

> Very few nations last a long time, of course. Nations rise and nations fall. One nation succeeds another in a given region, and then still another, and this process has been going on for centuries. All of this is taking place with the providence of God (and perhaps often by His direct intervention). As both Moses and Paul have reminded us (Deut. 32:8; Acts 17:24-26), the times and boundaries of the nations have been determined somehow by God, largely in reference to their individual faithfulness and effectiveness in carrying out His will for the nation.[1]

One of the great mysteries of Scripture is its scattered statements of God's sovereign predetermined control over the rise and fall of nations. "Known to God from eternity are all His works" (Acts 15:18). These plans and interventions throughout history appear to be related to how the various nations respond to the witness of God through the creation, and more specifically to the ministry of His prophets and spiritual leaders. The stated purpose for the "making" of these nations was that "they should seek the Lord, in

---

1.   Henry M. Morris, 2002, *God and the Nations*, Green Forest, AR: Master Books, 59.

the hope that they might grope for Him and find Him, though He is not far from each one of us; for in Him we live and move and have our being, as also some of your own poets have said, 'For we are also His offspring'" (Acts 17:27-28).

Therefore, it behooves us to pay attention to the role the nations have played and will play in the steadily unfolding plan of God.

The Nations of Japheth

Japheth was the eldest son of Noah. His seven sons recorded in Genesis 10 are Gomer, Magog, Madai, Javan, Tubal, Meshech, and Tiras. Four of these names should be well known to students of prophecy: Gomer, Magog, Meshech, and Tubal. Their descendants figure prominently in the battles outlined in Ezekiel 38 and 39, and again in Revelation 20. No wonder they are listed as important sons of Japheth!

But we must understand *where* these people groups settled if the biblical information is to be of any practical use as the last-days events prophesied in Scripture become more imminent. Some of this can be easily established.

Many of these family groups moved north and west after the incident at Babel. Japheth himself is frequently connected with the Iapheti, considered to be the ancestral name for the Greeks. That same name is also connected with the Aryans of India. Javan is connected with the Ionians, who are always identified as early Greek peoples. Many scholars strongly suggest that the bulk of the Indo-European populations came from Japheth's sons.

Herodotus, the noted Greek historian, insists that Gomer is the father of the Cimmerians. The Crimea today is located mostly around the northern shores of the Black Sea. It appears that some of these folks later migrated into Germany and Wales. Gomer's brother Magog seems to have had his name settle in Georgia, one of the former Soviet territories. Etymologists suggest that Magog means "the place of Gog."

Most historians agree that Madai is the one from whom the Medes came. The names of Tubal and Meshech surface early in southern Russia, apparently now preserved in the modern names of Moscow and Tobolsk. Meshech and Tubal appear together frequently in Ezekiel. There is some indication that "Muskovites" still represent Meshech. Tiras, the seventh son of Japheth, is probably the ancestor of the Thracians, who covered a large area of central and southeastern Europe.

Two of Japheth's sons, Gomer and Javan, have their sons listed in the table in Genesis 10. Ashkenaz, Riphath, and Togarmah are Gomer's sons. Elishah, Tarshish, Kittim, and Dodanim are Javan's sons. All seven are the grandsons of Japheth and in the third generation after the Flood.[2]

Ashkenaz is a name that has long been connected with German Jews. Even though some historians try to downplay or dispute the association, the "Ashkenazi" continue to use that title to describe themselves. Most of them settled in places like Bohemia, Hungary, Poland, Belarus, Lithuania, Russia, Ukraine, and Romania in Eastern Europe. William Albright suggests that the Ashkenazi are equivalent to the Scythians. Josephus equates the Scythians with the Magogites.

Josephus also insists that Riphath fathered the Paphlagonians, an ancient people-group that settled in the mountainous areas along the coasts of the Black Sea. Always mixing and mingling with the Greeks and later the Romans, these folks became assimilated into the Roman Empire and lost their identity. Togarmah may have followed his father Gomer into Germany. Some suggest that Togarmah's name is the source for the name Armenia, and that name seems to connect later to Turkey.

The Iliad mentions a people called the Eilesians, probably connected to Javan's son Elishah. It is also likely that Elishah is preserved in the Hellespont group the Hellenists—the same as the Greeks. The name Tarshish is famous in the Bible as the city toward which Jonah fled to keep from going to Nineveh. (The journey was interrupted

---

2. As indicated in the previous chapter, the generations referenced here are counted from the first family head given in each genealogical list.

when he got swallowed by the great fish.) Tarshish, son of Javan, is widely connected with seafaring peoples like the Phoenicians, the city of Carthage in North Africa, and Tartessus in Spain.

Two other grandsons of Japheth are given in Genesis 10. Kittim seems clearly to be connected with Cyprus. Occasionally, one runs across the term "Ma-Kittim" (Land of Kittim), which seems to designate the general region of Macedonia (Greece). Dodanim, the last-mentioned grandson, is likely preserved in the name Rodanim, and many suggest that term is probably found in the place names Dardanelles and Rhodes.

Please recall that these names are listed in Genesis for a reason. The stated purpose is that "from these the coastland peoples of the Gentiles were separated into their lands, everyone according to his language, according to their families, into their nations" (Genesis 10:5).

The Nations of Shem

The genealogical records given for Shem and his descendants are the most complete in the Bible. This is most certainly because it is from Shem that the nation of Israel is later formed, and through Israel came the Messiah. However, when Shem speaks of himself,[3] he considers another identity more important. He is "the father of all the children of Eber, the brother of Japheth the elder" (Genesis 10:21). Eber is a great-grandson to Shem—Shem to Arphaxad to Salah to Eber. It is unusual that the "recordkeeper" would single out a great-grandson of his—unless that great-grandson was a significant person in the events of the day.

Please recall that the events of Babel took place within the lifetime of the third generation after the Flood (counting from the sons of Noah), and that Noah and Shem (and many of the others) lived up until the time of Job and Abraham. Shem lived 502 years after the Flood (Genesis 11:10-11). That means he was still living when

---

3. Shem is considered to be the one who kept the genealogies from Genesis 10:2 through Genesis 11:10.

Abraham died some 467 years after the Flood. The recordkeeping was not a scattered collection of notes and memories; the birth dates and people mentioned were personally related and well known to those keeping the logs.

It should not be a surprise, therefore, that Shem would have bragged a bit on Eber. Eber seems to have been the king of Ebla, a major city of that era located in northern Syria that has provided a wealth of information about the early centuries after ancient Babel. Eber is also connected with the term "Hebrew" (the "h" sound is a common linguistic addition over time). Therefore, "the children of Eber" would include Peleg and direct descendants on down to Terah and Abram, the one whom God chose to begin the nation of Israel.

It may well have been that Abraham (or Terah) told Shem directly of the vision that God gave to Abraham. This would have dovetailed tightly with the prophecy that Noah spoke about Shem in Genesis 9:26, and Shem would have been thrilled to see one of his great-grandsons specifically called to "be a father of many nations" (Genesis 17:4). Shem would therefore have been proud to be called "the father of all the children of Eber."

Many of the Shemitic (or Semitic) nations had relatively short lives and are lost to antiquity. However, several were prominent and can be identified rather easily. Elam was the forebear of the Elamites, a group that later merged with the Medes, who themselves were descendants of Madai, one of Japheth's sons. Asshur's name became connected to the Assyrians. The early city of Asshur was eventually taken over by Nimrod and the Sumerian peoples. Lud is identified as the head of the Lydians, and Aram developed the Arameans, who later became the Syrians. The several other named descendants of Shem seem to have been absorbed by various people groups that settled in southern and eastern Arabia.

The most important descendant is, of course, Abram, who later became Abraham, the father of many nations. The son of promise, Isaac, produced both Jacob and Esau. Jacob was the father of the 12 sons who became the tribes of the nation of Israel. The son of the bondwoman Hagar was Ishmael. Abraham later married Keturah and that union produced six sons, seven grandsons, and three great-grand-sons who are named in the Bible (Genesis 25:1-4). Thus, the families of Ishmael, Esau, and the sons borne by Keturah (all related to Abraham) produced most of the nations that are thought of today as the Islamic people groups. And those are many nations, indeed.

The Nations of Ham

The record in Genesis lists four sons of Ham: Cush, Mizraim, Put, and Canaan. All of these sons founded well-known nations. Cush had at least six sons and two grandsons. Mizraim is recorded as having at least six sons, and Canaan is said to have had at least two sons—with nine "-ites" being named as descending from his line (Genesis 10:6-18). The Canaanites, of course, were the nations that inhabited the area promised to Abraham, the area that has been the source of so many battles and political concerns.

The description in Genesis of the land of the Canaanites reads almost like a Google map of Israel and portions of Lebanon today. It's funny how accurate the Bible's geographical and political records really are.

> And the border of the Canaanites was from Sidon as you go toward Gerar, as far as Gaza; then as you go toward So-dom, Gomorrah, Admah, and Zeboiim, as far as Lasha. These were the sons of Ham, according to their families, according to their languages, in their lands and in their nations. (Genesis 10:19-20)

Cush's most famous son was Nimrod, who developed the complex of cities centered on Babel. A longer discussion of the events at Babel was given in chapter 6. Those who remained with Nimrod at Babel after the dispersion later became known as the Sumerians (essentially synonymous with Babylonia), which became one of the great empires of that ancient world. Nimrod later conquered the city founded by Asshur (a descendant of Japheth), which became known as Assyria and was stilled called the "land of Nimrod" by Micah some 1,200 years later (Micah 5:6).

Cush and several of Ham's other descendants left after the language event at Babel and settled mostly in North Africa. Cush is typically translated "Ethiopia" by most Bible scholars, since it has been well-established that it was settled by the "Kashi," as the Cushites were called in the Tel el-Amarna tablets (also known as the Amarna letters). Those cuneiform tablets, written primarily in Akkadian, are composed of over 300 letters of commerce, and are a helpful source for the history of the development and spread of the Hamitic peoples. Many of the lesser descendants of Ham (Seba, Havilah, Sabtah, Raamah, Sabtechah, Sheba, and Dedan) seem to have settled in southern Arabia across the Red Sea from Ethiopia.

Mizraim is definitely the founder of Egypt. The Hebrew word *Mizraim* occurs at least 680 times in the Old Testament, 610 of which are translated "Egypt." The book of Revelation indicates that the Egyptian nation was the first of the seven empires that would develop under the "dragon" of prophecy.[4] Mizraim is most assuredly a major factor in the nations of history.

The name of Put (or Phut), the third son of Ham, appears seven times in Scripture, and is translated "Lybians," "Lybia," and "Lubim." That fits with other sources suggesting that the descendants of Put settled somewhat west of the descendants of Mizraim. Others have suggested that at least some of the Put peoples moved eastward toward Ethiopia and Somalia. Obviously, the bulk of the descendants of Mizraim and Put moved across the Red Sea to settle North Africa and eastward toward the horn of Africa.

Canaan appears to be the source of much of the biblical concerns related to the interchange between Israel and the nations living in the land of promise south of Syria. Canaan is the ancestor of the Phoenicians and the Hittites. The name of Sidon, Canaan's' firstborn son, is still preserved in the city by that name in what is now Lebanon.

---

4. See the notes for Revelation 12:3 and 17:10 in Henry M. Morris, 2012, *The Henry Morris Study Bible*, Green Forest, AR: Master Books, 2014, 2028.

Sidon, the chief city of the Phoenicians, and the companion city of Tyre formed the dual headquarters for that well-known nautical nation whose exploits are still being uncovered. Heth, Canaan's other named son, became the father of the Hittites. Through Canaan also came the many other "-ite" nations known by Moses and Joshua collectively as the Canaanites.

The Hittites have been verified as being strongly settled in Turkey. Herodotus makes mention of the famous king Midas as one of the peoples connected to the Hittites. Based on similarities between various monuments, the Sinites have been portrayed by some scholars as having migrated from Ararat and Babel into parts of Asia. That migration, these scholars would suggest, is the beginning of the Chinese nations. The term "Cathay" may have a linguistic connection to "Khittae," used by the Hittites in some of those ancient monuments. The notation in Genesis 10:18 simply says, "Afterward the families of the Canaanites were dispersed."

Other Issues

Obviously, the development of these 70 family nations listed in Genesis 10 becomes more difficult to trace as they broaden their territories, strengthen their political alliances, and eventually become absorbed into the more powerful nations as time progresses. There are nearly 200 politically identifiable nations today.[5] From the original 70 languages after the confusion of tongues at Babel, well over 6,000 languages and dialects can be identified as spoken within those nations.

Much study has gone into tracing the ethnic (genetic) connections of the descendants of the three sons of Noah. The bigger picture is more easily understood.

- Japhetic peoples are mainly the Caucasian groups of Indo-Europe.
- Shemitic (Semitic) peoples are the Jewish and Arab groups.
- Hamitic peoples are mostly related to the African and Eastern nations.

---

5. The United Nations claimed 193 nations as full voting members as of April 2012.

There is certainly a mingling of these groups today, but the individual lineages are still recognizable.

Cave Men

Part of the evolutionary story, of course, is that man slowly evolved through various stages until the modern *Homo sapiens* came on the scene. Every museum of natural history has some diorama showing "cave men" with a long-armed, low-browed, and stoop-shouldered stature, wearing animal-skin loincloths and huddled around a fire while drawing stick figures on cave walls next to them. These fanciful depictions were developed from tiny bits of fossilized material, some tools found near cave sites, and pictures and pictographs discovered in a few locations around the world.

Contrary to the impression given in news reports, TV programs, and other media, such discoveries are few. They appear in a recognizable "ring" around the European continent, with just enough evidence to establish that there was a "hunter-gatherer" culture around those sites. The locations show no evidence of a long residence. There is no evidence that these peoples consisted of large groups, but rather that they centered around a few shelters in a known area and then... disappeared!

And that is just what one would expect if the event at Babel transpired as the Bible teaches. Suddenly, the language of each "family" became gibberish to everyone else. The weaker and smaller families were either driven away by the stronger groups or voluntarily chose to find another location to "multiply" and "fill the earth." Instantly obeying the command of the Creator, and being forced to find another place to establish their homes, they were driven into a short "hunting and gathering" existence while they migrated. It is clear they had knowledge; they were part of the group at Babel who were building a city of brick and a worship tower.

But knowledge without resources was futile—until the resources could be located and developed for use. Even the first people of the great Egyptian nation had to migrate from Mesopotamia after their language was separated from the others. They had the knowledge to build the great pyramids, but must first have had to supply themselves on a long march through uninhabited wilderness, surviving in natural shelters to begin with and making use of minimal tools until the leadership began to take shape and organize the new "nation" into an effective society.

The Races

The concept of "race" has been the bane of many discussions and the source of many political efforts to redress injustices done over the centuries. Both Europe and the United States have struggled with slavery, the practice of which was often justified by a terribly incorrect interpretation of Genesis 9:24 as a "curse" on the black-skinned peoples of sub-Saharan Africa. Essentially, the Negro populations were considered inferior to lighter-skinned populations because of their supposed connection to Ham, whose name was touted to mean "dark." Therefore, the "dark" peoples who had descended from Ham were "cursed" and considered to be fair game for use as "servants." That false interpretation and its impact are more fully discussed in chapter 5.

It is no secret that Charles Darwin subtitled his famous book *Origin of Species* "The Preservation of Favoured Races in the Struggle for Life." In fact, the Negro "races" of Africa were deemed subhuman by Darwin as he tried to document examples of "natural selection." Thomas Huxley, one of Darwin's strongest proponents, insisted that the Negro was inferior to the "white man."

> No rational man, cognizant of the facts, believes that the average negro is the equal, still less the superior, of the white man. And if this be true, it is simply incredible that, when all his disabilities are removed, and our prognathous relative has a fair field and no favour, as well as no oppressor, he will be able to compete successfully with his bigger-brained and smaller-jawed rival, in a contest which is to be carried out by thoughts and not by bites.[6]

---

6. Thomas Huxley, 1871, *Lay Sermons, Addresses and Reviews*, New York: D. Appleton, 20.

The atrocities of Hitler were justified by a strong evolutionary belief, with his followers piously going about exterminating the "unfit" races that polluted Europe. Sir Arthur Keith, a well-known anthropologist and evolutionist, made this simple comment about Hitler: "The German Fuhrer…has consciously sought to make the practice of Germany conform to the theory of evolution."[7] Margaret Sanger, of Planned Parenthood fame, started the modern movement of eugenics, by which was meant the conscious elimination of the "unfit races" that were a burden to society.

The concept of "race" is now so ingrained in our consciousness that we use the term without thinking. What is normally meant is a correlation of ethnicity or an observable trait such as skin color and/or eye shape or some other physical feature. This has done and continues to do huge damage to social efforts of "integration" and "politicization" in our country. Sadly, the fight enters almost every facet of life.

How did the different ethnicities originate? God's intervention at Babel split humanity into 70 separate family groups. Since the genetic information of each group was now confined within a single family, it would not be long before dominant features began to surface among the early generations. And as time moved onward, the ruling families forced others to migrate elsewhere (all in accord with the overall plan of God), bringing to the forefront other dominant features that would physically set them apart from each other "nation."

People do the same thing with animals all the time. We call it "breeding," and the results are a special "breed" of dogs, cats, cattle, etc. We call such efforts a "science" and brag about how quickly we can establish a new breed that makes headlines at the pet show and money at the pet shop. God is much better at it, and does it without fanfare. He allows even the "wrath" of men to accomplish His purposes outlined so long ago in the Garden of Eden.

The Bible knows absolutely nothing about "race." "He has made from one blood every nation of men to dwell on all the face of the

---

7. Arthur Keith, 1949, *Evolution and Ethics*, New York: G. P. Putnam's Sons, 230.

earth" (Acts 17:26). What God intended to do was to divide humanity by language. And that was done at Babel for the protection of mankind so that the Satanic effort to enslave the entirety of the world's population would be hindered until the end of time.

CHAPTER EIGHT
LESSONS FROM JOB

Attached to the Wisdom Literature of the Psalms, Proverbs, Ecclesiastes, and the Song of Solomon, the book of Job is probably the oldest section of the Old Testament.[1] No one is absolutely sure who wrote it, but the internal references and allusions to the creation, the specific judgments given at the Fall of man, and the several references to the great Flood of Noah's day and the events immediately following the disbursement of the nations at Babel would suggest that Job himself authored this epic poem.

The main purpose for evaluating this book here is to gain a perspective on the young earth's condition at the time of Abraham. A straight event-to-event calculation of the birth records from Shem to Abram would put Abram's birth at 292 years after the Flood. The dispersal at Babel would have taken place sometime early in the second or third century, thus making the events described in the book of Job sometime during the fourth century, probably in the years before Abram left Ur of the Chaldees with his father Terah to go to Haran.

Thus, God has given us an insight to the character of the nations that had been displaced from the area around Babel. The book of Job

---

1. Apart from Genesis 1-11, which is no doubt older. Based on attributions in the text and other indications, the first 11 chapters of Genesis were evidently written by Adam, Noah, Noah's sons, and Terah, and later compiled by Moses.

offers contemporary knowledge of the difficulties faced by the families who were forced to leave the settled civilization of the Babel-Nineveh complex of cities, endure the hardships of survival, and develop cities, businesses, and trade relations of their own. The debate between Job and his friends gives keen insight into the theology of the day, and can help Bible students grasp the challenges facing Abram and Lot when they left the safety of the well-established city of Ur to travel north and west into a far less secure territory.

The Land of Uz

The book of Job takes place in the land of Uz (Job 1:1). Uz was one of the sons of Aram and a grandson of Shem (Genesis 10:22-23). Since Shem's first son, Arphaxad, was born only two years after the Flood, it is likely that his remaining sons would have been born in some reasonable sequence of time thereafter. And daughters would have been interspersed in between, as they were in the lineages of the other sons of Noah (Genesis 11:11, etc.), else there would have been no wives to produce the subsequent generations!

The average age of the fathers at which their named sons were born in the generations after Shem was around 36 years old—35 + 30 + 34 + 30 + 32 + 30 + 29 + 70 = 290 divided by 8 (Genesis 11:10-26). Aram, the father of Uz, may well have been the last born of the named sons of Shem (Genesis 10:22), but it is unlikely that he would have been born past the first century after the Flood. Please remember that the events at Babel took place sometime during the fifth generation (the generation of Peleg), and Uz would have been alive during that event.

The land of Uz is later associated with the territory of Edom (Lamentations 4:21), which is near the area southeast of the Dead Sea. That reference would indicate that Uz and his family migrated southwestward, either from the area around Babel (the central Tigris and Euphrates plateaus) or from the early settlements around the "mountains of Ararat." The land of Uz would have been toward the upper reaches of the Sinai Peninsula, east of Egypt and just north of the Red Sea. Although that area is not very pleasant now, at the time of Abraham it was "well watered everywhere (before the LORD destroyed Sodom and Gomorrah) like the garden of the LORD, like the land of Egypt as you go toward Zoar" (Genesis 13:10). Quite likely, this was one of the more beautiful spots that was safely away from the rule of Nimrod and farther away from the climate shifts that were leading to the coming Ice Age.

Job and Friends

By the time the epic poem begins, Job had established himself as one of the more well-known leaders in the area. He was wealthy by any standards, in possession of "seven thousand sheep, three thousand camels, five hundred yoke of oxen, five hundred female donkeys, and a very large household" (Job 1:3). It is likely that Job was a tradesman, something of an import-export businessman, accumulating an enormous stock that he could sell for seed stock, wholesale food supplies, and equipping distance caravans for himself and others.

It is quite likely that the four friends cited in the book were connected to Job's business in some way, since they lived at different points across the Arabian Peninsula. Eliphaz was from Teman, a city in the northern part of the land that later became known as Edom. Bildad was from Shuhu, somewhat south of Haran near the southern borders of what is now Turkey. Zophar was from Naamah, which was likely located to the east in the south of Canaan. Elihu, the young man who speaks in the later chapters of the book, was from Buz, located in northern Arabia. None of these men were "next door neighbors." They came to comfort Job from some distance. Their relationship to Job is not given, but it is obvious that they knew Job over both distance and time.

The two war-party bands that destroyed Job's family and rustled his livestock were the Sabeans and the Chaldeans. The Sabeans had settled in the southwest tip of the Arabian Peninsula in the area that is now known as Yemen. The Chaldeans were the people group that remained at Babel and developed the Babylonian nation in the middle of the Tigris-Euphrates River Valley. It is obvious that they were aware of Job's success or they would not have sent raiding parties such distances. Even though the world was still developing after the Flood's devastation, the population was growing and breeding programs for domestic animals were burgeoning.

The book clearly indicates that Job was a person of note in his world. In one of the sessions with his friends, Job was accused of having a secret sin of some sort. In his defense, Job described the respect that he had among the nobility of the region before his downfall.

> "When I went out to the gate by the city, When I took my seat in the open square, the young men saw me and hid, and the aged arose and stood; The princes refrained from talking, And put their hand on their mouth; The voice of nobles was hushed, and their tongue stuck to the roof of their mouth." (Job 29:7-10)

The next several verses tell of his generosity and charity work. Job was indeed one of the more righteous men living at the time.

> "When the ear heard, then it blessed me, And when the eye saw, then it approved me; Because I delivered the poor who cried out, The fatherless and the one who had no helper. The blessing of a perishing man came upon me, And I caused the widow's heart to sing for joy. I put on righteousness, and it clothed me; My justice was like a robe and a turban. I was eyes to the blind, And I was feet to the lame. I was a father to the poor, And I searched out the case that I did not know. I broke the fangs of the wicked, And plucked the victim from his teeth." (Job 29:11-17)

Memories of the Flood

Job contains many references to the Flood, couched in the language of those who had personal knowledge of the event—not like the later legends and stories drawn from misty memories.

"He removes the mountains, and they do not know When He overturns them in His anger; He shakes the earth out of its place, And its pillars tremble; He commands the sun, and it does not rise; He seals off the stars; He alone spreads out the heavens, And treads on the waves of the sea." (Job 9:5-8)

The word choices in this little section depict the creation being shaken to the core, "trembling" at the force of the awful judgment that was released on the earth. Modern creationist and Flood geologists can only surmise what may have happened during the year of the Flood. Job and his friends were living during the lifetime of Noah and his sons, and would have had access to those with a direct knowledge of the earth being moved "out of its place," as well as firsthand experience with the unfathomable power of God and the scope of His judgment.

"If He breaks a thing down, it cannot be rebuilt; If He imprisons a man, there can be no release. If He withholds the waters, they dry up; If He sends them out, they overwhelm the earth." (Job 12:14-15)

The "world that then existed," the apostle Peter notes, "perished" (2 Peter 3:6). Once the evil of the First Age had become intense and widespread, the gracious and omnipotent Creator offered 120 years of opportunity for mankind to repent and turn from wickedness. But when that opportunity ran its course and Noah, the "preacher of righteousness," had given his last invitation, God "shut the door" to the Ark and the judgment waters came and overwhelmed the earth.

"Will you keep to the old way Which wicked men have trod, Who were cut down before their time, Whose foundations were swept away by a flood? They said to God, 'Depart from us! What can the Almighty do to them?'" (Job 22:15-17)

The friends of Job were direct descendants of the sons of Noah. They had heard the account of the Flood—if not directly from the mouth of Noah or one of his sons, each had surely heard it from his own father or his father's father who had received a direct telling. Noah lived for 350 years after the Flood. Shem lived 502 years beyond the day he and the rest of Noah's family disembarked from the Ark. Shem outlived Abraham! Job and his friends lived during the same time as Terah and Abraham. They were no strangers to the information regarding the end of the First Age. They knew that the evil people living prior to the Flood had been in full rebellion against the Almighty. They knew!

> "The pillars of heaven tremble, And are astonished at His rebuke. He stirs up the sea with His power, And by His understanding He breaks up the storm. By His Spirit He adorned the heavens; His hand pierced the fleeing serpent. Indeed these are the mere edges of His ways, And how small a whisper we hear of Him! But the thunder of His power who can understand?" (Job 26:11-14)

Our generation mocks the authority and power of God. But these men lived in the days when the evidence of God's anger at sin was still fresh in the minds and memories of everybody. Eliphaz the Temanite, Bildad the Shuhite, and Zophar the Naamathite were certainly not born past the seventh generation after the Flood. So impressed were they at the horrible consequences that came on those who sinned against the Creator, they were convinced that Job's awful sickness and tragic losses must be the result of sin. If the "pillars of heaven" were shaken by God's judgment, then Job ought to "come clean" before God destroyed him like He did the prior cosmos.

Memories of Babel

One would suspect that Job and his friends would also show direct knowledge of the rebellion of Nimrod and the events at Babel. Although the language in Genesis 10 and 11 is somewhat limited, the text does insist that the whole earth was impacted by those events—at least as far as human language was concerned. That could not have happened without resulting in widespread knowledge of what had occurred.

But the book of Job doesn't reflect any trace of the worship of the "host of heaven" that dominated Babel. Neither Job nor any of his friends give allegiance to "mystical" powers, but freely acknowledge the sovereign power of the Creator. There is no hint of polytheism or pantheism, but only a somewhat confused idea about God's justice. It is possible that the people groups that later founded these extended settlements could have been isolated from the distorted worship under Nimrod—perhaps because of Shem's resistance to Nimrod's rebellion. Then, when the world was "reshuffled" after Babel, they took their knowledge of the Creator with them to their new homes.

Job, along with his friends, could have been born after his forebears had survived the trek from Babel following the confusion of languages. The stories and memories of those awful days would have still been fresh. One of Job's responses to his friends provides a summary that seems to be an overview of the experiences many people would have had in finding new places to live after the terrible disruption of their lives at Babel.

> "He deprives the trusted ones of speech, And takes away the discernment of the elders. He pours contempt on princes, And disarms the mighty. He uncovers deep things out of darkness, And brings the shadow of death to light. He makes nations great, and destroys them; He enlarges nations, and guides them. He takes away the understanding of the chiefs of the people of the earth, And makes them wander in a pathless wilderness. They grope in the dark without light, And He makes them stagger like a drunken man." (Job 12:20-25)

Following the awful confusion and subsequent physical disbursement of the families around the lush area of the fertile valley in between the Tigris and Euphrates Rivers, at least some of the families (no doubt the weaker and smaller ones) would have been required to live off the land as they traveled. For a short season, they would be forced to live as the so-called "hunter-gatherers" of ancient history.

Their plight is remembered by Job as he bemoans his own sorrow and exile. Now in poverty and pain, Job likens himself to those who were driven out from the relative security of Nimrod's empire into the caves and wild lands where no human had gone before. It is no wonder that modern archaeologists find remnants of such an existence. Cave men really did exist—but they were not the beetle-browed savages of evolutionary development, they were merely the "rejects" and refugees of a savage ruler who drove from his domain those who could not understand his language!

> "They are gaunt from want and famine, Fleeing late to the wilderness, desolate and waste, Who pluck mallow by the bushes, And broom tree roots for their food. They were driven out from among men, They shouted at them as at a thief. They had to live in the clefts of the valleys, In caves of the earth and the rocks. Among the bushes they brayed, Under the nettles they nestled. They were sons of fools, Yes, sons of vile men; They were scourged from the land." (Job 30:3-8)

This was recent history to Job and his friends. They knew those who had made the journey. They were no doubt aware of some family members who had died as a result of that terrible judgment. This was not rumor or legend. This was as vivid to them as the memories of parents and grandparents.

Theological Considerations

The book of Job contains some unique information. Once the biblical record reaches the history of Abraham, it provides a wealth of insight about the choosing of Abraham and the founding of the nation that would be the human agency through which the blessing of the Redeemer would come. This section of Genesis and the later Old Testament books of history and prophecy offer lessons of faith, obedience, disdain, and rebellion in the lives of the patriarchs and the kings, prophets, and warriors of Israel. The intervention of Jehovah is declared and demonstrated again and again—but the nature of the spiritual Enemy, Satan, is more often than not shrouded in mystery.

We know from the early chapters of Genesis that Satan was behind the successful temptation of Eve and the knowledgeable rebellion of Adam. But even there, if it were not for the subsequent details provided in the New Testament book of Revelation—which show the connection between the serpent in the beautiful Garden of Eden and the serpent of seven heads and ten horns[2]—it would be difficult to tie the archangel to the cunning creature that instigated the Fall.

Not so in Job.

Satan's Proposition

It is not clear if it was Job who described the interchanges between Satan and God in the first and second chapters of the book. There is nothing in the body of the epic that would indicate Job knew what had taken place in the heavens. Perhaps God gave Job the insight as the poem was inspired, or perhaps Moses wrote the preamble as he completed Genesis. (The book of Job predated the editing of Genesis.) But whatever the case, the dialogue between the Creator of heaven and earth and the "the anointed cherub who covers," the one who was perfect "from the day [he was] created" (Ezekiel 28:14-15), is only found in the first chapters of Job.

> Now there was a day when the sons of God came to present themselves before the LORD, and Satan also came among them. And the LORD said to Satan, "From where do you come?" So Satan answered the LORD and said, "From going to and fro on the earth, and from walking back and forth on it." (Job 1:6-7)

This is a startling piece of information. To begin with, it does not seem to fit with the common idea that Satan was cast out of heaven prior to Genesis 3. Most Bible commentators would suggest that when the Jesus said that He "saw Satan fall like lightning from heav-

---

2. See the note for Revelation 12:9 in Henry M. Morris, 2012, *The Henry Morris Study Bible*, Green Forest, AR: Master Books, 2015.

en," He was referring to Satan's ejection from heaven prior to the Fall of man (Luke 10:18). Also, many would suggest that when Michael led the battle against Satan recorded in Revelation that culminated when Satan "was cast to the earth, and his angels were cast out with him," the same event was being described (Revelation 12:7-9).

Furthermore, most theology presumes that when Satan was cast out of heaven, he became "the prince of the power of the air" (Ephesians 2:2) and has been confined to earth, working feverishly to assemble the ultimate human army to defy and defeat the Creator. If that is so, then the rather nonchalant appearance of Lucifer in Job 1:6 among the "sons of God" in the throne room seems very much out of place.

Perhaps, as Job's account would imply, the arrogance of Satan is based on the "freedom" he believes he has as one of the chief angels, "going to and fro" with apparent impunity "seeking whom he may devour" (1 Peter 5:8). Whatever may be the actual state of Lucifer's freedom under the sovereignty of Almighty God, here, in the early years after the Flood, Satan responds to God's question regarding Job and dares to make a proposition.

> Then the LORD said to Satan, "Have you considered My servant Job, that there is none like him on the earth, a blameless and upright man, one who fears God and shuns evil?"
>
> So Satan answered the LORD and said, "Does Job fear God for nothing? Have You not made a hedge around him, around his household, and around all that he has on every side? You have blessed the work of his hands, and his possessions have increased in the land. But now, stretch out Your hand and touch all that he has, and he will surely curse You to Your face!"
>
> And the LORD said to Satan, "Behold, all that he has is in your power; only do not lay a hand on his person." So Satan went out from the presence of the LORD. (Job 1:8-12)

Several points must be noted. First, Satan acknowledges the sovereign power of God (whether in pretense, flattery, or acknowledgment). Satan concedes that *God* has "made a hedge" around Job and that *God* has "blessed the work of his hands." Second, the challenge (or proposal) required that *God* "touch" all that Job had, with Satan's assumption that Job would then curse the One who had blessed him. Finally, although Satan had the power to do the damage (and he does have great power), he appears to understand that no damage could be done to Job unless the Creator Himself gave the permission.

God's protective authority is verified in the New Testament.

> No temptation has overtaken you except such as is common to man; but God is faithful, *who will not allow you to be tempted* beyond what you are able, but with the temptation will also make the way of escape, that you may be able to bear it. (1 Corinthians 10:13)

No explanation is given with the stunning account in Job 1. Job had proven his righteousness and his trust in the Lord. And even when suddenly plunged into total poverty and riven of his children, Job did not curse or blame God. Instead, the Bible says that he worshiped!

> Job arose, tore his robe, and shaved his head; and he fell to the ground and worshiped. And he said: "Naked I came from my mother's womb, And naked shall I return there. The Lord gave, and the Lord has taken away; Blessed be the name of the Lord." In all this Job did not sin nor charge God with wrong. (Job 1:20-22)

God, apparently, was willing to allow His "servant" Job, whom He considered to be "blameless and upright," to suffer the loss of all of his possessions and all of his children—to prove a point! And to make matters appear to be worse, after Job has lost everything in a single day, Satan returns to double down on the bet!

> Again there was a day when the sons of God came to present themselves before the Lord, and Satan came also among them to present himself before the Lord. And the

LORD said to Satan, "From where do you come?"

So Satan answered the LORD and said, "From going to and fro on the earth, and from walking back and forth on it."

Then the LORD said to Satan, "Have you considered My servant Job, that there is none like him on the earth, a blameless and upright man, one who fears God and shuns evil? And still he holds fast to his integrity, although you incited Me against him, to destroy him without cause."

So Satan answered the LORD and said, "Skin for skin! Yes, all that a man has he will give for his life. But stretch out Your hand now, and touch his bone and his flesh, and he will surely curse You to Your face!"

And the LORD said to Satan, "Behold, he is in your hand, but spare his life." So Satan went out from the presence of the LORD, and struck Job with painful boils from the sole of his foot to the crown of his head. (Job 2:1-7)

Obviously, some time had passed after the first "report" of Satan before the throne. Job had proven God's point. Once again God confronts Satan with the stellar character of Job, and once again Satan arrogantly suggests that if God "stretches His hand" against Job—this time by ruining his health—Job would rebel and disavow his relationship with God.

The marvel in this account is that God seems to be willing to go along with Satan without any apparent care for what happens to Job. God is supposed to be a God of love, and yet He appears callous toward Job's plight. From our perspective on this side of heaven, the account is both surprising and a bit unnerving. Why is God so indifferent to Job? What guarantee is there that God would not allow Satan to run such a "test" again with someone else? How does that square with the issue of pain and suffering being permitted by a loving God?

Pain and Suffering

Theologians and philosophers have wrestled with this question for ages. On the one hand, if God is sovereign and omnipotent, why does He permit "bad" things to exist? On the other hand, since pain and suffering do exist, does that not prove that God is not omnipotent, or not "good," or both? Logic would seemingly demand one conclusion or the other. Usually, those who are personally hurt by the existence of evil (pain and suffering) insist that God either does not exist or cannot stop evil, and therefore does not deserve allegiance. Charles Darwin disavowed the existence of God because of this problem.

Although the debate will not be settled in this short chapter, there are some Bible facts that must be considered.

When Adam and Eve chose to embrace the lie of self-determination and reject the rule of the Creator over them, God pronounced the sentence of death on all life and the sentence of disorder on all functioning systems in the universe. Death, of course, is the source of all pain and suffering, and "thorns and thistles" represent the ultimate decay of function and order in everything else (Genesis 3:17-19; Romans 8:22). Pain and suffering (that which man calls evil) is the *result,* not the *cause,* of evil.

Furthermore, God presents Himself throughout the Scriptures as sovereign over the affairs of men. Debates over a Calvinistic or an Arminian view of theology notwithstanding, "Will the thing formed say to him who formed it, 'Why have you made me like this?' Does not the potter have power over the clay, from the same lump to make one vessel for honor and another for dishonor?" (Romans 9:20-21). When theology or philosophy differs from Scripture, the choice is either one or the other. The amalgamation of the differences always leads to error.

And that is what happened to Job's friends. Since Job was suffering and God was sovereign, the only solution in their minds was that Job had violated one of God's laws and was therefore suffering *because* he had sinned. Logic dictated that God was good and right, therefore

Job was wrong and evil. The trouble was, of course, that human logic could not take into account the inscrutable omniscience of an omnipotent Creator.

The great mystery of the human will and the choice God gives us to submit and love Him is beyond our ability to explain. Satan needed a lesson in sovereignty, but also a lesson in love. Satan's logic would have it that all love was self-serving. He (Satan) was the deceived Deceiver. He had deceived himself into believing that he could overthrow the Creator—that he could win the worship of the human race by throwing his largess of power and brilliance on those who follow his leadership. (That sounds suspiciously like the human history of political manipulation over the millennia.)

What Satan could not understand, and what he needed to be taught, was that some of the human race were "blameless and upright" like Job, and loved and trusted God for their eternal destiny. That kind could not be "bought" by possessions or circumstances, but would declare—as Job later did—that "though He slay me, yet will I trust Him" (Job 13:15).

Satan has twisted the judgment of God against sin into an unfair condition that can be reversed by health and wealth. His original lie to Adam and Eve was that they could obtain the power of God by grasping the "secret" of evil. His effort to take over the human race using the duplicity of angelic power and human procreation described in Genesis 6 was destroyed by God with the great Flood. Satan tried again with Nimrod at Babel, and was defeated by God when human language was confounded. Now Lucifer attempts to "trick" God into taking away His blessing on Job so that Satan would have an "example" to show of God's capricious care. All Satan got for his efforts was the testimony of this great man that has been enshrined in Scripture, encouraging the rest of humanity with its depiction of the almighty God of creation.

Pain and suffering do indeed exist, but they are the result of sin, not the cause of it. Satan would have mankind believe that God cannot relieve it, and that the only "cure" is the pursuit of health and wealth. God will sometimes allow Satan to use his angelic prowess to injure the godly, but in doing so—every time—the grace and power of God is demonstrated by those who love and trust in God.

God's Plan for Israel

There is no mention of the nation of Israel in the book of Job. There is no reference to the Ten Commandments. And although there is reference to sacrifice, there is no hint that a system of formal liturgical tabernacle or temple worship was known. Everything in the book suggests that its authorship is long before the nation of Israel existed. References to law demonstrate a general knowledge of God's will similar to what Abraham knew from personal interaction with the Creator. "Abraham obeyed My voice and kept My charge, My commandments, My statutes, and My laws" (Genesis 26:5). Job said essentially the same thing: "I have not departed from the commandment of His lips; I have treasured the words of His mouth More than my necessary food" (Job 23:12).

Up until the codification of the Law under Moses, personal sacrifices were performed by the head of the family, not by a delegated and ordained priest. Noah and Abraham both followed the earlier practice (see Genesis 8:20 and 22:13). This was clearly the practice of Job and his three friends (Job 1:5 and 42:7-9). Although these offerings were connected to atonement for sins committed, Job's friends give a hint of a doctrine of salvation through works. The main thought among these friends concerning righteousness seemed to be reciprocity. That is, if you are good, good things will happen to you. If you are bad, bad things will happen.

Job's Gospel

However, it is very clear that this reciprocity was not the belief system that motivated Job. His friends may well have bought into the growing philosophy of "works" that would suffice for salvation, but not this "blameless" and "upright" servant of God. Although Job continually protested that he had lived a righteous life and was mystified why God had allowed the calamities to descend on him, Job still understood that he was a sinner by nature and needed the cleansing that only God could provide.

> "What is man, that You should exalt him, That You should set Your heart on him?" (Job 7:17)

> "But how can a man be righteous before God?" (Job 9:2)

> "Who can bring a clean thing out of an unclean? No one!" (Job 14:4)

The "mystery of godliness" revealed in the New Testament—the simplicity of the gospel of salvation through the death of Jesus Christ (1 Timothy 3:16)—may not have been clear to Job. Job's contemporary, Abraham, "believed God" at the simple level of promised nations, and God "accounted it to him for righteousness" (Genesis 15:6). Whatever insight God had revealed to Job through the lives of Noah and the rest of Job's forebears, Job expressed one of the most solid comments about the resurrection in the entire Old Testament.

> "For I know that my Redeemer lives, And He shall stand at last on the earth; And after my skin is destroyed, this I know, That in my flesh I shall see God, Whom I shall see for myself, And my eyes shall behold, and not another. How my heart yearns within me!" (Job 19:25-27)

Even God Himself said of Job: "Have you considered My servant Job, that there is none like him on the earth, a blameless and upright man, one who fears God and shuns evil?" (Job 1:8). Job knew the "good news" of a holy, loving, saving Creator and coming King.

The Witness of Creation

The last five chapters of the book of Job are a magnificent look at the creation and at God's sovereignty over it. The self-righteous friends had attempted to justify their understanding of God by blaming Job for the pain that he was enduring. Job had consistently insisted that although he knew that he was born in sin, he had not knowingly violated anything that God had required of him, and begged God for an answer to his dilemma. Why, when he had tried to live a godly life, had God brought such calamity in his life?

God's answer is most interesting. Not once did God explain Himself. Not once did He give Job an insight into the "why" question. God simply asked a series of rhetorical questions, with some questions designed to elicit the admission that only God could know their answers, and other questions designed to highlight man's lack of knowledge regarding many areas of his world. Some of these questions are genuine avenues for research. That is, a genuine effort to fulfill the initial mandate to subdue and rule the earth would involve finding the answers in order to fulfill the stewardship role delegated to humanity. Others were obviously outside man's ability to answer—except by acknowledging that God's authority and power are the answer.

Questions about the Beginning

> "Where were you when I laid the foundations of the earth? Tell Me, if you have understanding. Who determined its measurements? Surely you know! Or who stretched the line upon it? To what were its foundations fastened? Or who laid its cornerstone, When the morning stars sang together, And all the sons of God shouted for joy?" (Job 38:4-7)

Origins do matter! How one perceives his or her origin makes a huge difference in how faith and actions are developed. Rather than answering the plaintive cry of "why," God forced Job to consider how he came to be. To any honest person, the answers to these questions could only be a combination of "I don't know" and "God did it." Yet ever since the rebellion in the Garden, man has followed the insinuations of Satan and tried to invent preposterous stories about how "things" came to be.

Since the ancient Babylonian Enuma Elish creation myth, priests and shamans, scientists and theologians have fostered tales of "gods" or "forces" evolving the present universe out of the chaos of the unknown. Some tales are more fanciful than others. Some are more sophisticated. But all of the myriad "theories" are variations of the same theme—that the random, purposeless, or capricious interplay of "nature" has, over unthinkable eons of time, resulted in the "apparent" design and order of today.

The questions of God to Job still remain unanswered. The basis of all science is observation. How can thinking man observe the chaotic past when there was no human present? What test can be devised that can re-create the creation? To ask such questions is to know the answer! The observable evidence is overwhelming. Only a Being with omniscience and omnipotence could possibly "lay the foundations of the earth." Yet in spite of such knowledge, men persist in their willful denial of the Creator:

> Although they knew God, they did not glorify Him as God, nor were thankful, but became futile in their thoughts, and their foolish hearts were darkened. Professing to be wise, they became fools, and changed the glory of the incorruptible God into an image made like corruptible man—and birds and four-footed animals and creeping things....[They] exchanged the truth of God for the lie, and worshiped and served the creature rather than the Creator. (Romans 1:21-23, 25)

Just like Satan, who was among the "morning stars" that sang when they watched the earth being "hung upon nothing" (Job 38:7; 26:7), these men denied and distorted the evidence before their own eyes so that they might worship the "creature" rather than the Creator.

Questions about the Flood Judgment

> "Or who shut in the sea with doors, When it burst forth and issued from the womb; When I made the clouds its garment, And thick darkness its swaddling band; When I fixed My limit for it, And set bars and doors; When I said, 'This far you may come, but no farther, And here your proud waves must stop!' Have you commanded the

morning since your days began, And caused the dawn to know its place, That it might take hold of the ends of the earth, And the wicked be shaken out of it?" (Job 38:8-13)

None alive today have observed anything like the horrific cataclysm of the global Flood. Job would certainly have heard about it. Noah and Shem would have told and retold the terror of that judgment, but Job and those who followed could only observe the results of those awful energies. Yet just like the obvious answers to the questions about the creation, the evidence of the Flood judgment does not "fit" the stories of natural evolution. Those who reject the creation must also, by necessity, reject the global Flood. Those who believe that the God of Scripture exists, however, have no trouble answering the questions about the Flood.

Questions about Physics

"It takes on form like clay under a seal, And stands out like a garment. From the wicked their light is withheld, And the upraised arm is broken. Have you entered the springs of the sea? Or have you walked in search of the depths? Have the gates of death been revealed to you? Or have you seen the doors of the shadow of death? Have you comprehended the breadth of the earth? Tell Me, if you know all this. Where is the way to the dwelling of light? And darkness, where is its place, That you may take it to its territory, That you may know the paths to its home? Do you know it, because you were born then, Or because the number of your days is great?" (Job 38:14-21)

All of these are legitimate questions for science to explore. Much has been learned about these processes over the centuries—but no honest scientist would dare declare that the ultimate answers are known. Humanity scratches the edges of this knowledge, and is amazed as some pieces become clear, but the whole of the picture is far from visible. Millions, indeed billions, of dollars and untold man-hours are spent in an effort to peer into these depths. An honest scientist admits that only omniscience can approach these answers.

Questions about Water

"Have you entered the treasury of snow, Or have you seen the treasury of hail, Which I have reserved for the time of trouble, For the day of battle and war? By what way is light diffused, Or the east wind scattered over the earth? Who has divided a channel for the overflowing water, Or a path for the thunderbolt, To cause it to rain on a land where there is no one, A wilderness in which there is no man; To satisfy the desolate waste, And cause to spring forth the growth of tender grass? Has the rain a father? Or who has begotten the drops of dew? From whose womb comes the ice? And the frost of heaven, who gives it birth? The waters harden like stone, And the surface of the deep is frozen." (Job 38:22-30)

Yes, mankind has uncovered some of these answers, but far more is known about the symptoms and the effects than the causes. The core of these questions demonstrates how little is known about the source of the rain and snow. Some have suggested that God is asking Job to consider the beginnings of the Ice Age that was starting to creep southward from the northern edges of his world. Perhaps, but all the questions remain mysterious. Nimrod personified the forces of nature and called the world to worship the "host of heaven." Modern man eulogizes the chaos of nature and worships the result. God demands acknowledgment that He alone is capable of providing the truth.

Questions about the Stars

"Can you bind the cluster of the Pleiades, Or loose the belt of Orion? Can you bring out Mazzaroth in its season? Or can you guide the Great Bear with its cubs? Do you know the ordinances of the heavens? Can you set their dominion over the earth?" (Job 38:31-33)

Astronomers have plotted the positions of the stars over much of the Milky Way galaxy, and the positions of thousands more galaxies. But none would be fool enough to say that they can control them. The majesty and beauty of the universe is stunning, to say the least, but all that can be done...is watch! Only a fool says, "There is no God" (Psalm 14:1)! Yet that is precisely what many do say. What arrogance to suggest that the order and precision of the known universe "just happened." No one has seen a star being born. No one knows how, much less why, the galaxies keep to their circuits. Honest answers demand an omnipotent Creator!

Questions about Animals

Three chapters in Job are given over entirely to the wild creatures of earth. Question after question is spun from the mind of God concerning a realm that should be under man's dominion. These are questions that man is expected to be able to answer, since they are part of the original authorization by the Creator. Man—even as inconsequential as he may appear to the vast reaches of the angelic host—is responsible to know these things.

> What is man that You are mindful of him, And the son of man that You visit him? For You have made him a little lower than the angels, And You have crowned him with glory and honor. You have made him to have dominion over the works of Your hands; You have put all things under his feet, All sheep and oxen—Even the beasts of the field, The birds of the air, And the fish of the sea That pass through the paths of the seas. (Psalm 8:4-8)

Yet reading through the questions of God's monologue with Job only brings the humbling admission that even today little is known of the "beasts of the earth."

These questions are of special interest in grasping the environment of these early centuries after the Flood. Please recall that Job and Abraham were likely contemporaries who lived during the same time period. As mentioned before, a simple addition of recorded events allows for only 292 years to elapse from the Flood to the birth of

Abraham. His father, Terah, lived another 135 years before he died in Haran in the northern part of Mesopotamia.

Most archaeologists and biblical scholars believe that Abraham lived around 2100 B.C. If that is correct, then the animals that God demanded that Job recognize would have been known to Abraham as well. The ancestors of those animals would have been taken on board the Ark barely 350 to 400 years before.

God gave two of those animals special emphasis—behemoth (Job 40:15-23) and leviathan (Job 41:1-34). It is interesting to note that God spent a large amount of His declaration citing the behavior and descriptions of these two very large animals. God mentioned lions, wild goats, unicorns, peacocks, the ostrich, the horse, hawks, and eagles—all in the space of 32 verses. Then, as though Job needed to pay special attention, God takes 44 verses in two chapters to talk about just two animals. Why the interest in these creatures? Why should it matter?

To begin with, behemoth was "made along with you." Whatever this animal was, it was created by God contemporaneously with man. Furthermore, behemoth was a very large animal that "moves his tail like a cedar" and had bones "like beams of bronze" and "ribs like bars of iron." This large animal had a specific purpose: "He is the first of the ways of God; Only He who made him can bring near His sword" (Job 40:15-19). This animal was designed by God to express something of the enormous power of the Creator and give evidence that only God could control it.

Today, with only fossil bones to give some idea of the enormity of this animal, science would call behemoth an *Apatosaurus*. There is abundant evidence that this creature really lived in the past. The fossils indicate it was between 70 and 90 feet long and nearly 15 feet high at the hips. The tail was about 50 feet long (remember the cedar tree) with peg-like teeth that suggest a plant diet. The legs were like columns. Estimates suggest that the animal weighed around 35 tons. With this kind of known evidence, it is mystifying to see the notes in the margins of many Bibles suggesting that the behemoth was either an elephant or a hippopotamus.

The other special creature that God points out to Job is the leviathan. Again, whatever this animal was, it is no longer with us—but Job (and Abraham) were familiar with it. Apparently it was a marine animal, with such a fierce character and strong body that "no one is so fierce that he would dare stir him up." In fact, God says that this animal is a good reference for His own power. "Who then is able to stand against Me?" Leviathan has "graceful proportions" and precision "scales" with the ability to withstand attacks by "spear, dart, or javelin" (Job 41:9-15, 26).

One of the mysteries of this creature was its ability to shoot some sort of fire from its nose and mouth. "Out of his mouth go burning lights; Sparks of fire shoot out. Smoke goes out of his nostrils, as from a boiling pot and burning rushes. His breath kindles coals, And a flame goes out of his mouth" (Job 41:19-21). Some have suggested that this animal was a crocodile, but that hardly seems sufficient for the language that God Himself uses. Either God is an awful exaggerator, or man is trying his best to ignore the message of Scripture.

Other Evidence

The book of Job is a cameo look into the age of Abraham. The knowledge shared is in diametric opposition to the legends and theories of evolutionary development, but it is in sync with the carvings, pictographs, writings, and archaeological discoveries all over the globe.

Several recent books have been published that document the current evidence of these findings, both in the remnants of past civilizations and in the fossil record. More detailed information can be gained from *Dragons: Legends & Lore of Dinosaurs* by Diana Bogardus and Terry White (Master Books); *Bones of Contention: A Creationist Assessment of Human Fossils* by Marvin L. Lubenow (Baker Books); and *The Fossil Record: Unearthing Nature's History of Life* by John Morris and Frank Sherwin (Institute for Creation Research).

CHAPTER NINE
ABRAHAM'S WORLD

> And Terah took his son Abram and his grandson Lot, the son of Haran, and his daughter-in-law Sarai, his son Abram's wife, and they went out with them from Ur of the Chaldeans to go to the land of Canaan; and they came to Haran and dwelt there. (Genesis 11:31)

Almost everyone knows the name Abraham. He is, indeed, the father of many nations. The Muslim world knows him as Abrahim, the father of Ishmael. Haram ash Sharif, the famous mosque in Jerusalem also known as the Dome of the Rock, is purported to be the spot where Mohammad ascended into heaven with the angel Gabriel. Jewish tradition holds that the stone over which the mosque is built marks the exact location of the Holy of Holies in the ancient temple of Solomon. Many Bible scholars place the location of Mount Moriah, the place where Abraham bound Isaac and prepared to sacrifice him (Genesis 22:1-19), at the Temple Mount in Jerusalem.

Obviously, that spot on earth is the focal point for much of history. And God's redemptive history as carried forward through Abraham begins at the end of Genesis 11.

A casual reading of the first 11 chapters of Genesis does not seem to convey much of an active world. The first six chapters, of course, record only the key points of the First Age of the earth. Those nearly 17 centuries race by with mere flashes of information, culminating with the horrible global destruction by water. The next five chapters spend much of their focus on the specifics of the Flood, and then plunge through some 400 years of history with little tidbits about Nimrod and Peleg, a few verses on the Tower of Babel with the resulting confounding of language, and a listing of the main descendants of Noah's sons, Shem, Ham, and Japheth. Were it not for the epic poem about the trials of Job, interested historians would not have much insight into the setting of Abraham's world.

With Genesis 11:31, the biblical narrative suddenly shifts into high gear to chronicle the lives of the patriarchs of Israel. Abram (later renamed Abraham) leaps onto the stage of history, gets married, moves north from Ur into Haran, then treks to the other side of the Fertile Crescent and temporarily settles at Bethel. From there, he moves with his nephew Lot and an entourage of people and possessions into Egypt, where we find a thriving civilization governed by a pharaoh—all in the space of 34 verses!

Historical Records

Secular history can be helpful in shedding light on the biblical narrative. There are written records preserved in various forms that carry a student of history back some 5,000 years—to somewhere in the neighborhood of 3000 B.C. However, historical records as they are written today normally began at a much later time period. Herodotus (484–425 B.C.) is often called the father of history. He was part of the Persian Empire and wrote a history of the Persian Wars. Manetho, who lived in the third or fourth century B.C., is called the Father of Egyptian History. He was an Egyptian priest who segregated the early kings of Egypt into "dynasties" and started the classification system of pharaonic rule that is still used today. The Jewish historian Josephus, who is often cited by biblical scholars, lived and wrote during the first century A.D.

There are others, of course, but it can be easily seen that much of *written* history comes from a perspective over a thousand years after the time of Abraham. The information about that era is preserved mainly on monuments, steles, obelisks, temple and palace walls, memorial tablets, prisms, and cylinders of clay or alabaster. Modern historians, using the limited information recorded on those various monuments and artifacts, attempt to fit together the historical bits and pieces and interpret them in the light of archaeological discoveries. Much of that material has been assembled since the 1700s A.D.

The difficulty in putting together a complete picture of ancient history is twofold. First, monuments from that time usually commemorate the early kings and pharaohs, who tended to view themselves as god-like viceroys of the deities that their cultures worshiped. Thus, the stories of their rule were colored by an assumed heavenly authority. Many of the inscriptions related to their reigns were dedicatory citations with flowery language about the opening of a canal or the victory of a certain battle. The completion of a palace or temple is couched in religious tones, praising the ruler and the god(s) that they represented. Hunting expeditions are noted with nearly the same level of honor as a military campaign. This is selective history, to be sure.

Second, the day-to-day recordings of business transactions, property transfers, and wholesale mercantile purchases—which comprise the majority of ancient records that have survived—do not add much to the broad picture of history. They are interesting insights into the daily life of those early cultures, but they seem oddly out of place with the "heavenly" exploits of the kings. These mundane transactions number in the thousands, preserved mainly on clay tablets. They rarely make the public news when found, and are often relegated to the arcane musings of scholars who attempt to develop somewhat fictional stories about their significance. Coupling these two ends of the historical spectrum together often produces a historical novel, but the truth of those days remains elusive.

This is especially so since many of the archaeological and anthropological teachings of the major universities are steeped in evolutionary philosophy. When the presuppositional basis for interpretation is a naturalistic development over eons, then the "ages" of history tend to become stretched quite a bit. For instance, the biblical timeline from the exit of the Ark to the death of Abraham is less than 500 years. Secular history and biblical history both place the life of Abraham around 2100 B.C. Secular history becomes more speculative regarding the time before Abraham, with some historians suggesting that Egypt began some 700,000 years ago. Many scholars insist that the first pharaoh of Egypt reigned around 3100 B.C.

The differences in the dating of early history are obviously a matter of personal opinion and presupposition. The Bible's record is a simple event-to-event history from Adam through Abraham. That history strongly attests to a little more than 2,100 years from creation to Abraham. Secular history insists on more than a million years for the start of fully human *Homo sapiens*, and if the biblical Flood is alluded to at all, it is assumed to be a regional flood in the Mesopotamian area more than 5,000 to 8,000 years ago.

For purposes of this chapter, this author will assume that the biblical timeline is correct, but will use the documented evidence about the early cities, kings, and nations to help color the world of Abraham.

Ur of the Chaldees

For many years during the height of the school of "higher criticism," Ur was considered a mythical city. Then in the mid-1800s, John G. Taylor began excavations in what is now known as Tell al-Muqayyar, halfway between the Iraqi capital of Baghdad and the northern shores of the Persian Gulf. Later, in the early 1900s, the British Museum funded an extensive effort under the leadership of Reginald C. Thompson and H. R. H. Hall. That excavation stopped for a few years, but was later re-doubled under funding from the British Museum and the University Museum of the University of Pennsylvania. Sir Leonard Woolley was the archaeologist in charge of hundreds of laborers. That expedition ended in 1934.

Layers of remains were uncovered that indicated the city developed from a small farming community in its early days to a thriving city of nearly 200,000 at its peak. During the several excavations, it was discovered that the Persian Gulf had extended much farther during the time of Ur, and it is very likely that Ur was one of the major port cities of the Sumerian empire for a century or more. Now the ruins are much farther inland.

Perhaps the more significant discovery by Taylor was the uncovering of the famous ziggurat at Ur. In that temple site, Taylor found cuneiform cylinders, several of which identified the city as "Ur of the Chaldeans." The biblical name was confirmed, and the evolutionary scholars who had insisted that such a city never existed were exposed for the biased academics that they were. In fact, until those cuneiform cylinders were found, it had been the position of such scholars that writing had not yet been invented that "early" in man's history, and Abraham, if he existed, could have been nothing more than a wandering illiterate goat-herd.

Much more was discovered, of course, and Tell al-Muqayyar has become one of the most valuable sites of antiquity. Sir Woolley found over 1,800 gravesites, with 16 sites known to be tombs of royalty. Those royal bodies were dated by scholars as having been buried prior to the birth of Abraham. The more famous of the royal burial sites, that of Queen Puabi, had not been looted and yielded quite a cache of art and valuable personal items. Her tomb, along with the attendants who were buried with her, gave a clearer picture of her life and the practices of that culture.

Sir Woolley surmised that this stunning tomb was a "death pit." The bodies were in formal dress and positioned in careful rows, indicating that they willingly died with the king and queen that they served. The king was buried first (and was looted), the queen on top of him, and the 74 bodies of six men and 68 women followed in sequence on top of the queen. The bodies of the men were warriors or royal guards buried with their weapons near the entrance to the pit. Most of the women were in four rows across one corner of the tomb. Six other women were under a canopy in the opposite corner. Another six were near the southeast wall. Almost all of them wore fragile headdresses of gold, silver, and lapis, mimicking the headdress of Queen Puabi.

A good summary of these findings is documented at the University of Pennsylvania Museum of Archaeology and Anthropology.

> Many of the stone vessels found in the Royal Cemetery were made of alabaster, a light-colored calcareous stone found on the Iranian Plateau. The most common shape is a cylinder with a flat rim that is paralleled at Iranian sites where workshops have been found (Shahdad, Konar Sandal South, Shahr-i Sohkta). Similarly, a dark greenish gray soft stone (chlorite or steatite) was also commonly used for bowls that nested inside one another for efficient storage and travel. The most distinctive example is the carved canister from Puabi's tomb, which is decorated with a pattern identical to ones found in south central Iran (Tepe Yahya), the ancient Land of Marhashi.

> Shell, used for cosmetics cases, pouring vessels, and cylinder seals, came from the Persian Gulf. Carnelian, a semi-precious stone used extensively for beads, came from eastern Iran and/or Gujarat in India. Lapis lazuli was used for jewelry, cylinder seals, and inlays, and came from northeastern Afghanistan. Mentioned in Mesopotamian myths and hymns as a material worthy of kings and gods, lapis would arrive in small, unfinished chunks to be worked locally into beads, cylinder seals, or inlays. Similar beads of agate and jasper came from Iran's mountains and plateau.[1]

Much, much more was uncovered in those years. Unfortunately, the site has not been further excavated since Sir Woolley ended his work in 1934. Suffice it to say, however, that Ur of the Chaldees was not a myth, but a vibrant, bustling, pagan port city by the time that Abraham was born. It is likely that Job had commercial interchange

---

1. Iraq's Ancient Past: Rediscovering Ur's Royal Cemetery. University of Pennsylvania Museum of Archaeology and Anthropology. Posted on www.penn.museum.

with Ur, although he lived a considerable distance to the west of Ur. Whether Job and Abraham ever met is purely speculative, but the differences in their cultures were significant. Ur was most certainly connected to the culture of Babel and its polytheistic worship. The biblical information about Job and friends indicates that they were still keeping faith in Jehovah.

The calling of Abram, still living in Ur and most likely under the pagan influence of Babel, makes the record of God's choice of him all the more remarkable.

Haran

Information on the place named Haran is not plentiful. Abraham was one of three named sons of Terah. The others were Nahor and Haran (Genesis 11:27). Although it is possible that the place Haran is named after the person Haran, it is unlikely, since Haran the person died in Ur before the family left (Genesis 11:28). Haran is later called the "city of Nahor" (Genesis 24:10) and the place where Laban lived (Genesis 27:43). Centuries later, during the reign of King Hezekiah of Judah, the Assyrian general Rabshakeh boasted that he had destroyed Haran (2 Kings 19:12), and in a prophetic warning to Tyre, Ezekiel cites Haran as one of many merchant cities (Ezekiel 27:23).

There is a modern city in southern Turkey named Harran in which lies an archaeological site suggesting earlier occupation near the time of Abraham. Secular data, however, are sparse. The general consensus (mostly relying on biblical data) is that Haran was a central commercial center on the major trade route through the Mesopotamian crescent. Ur would be at the southern tip on or near the seacoast of the Persian Gulf. Traveling northwest nearly 500 miles would bring the caravan to Haran. Traders from the east would meet the southern caravans in Haran. Those with goods for Syria would then travel west to Ebla or Damascus (Genesis 14:15).

Haran was a pagan city much like Ur of the Chaldees. The commercialism of the trade routes would have emphasized secular behavior, but the astrology of Nimrod and Babel was strongly practiced in both Ur and Haran. The main deity seems to have been a moon god named Sin or Nanna, depending on the city or the temple where inscriptions and descriptions were found. The crescent moon is often associated with both Sin and Nanna, and appears frequently over the millennia with names like "father of the gods" and "chief of the gods," and sometimes "creator of all things." There have been several attempts by various authors to trace the Babylonian worship of astrology throughout the centuries; the most notable is *The Two Babylons* by the Presbyterian theologian Alexander Hislop, published in 1853.

Like Ur, Haran was a thriving city of trade, heavily influenced by the pagan worship started under Nimrod. Terah moved his family (and probably a family-owned business) to Haran. When Abram left Haran, he was 75 years old and a wealthy and well-established businessman.

Canaan and Bethel

> Then Abram took Sarai his wife and Lot his brother's son, and all their possessions that they had gathered, and the people whom they had acquired in Haran, and they departed to go to the land of Canaan. So they came to the land of Canaan. (Genesis 12:5)

The reason given for Abram's departure from Haran is God's promise of "a land that I will show you." God also stated that He would make Abram a great nation, and that in him "all the families of the earth shall be blessed" (Genesis 12:1-3). The record of Abram's initial move to Bethel has little to mark it other than to specifically identify the Canaanites who were then in the land—the land that God had promised to give to Abram and his descendants. The biblical emphasis on the various "-ites" of that period gives some insight to the people-groups who had already settled in the area. They reached as far north as Damascus in Syria and the eastern side of the Jordan River (modern Jordan today), down to the southern reaches of the Dead Sea and the edges of the Sinai Peninsula.

> Canaan begot Sidon his firstborn, and Heth; the Jebusite,

the Amorite, and the Girgashite; the Hivite, the Arkite, and the Sinite; the Arvadite, the Zemarite, and the Hamathite. Afterward the families of the Canaanites were dispersed. And the border of the Canaanites was from Sidon as you go toward Gerar, as far as Gaza; then as you go toward Sodom, Gomorrah, Admah, and Zeboiim, as far as Lasha. (Genesis 10:15-19)

Much of the archaeological information on the Canaanites comes from the excavations of the city of Ebla in northwest Syria, which at its peak held over 250,000 people. Nearly 20,000 tablets were uncovered from a building next to the royal palace. Many of the biblical city names are verified by these records, along with geographical locations. Sodom and Gomorrah were repeatedly noted as important trading partners to the south of Ebla. The many names and transactions help to date the city to the time of Abraham.

The Hittites were also present during the life of Abraham. At the death of Sarah, Abraham purchased a cave and its associated plot of land from Ephron the Hittite (Genesis 23:10-16). Ephron was "among the sons of Heth," one of the sons of Canaan, son of Ham, son of Noah. Recall that this period is barely 400 years after the Flood—perhaps around 2000 B.C or a bit earlier. By this time, the sons of Heth (the early Hittites) recognized Abraham as "a mighty prince among us" (Genesis 23:6). It is unfortunate that many of the extra-biblical depictions of Abraham and the many "-ites" of that day give the impression of nomadic Bedouins who wandered from place to place eking out a bare existence from the open range. As was the case with Ur and Haran, the major cities of the Canaanites were large, sophisticated—and wicked.

Before Abram and Lot went down into Egypt with their families due to the famine in the territory of the Canaanites, Abram stopped for a while at a "mountain east of Bethel, and he pitched his tent with Bethel on the west and Ai on the east; there he built an altar to the LORD and called on the name of the LORD" (Genesis 12:8). That description was probably necessary because the place was likely unpopulated at the time. Jacob was the one who later named the spot when he had the encounter with the Lord as he made his way from the head-quarters of Isaac to his exile in Haran working for Laban (Genesis 28).

Abram had been traveling south from the region of modern Syr-ia, through the middle of the land that later became Israel, and set up a temporary "ranch" in an area some 25 miles east of the Jordan River, northeast of Jericho and almost 15 miles north of Jerusalem. It is entirely likely that both Jericho and Jerusalem were occupied and fortified cities then, and it is quite probable that Abram, with his large entourage gained in Haran, wanted to "settle down" in an area that could support his "possessions that they had gathered, and the people whom they had acquired" (Genesis 12:5).

As a recognition of the Lord who had appeared to him in Ur and again as he entered the land of Canaan, Abraham built an altar and "called on the name of the LORD" (Genesis 12:8). This is the first in-dication that Abram had "converted" to the worship of Jehovah. His family and business in Ur and Haran had not been cited for their sub-mission to *Yahweh*. The Scriptures do not ascribe a "salvation" expe-rience to Abraham until sometime later (Genesis 15:6; Romans 4:3). But at this Bethel ("the house of God") in the open country north of Jerusalem, Abram began to focus his life on the promise given to him earlier in Ur of the Chaldees.

The Land of Egypt

But a famine in the land of Canaan challenged Abram's welfare and success. His choice to go down to Egypt would have required serious consideration and careful planning. Remember that his "pos-sessions and people" were large and this journey involved more than a mere packing of a U-Haul and driving down a freeway for a few hours. Even with modern transportation, the moving of a business is a major undertaking. Later, after his return from Egypt, we are given a specific record of Abram's household when he went in pursuit of the five kings who had taken Lot's family captive. Abram "armed his three hundred and eighteen trained servants who were born in his own house" (Genesis 14:14).

Perhaps the size of Abram's household in this later stage of his life was more significant than when he went into Egypt, for he gained "sheep, oxen, male donkeys, male and female servants, female donkeys, and camels" while he was in Egypt (Genesis 12:16) and entered Canaan again "very rich in livestock, in silver, and in gold" (Genesis 13:2). But in any case, the move of a substantial agricultural business was not easy, and the decision to leave a reasonably settled area in Canaan would not have been made lightly.

The First of the Dragon's Heads

> And it came to pass, when he was close to entering Egypt, that he said to Sarai his wife, "Indeed I know that you are a woman of beautiful countenance. Therefore it will happen, when the Egyptians see you, that they will say, 'This is his wife'; and they will kill me, but they will let you live. Please say you are my sister, that it may be well with me for your sake, and that I may live because of you." (Genesis 12:11-13)

Having made the decision to move and gotten the relocation underway, Abram began to be anxious about the reception he might get when he arrived. With his wealth and followers, he was not merely one of the many common refugees that must have been coming into Egypt from Canaan as the famine worsened. Abram no doubt would have expected word of his coming to be related to the pharaoh. Through his participation in the normal course of business throughout the land, Abraham would surely have learned of the growing wealth and power of Egypt. His fear for his life (whether the threat was real or not) indicated that the reputation for the dictatorial power of Pharaoh was not undeserved.

Egypt was the first of the world empires of the seven-headed dragon of Revelation. Much of what is known about the development of the nation of Egypt is from the tombs and temples that have survived the efforts of looters and black-market archaeologists. One of the reasons that Egypt holds such fascination for the modern world is that famous discoveries like Tutankhamun's tomb held such fabulous wealth.

From a biblical perspective, Egypt was settled beginning in the 22nd century B.C. by the descendants of Noah's son Ham. Secular historians would suggest that the earliest pharaohs ruled as far back as 3100 B.C. This dating is primarily based on the exaggerated inscriptions of rulers who considered themselves divine. The missing gaps are then filled in with a predisposition to follow a timeline based on a slower evolutionary development than would be considered by a biblical archaeologist. Therefore, for the purposes of this chapter on the world of Abraham, the differences of time will not be considered. The empirical evidence is stunning enough!

Pharaoh's House

Secular historians follow the dynastic system established by Manetho, the Egyptian priest who is generally thought to have lived in the third century B.C. He wrote the *Aegyptiaca* (History of Egypt). Although many scholars have struggled with the disparities among the writings of Egyptian, Jewish, and Greek historians over which society deserves the "honor" of being designated the oldest civilization, such arguments seem a bit childish and throw the various secularly assigned dates into debate.

Further complicating the dating of the pharaonic "dynasties" is that the original manuscripts of *Aegyptiaca* are not known, with the earliest quotations coming from Josephus, who wrote nearly four centuries after Manetho. Egyptians, of course, swear by Manetho and insist that disparities between his dynastic listings and any other chronological system are inconsequential. The result of all of this bickering tends to make an honest scholar somewhat dubious about the integrity of the various interpretations of the dates of this historical era.

What can be done, however, is to gather the facts from the archaeological discoveries and let the questions of "when" and "how long" be less of a consideration. The artifacts from the tombs are astounding.

The frescoes and sculptures on the walls of the tombs and temples are magnificent, and the wealth and power that they portray—even if incorrect by half—still show a rise to prominence and prestige that is both swift and difficult to imagine happening today. Modern engineers marvel at the pyramids of Giza. The precision of the construction and the placement of the foundations to align with astronomical phenomena still puzzle everyone.

No wonder Abram felt a bit intimidated as he approached the greatest empire of his day. Even though he was wealthy by any standards, he was overshadowed by the pomp and power of the ruler of Egypt. If the depictions of the inscriptions and the sampling of the artifacts are any indication, Pharaoh's court would have struck awe into anyone. Perhaps the only record that can compare is the reaction of the Queen of Sheba to her visit at Solomon's court.

> And when the queen of Sheba had seen the wisdom of Solomon, the house that he had built, the food on his table, the seating of his servants, the service of his waiters and their apparel, his cupbearers and their apparel, and his entryway by which he went up to the house of the LORD, there was no more spirit in her.
>
> Then she said to the king: "It was a true report which I heard in my own land about your words and your wisdom. However I did not believe their words until I came and saw with my own eyes; and indeed the half of the greatness of your wisdom was not told me. You exceed the fame of which I heard." (2 Chronicles 9:3-6)

Pharaoh's Rule

All records in every dynasty insist that the pharaoh held absolute power in the empire. Although he implemented his authority through layers of bureaucracy, each of the various viziers, governors, treasurers, and so forth, served totally at the pleasure of a ruler who could demote or execute them at a moment's whim. Some pharaohs were more benign, like the ruler who placed Joseph in power. Others, like the pharaoh who ruled Egypt when Moses brought God's command to free the children of Israel, were moody and capricious, ruling by fear rather than by wisdom.

Abram's anxiety that he might be killed and his beautiful wife taken into Pharaoh's harem was well founded. Not only did the pharaoh have such power, but he often implemented just such atrocities to demonstrate his power and surround himself with physical beauty. Exquisite beauty has always been a symbol of wealth, and the "trophy wife" is no stranger to powerful men today. Multiply that by the guarantee of absolute power—even the expectation of the power of a god—and such psychological and physiological manipulation could be anticipated by anyone.

Egypt's economic engine was agriculture. Population estimates of Egypt at the time of Abraham vary widely, but if the city of Ur had some 200,000 and Ebla in Syria had 250,000, it is not at all unreasonable to suggest that Egypt's population would have been in the millions. The profusion of gold and precious stones that surrounded the pharaoh was stunning, but the true wealth of Egypt was in its natural resources. In order for a pharaoh to stay "favored" by the gods, he must feed his land. Many members of the pantheon of Egyptian gods were related in one way or another to the productivity of the land. As the divine emanation of the greatest god, Pharaoh must order all things so that life can continue.

Thus, government was totally controlled by the brokers of power. All power flowed from the pharaoh to his vassals, who implemented his authority throughout the nation. Prosperity resulted from the favor of the pharaoh. Punishment for disobedience was swift and terrible. Taxes were enormous, but cradle-to-the-grave provisions were the promise of government, and a docile or subject people provided the labor that powered the engine of the economy. Laborers were paid in grain. Housing was assigned. Clothing reflected one's station in life. Everything had its place, and every place had its purpose.

Court documents that survive from ancient Egypt do not demonstrate a defined legal code such as the Code of Hammurabi or the Ten Commandments. Rather, they appear to be based on custom or some sense of fairness at the local level. Punishment involved fines for minor infractions, imprisonment for some offenses, but physical mutilation for property or personal crimes (theft, embezzlement, rape, murder). Punishment for crimes among the nobility (those individuals who rose to the knowledge of Pharaoh) was both capricious and vicious. Recall the baker and the butler who served the pharaoh of Joseph's day. The baker was hung, the butler was restored. The closer one was to the person of Pharaoh, the more precarious was one's position.

Abram knew all this and was justifiably concerned.

Pharaoh's Religion

The religious practice of Egypt during Abraham's life involved a curious mixture of ritual piety and flagrant polytheism. There was usually a supreme god. Ra (or Re, or sometimes Amun-Ra) was the god normally associated with the sun, and was, therefore, ruler of all things. This is the god most often associated with Pharaoh. However, other deities by the dozens ruled over various aspects of nature. Most of the major deities had cult temples that held the "secrets" of various rites that were to guarantee fertility or a good harvest, cure diseases, bring the annual flooding of the Nile, and many, many other needs and blessings.

Sometimes, the gods were combined. For instance, Amun-Ra was considered the "the hidden one," an invisible creator deity with a cult temple in Thebes whose earthly manifestation was the sun. The priests of these many gods and goddesses held a mystical power over the populace, and often vied for political power with the pharaohs. The influence of Nimrod's Babel is fairly obvious. The sovereignty of the Tri-une Creator was distorted and fragmented through the personification of natural forces, luring many into demon worship and degrading religious rites. While this book does not have room to explore the details, the ten plagues of *Yahweh* under Moses were directed specifically at the power of the main "gods" of the Egyptian pantheon.

On its surface, the religious worship of Egypt was clean and moral. Personal hygiene was constantly practiced. Ritual bathing was performed daily. Men shaved their entire bodies to keep clean, and those who could afford it used perfumes and body oils. Those caught in adultery (emphasis on *caught*) were usually executed. Monogamous marriage was the custom, but concubines were permitted for those with wealth and power. Children of the wife would inherit the estate. Children of concubines were cared for and sometimes given positions of authority, but only the legitimate children were recognized and favored.

Foreigners like Abram, Sarai, and Lot were often forced to embrace the gods of Egypt, particularly the deification of the pharaoh. Those who refused were sometimes forced into slavery and their property confiscated. Recall that the young nation of Israel later became enslaved in Egypt and was isolated into a region away from the rest of the population.

The actions taken by Abram as he approached Egypt may seem incomprehensible to the modern generation, most of whom cannot relate to the pressures and very real threat Abram faced as he approached the realm of a ruler who not only had absolute authority, but also considered himself to be a god. Abram had more than enough reason to be apprehensive and feel that he needed to take measures to protect himself.

Thoughts to Ponder

It is not within the scope of this book to think through the sacrifices and difficulties of the patriarchs, or to detail the unique contributions each of them made to God's purpose to provide for the salvation of the world. It should be noted here, however, that God specifically chose Abraham to be an avenue of blessing: "I will bless those who bless you, and I will curse him who curses you; and in you all the families of the earth shall be blessed" (Genesis 12:3).

All who read this book have the completed "Book" to inform their view of history. Each of us can know that the fearful Abram of

Egypt became the fearless and obedient Abraham of Mount Moriah. We are privileged to know that Abraham was ultimately known as "the friend of God" (James 2:23). When the writer of the book to the Hebrews listed the great men and women of faith, Abraham and Sarah are firmly settled among them (Hebrews 11:8-12).

History has given us enough of a picture to know that Abraham faced a formidable world that was dominated by false gods and evil societies. We should be encouraged that there were men and women like Abraham and Sarah who faced challenges that we can scarcely relate to, yet remained fixed on God's promise, obedient with the light given them, wavering from time to time, but not failing at the crucial moments. We can learn much from them.

History is a good teacher. Yet history can be distorted if we struggle to fit the interpretations of secular historians within the framework of biblical information. If history has taught us anything, it is that the majority is seldom right and that the majorities of all nations have chosen to move away from God rather than to submit to His authority. Perhaps it would be well to remember the words of the Lord Jesus:

> "If the world hates you, you know that it hated Me before it hated you. If you were of the world, the world would love its own. Yet because you are not of the world, but I chose you out of the world, therefore the world hates you. Remember the word that I said to you, 'A servant is not greater than his master.' If they persecuted Me, they will also persecute you. If they kept My word, they will keep yours also. But all these things they will do to you for My name's sake, because they do not know Him who sent Me." (John 15:18-21)

Even though the secular world's thinking will always be alien to the long-term sovereign plan of our Creator, and though sometimes we will struggle to comprehend the differences and counteract the distortions that come with that alienation, we can be assured that our work for the Lord will stand if we keep our faith in Him.

Do not fret because of evildoers, Nor be envious of the workers of iniquity. For they shall soon be cut down like the grass, And wither as the green herb. Trust in the LORD, and do good; Dwell in the land, and feed on His faithfulness. Delight yourself also in the LORD, And He shall give you the desires of your heart. (Psalm 37:1-4)

CHAPTER TEN
GOD'S PLAN AND PURPOSE

Beloved, I now write to you this second epistle (in both of which I stir up your pure minds by way of reminder), that you may be mindful of the words which were spoken before by the holy prophets, and of the commandment of us, the apostles of the Lord and Savior, knowing this first: that scoffers will come in the last days, walking according to their own lusts, and saying, "Where is the promise of His coming? For since the fathers fell asleep, all things continue as they were from the beginning of creation." (2 Peter 3:1-4)

One of the bigger mistakes that Bible students make is to so enmesh themselves in the details of a specific prophecy or biblical event that they misplace the sequence of the event or the application of the prophecy because they've lost sight of the big picture. The details are important, of course, but their significance may well be skewed if the subject they concern is not understood in its proper context in God's overall plan for the ages.

The third chapter of Peter's second letter is, perhaps, the clearest single picture in all of Scripture of a "beginning to end" sequence of God's design for the ages. It is important not only because of the sequence of "ages" that are given, but also for its specific clarification and verification of the promise of preservation given by the Lord to Noah when he, his family, and the animals set foot in the new world after the first world was destroyed.

Peter includes all of the Old and New Testament writers when he speaks of "the words" of both the prophets and the apostles of the Lord Jesus. The "prophets" were the human writers of the Old Testament from Genesis to Malachi. The "apostles" of the Lord Jesus were most of the writers of the New Testament from Matthew to Revelation. All of these writings are rejected by the "scoffers" who dominate the "last days." They mock the promise of the Lord's return, citing the "no show" of Jesus and insisting that everything is running at the same rate and with the same results that were present at "the beginning of creation."

Please note—the processes that the scoffers embrace were (according to them) established at "the beginning" of the creation, not at its completion. Herein lies the core of the argument, of course: that there was nothing *super*natural about the creation itself—that the processes of creation are exactly the same processes that we can see and measure today. And if that is so, then all the rest of history must be understood by a natural methodology, not by or with supernatural or miraculous events interposing themselves in the process.

The First World

If the scoffer's view is correct, then the first *kosmos* was no different from the world we see now—even though the Bible insists that it "perished" by a *catakustheis* of water.

> For this they willfully forget: that by the word of God the heavens were of old, and the earth standing out of water and in the water, by which the *world* that then existed perished, being *flooded* with water. (2 Peter 3:5-6)

If the biblical record is accurate, then the "world that then existed" is closed to modern scientific efforts to test and verify empirical conclusions. The processes that operated in that cosmology are no longer functioning at the same rate and with the same focus as are now observed in "the heavens and the earth which are now" (2 Peter 3:7). To reiterate, if the Bible is true, a scientist living after the Flood of Noah's day would be unable to re-create the energies and circumstances that brought about the destruction of that era—leaving for study only that which survived and remained for further examination.

There can be little question from a biblical standpoint that "the word" cited in 2 Peter 3:5 is a reference to the Lord Jesus Christ. John, the book that features the deity of the Lord Jesus more than any other book, opens with:

> In the beginning was the Word, and the Word was with God, and the Word was God. He was in the beginning with God. All things were made through Him, and without Him nothing was made that was made. (John 1:1-3).

Jesus created all things "that are in heaven and that are on earth, visible and invisible, whether thrones or dominions or principalities or powers. All things were created through Him and for Him" (Colossians 1:16). Furthermore, God "has in these last days spoken to us by His Son, whom He has appointed heir of all things, through whom also He made the worlds" (Hebrews 1:2).

When Jesus was on earth, He demonstrated this power to instantly create new, complex matter and systems in the seven great miracles recorded in the gospel of John. Each of those miracles is a wonderful example of God's *ex nihilo* creation power. Any one of them could be sufficient proof of his omnipotence and omniscience. But perhaps the creation of wine out of water at the marriage of Cana will suffice.

> Now there were set there six waterpots of stone, according to the manner of purification of the Jews, containing twenty or thirty gallons apiece. Jesus said to them, "Fill the waterpots with water." And they filled them up to the brim. And He said to them, "Draw some out now, and take it to the master of the feast." And they took it. When the master of the feast had tasted the water that was made

wine, and did not know where it came from (but the servants who had drawn the water knew), the master of the feast called the bridegroom. And he said to him, "Every man at the beginning sets out the good wine, and when the guests have well drunk, then the inferior. You have kept the good wine until now!" (John 2:6-10)

Jesus took no action. He gave no command to the elements. He merely instructed the servants to fill the water pots with H_2O and then draw out a sample for the host of the feast to taste. The response of the host indicated that much more than water was gratifying his palate. He was tasting some of the following new sugars and organic chemicals that had been created by the mere thought processes of the Lord Jesus.

Anthocyanidin-caftaric acid adducts	Astilbin
Astringin	B type proanthocyanidin dimers
B type proanthocyanidin trimers	Catechin
Caffeic acid	Caftaric acid
Coumaric acid	Coutaric acid
Cyanidin	Cyanidin 3O-glucoside
Cyanidin acetyl 3O glucoside	Cyanidin coumaroyl 3Oglucoside
Delphinidin	Delphinidin 3Oglucoside
Delphinidin acetyl-3Oglucoside	Engeletin

There were many more sugars, fibers, and various acids involved— all of which did not exist in the universe before the Lord Jesus created them in the six water pots. Even if it can be presumed that Jesus merely "translocated" each element to the water pot from some other place in the universe, in just the right amount and in just the right mixture, the miracle is hardly sleight-of-hand "magic." Such power and display of omniscience could only come from the Creator Himself. And indeed, that is just what Jesus said to the stunned but still rebellious crowd of that day.

"If I do not do the works of My Father, do not believe Me; but if I do, though you do not believe Me, believe the works, that you may know and believe that the Father is in Me, and I in Him." (John 10:37-38)

Modern paleontology has uncovered some very interesting fossils. The majority of them are marine invertebrates (ammonites, clams, coral, jellyfish, starfish, etc.) that are just like the sea creatures we see today, although a few are no longer available for study because they've gone extinct. What does stand out, however, is the abundance of the fossil record. Even casual measurements would indicate that some 100 times more biological material is preserved in the fossil record than is alive on the surface of the earth today. Essentially, that means that the past environment was more conducive to life than today's, and the various biological forms flourished in places that are now mostly sterile.

Vast coal beds are under the surface of the Antarctic continent. Modern warm-blooded animals are found fossilized in areas of the northern and southern hemispheres where they could not exist at all now. Sea levels are higher today by 600 feet or so, apparently due to the melting of the ice sheets and glaciers that formed during the Ice Age following the Flood. Something was very different in the past. Just what those forces or processes was is not testable today. Guesses and theories abound, but empirical evidence is very scarce indeed.

Much of this was discussed more thoroughly in the first book of this series, *The Book of Beginnings, Volume One: Creation, Fall, and the First Age*, and alluded to in chapters 1 and 3 of this book. The conditions that are cited in the early chapters of Genesis could not be possible in the environment of this day. Humans lived for centuries then, and the entire complex of earth processes was under a functionally flawless design that had begun to deteriorate because of the rebellion of Adam. But those ages and functions rapidly changed after the Flood.

The apostle Peter cites the earth "standing out of water and in the water" as part of the information that last-days scoffers "willfully forget." That is a reference, of course, to Day Two of creation, when God separated the waters by an "expanse" that split the dark, watery matrix of Day One. That upper body of water is no longer there. Our world has no access to test or analyze what form it may have taken and what it had been designed to do. Whether it was a canopy of vapor or a shield of distributed ions, current speculation is just that—speculation. All that we can do today is evaluate what can be seen, defined, tested, and verified. Those data do not provide insight to what existed in the First Age. However:

- We do have the insight from the biblical account.
- We do have the massive fossil record.
- We do have geological data that verify the global Flood.

The observable evidence that is available tells us of a vastly different cosmological system that permitted flora and fauna to thrive worldwide, living much longer than is the norm today. Something was very different before. Theories abound, but each of them lacks the data necessary to re-create the conditions in a laboratory setting. Scientists (both creationist and evolutionist) are stuck with the presuppositional belief systems that anchor their individual worldviews.

The Second World

> But the heavens and the earth which are now preserved
> by the same word, are reserved for fire until the day of
> judgment and perdition of ungodly men. (2 Peter 3:7)

This is the world that all of us are now living in. This world (the second world) began with Noah and his three sons and their wives leaving the Ark. It will continue until the universe is melted down in the final judgment against the ungodly. There are some important criteria that must be noted about this world, however. First, the "same word" that created the first world is now causing the current world to be "preserved." Right after Noah and his family had disembarked from the Ark, God pronounced a new covenant with Noah, and with the animals and the earth itself, that He would keep everything stable and working properly until the end.

> Then the LORD said in His heart, "I will never again curse the ground for man's sake, although the imagination of man's heart is evil from his youth; nor will I again destroy every living thing as I have done. While the earth remains, Seedtime and harvest, Cold and heat, Winter and summer, And day and night Shall not cease." (Genesis 8:21-22)

That promise and its worldwide ramifications were discussed in chapter 4. But in addition to the promise given through Peter about this second world, there are two other references in the New Testament that give us insight.

> And He [the Lord Jesus] is before all things, and in Him all things consist. (Colossians 1:17)

> God through His Son is "upholding all things by the word of His power." (Hebrews 1:1-3)

Three important verbs are the key to understanding what is happening in this second world. The first world was created and judged, and then began deteriorating rapidly under that judgment. This world (the second world) is now being "preserved," and is "consisting" and being "upheld" by the "same word" that brought it into existence.

- Preserved—Greek *thesaurizo* = treasured, or stored up, or kept in store

- Consist—Greek *sunistao* = to bring or band together, establish, composed

- Uphold—Greek *phero* = to carry, endure, to preserve

Without going into the technical aspects of physics, the energies that bind the mass of everything that exists in this universe are held together in various configurations. Scientists have done a marvelous job of peeking inside the molecules and atoms to search for the intricacies of our universe, but they are still struggling to explain what holds everything together. At the basic level of the atom, there is a question about what holds the nucleus together. Protons carry like charges and should repel—but they don't. Therefore, scientists postulate a "strong nuclear force." We don't know what it is and can't measure it, but it must be there, since the nucleus holds together.

Many scientists believe our universe started with the Big Bang. But this event did not, for some reason, generate enough energy to account for all that can be measured. To make up for that deficit, scientists have developed various theories about "cold dark matter." Matter, as it is able to be measured, is neither dark nor cold. But, since the Big Bang did not produce enough "normal" matter, scientists speculate that there must be some other form of exotic matter that cannot be seen or measured, but must be there—just because it must!

Even many creationist scientists are reluctant to attribute "mystical" or "supernatural" power to the observed stability of the universe. For instance, they often try to fit "natural selection" into the functions of nature, rather than trying to understand how the Creator designed the ability to adapt within each living thing. The observable evidence shows that it is the creature that does the "selecting" and "fitting," rather than a blind, lifeless, and impotent environment. To merely say that all physical laws operate well because God designed them that way is to relegate God to a passive, disconnected role, as the deists did. They said and still hold to a philosophy that God somehow "started" everything, and then let nature take over—like a clock that was wound up and has been ticking away on its own ever since.

That is not the message of Scripture.

Perhaps the problem lies in not considering the "word" that created the universe in the first place. One of the basic laws of all science is that energy can neither be created nor destroyed. Energies can be manipulated and changed from one form into another, but energy does not create itself. Nor can scientists create energy—no matter how hard they try. However, in spite of the fact that energy creation is "impossible," the universe is functioning quite well, thank you.

This world, our world, the world that began after the great global Flood, is being overseen and "preserved" by the same Creator who made it in the first place. His purpose for keeping it together and maintaining the functioning cycles of the planet is stated simply by the apostle Peter:

> But, beloved, do not forget this one thing, that with the Lord one day is as a thousand years, and a thousand years as one day. The Lord is not slack concerning His promise, as some count slackness, but is longsuffering toward us, not willing that any should perish but that all should come to repentance. (2 Peter 3:8-9)

Although this second cosmos has been functioning for some 4,500 years, God is not bound by our time references. He can wait for a thousand years when our feeble minds and passions would demand immediate action—or He can perform in a day what our finite minds could not conceive of developing in more than a thousand years. It is that very timelessness that keeps the great Creator patient for our sakes—"not willing that any should perish." He has promised to return, and indeed He shall, but our impatient and selfish whims lead us to forget why God created in the first place, and to smugly dare to ask to be "taken away" from all this mess, overlooking the millions who have not yet "come to repentance."

The Third World

Just as the first world was destroyed, so this second world will also be destroyed. The differences will be the method of destruction and extent of the destruction. The first world was annihilated by water. All air-breathing, land-dwelling life not housed on the Ark was killed, and all evidence of that age was obliterated. All that is left are the massive fossil graveyards encased in the hundreds of feet of water-deposited mud and sediment. The planet has been ripped and torn by the wrath of its Creator, leaving only the residue of the former magnificent earth. But even in that residue, the mercy of God is extended to keep the planet functioning so that men will have the opportunity to find repentance and salvation.

But the day will come when even God's longsuffering will cease.

> But the day of the Lord will come as a thief in the night, in which the heavens will pass away with a great noise, and the elements will melt with fervent heat; both the earth and the works that are in it will be burned up. Therefore, since all these things will be dissolved, what manner of persons ought you to be in holy conduct and godliness, looking for and hastening the coming of the day of God, because of which the heavens will be dissolved, being on fire, and the elements will melt with fervent heat? (2 Peter 3:10-12)

This time, the entire universe will be "dissolved" and the very "elements" will melt under the awful and final judgment of a holy God on a world in total rebellion. This time, a "new heavens and a new earth" will re-make or re-create a perfect universe in which the redeemed will live eternally with their Redeemer.

> Nevertheless we, according to His promise, look for new heavens and a new earth in which righteousness dwells. (2 Peter 3:13)

> Now I saw a new heaven and a new earth, for the first heaven and the first earth had passed away. Also there was no more sea....And I heard a loud voice from heaven saying, "Behold, the tabernacle of God is with men, and He will dwell with them, and they shall be His people. God Himself will be with them and be their God. And God will wipe away every tear from their eyes; there shall be no more death, nor sorrow, nor crying. There shall be no more pain, for the former things have passed away." (Revelation 21:1, 3-4)

The Rich Harlot Astride the Beast

Obviously, this is not a book on prophecy. It is always wise, however, to study history in the light of what is to come. Much of the Bible records history. It covers the first world from the time of its creation until its destruction by a global flood. It covers the second world from the time of the early nations and the Tower of Babel until the incarnation of the Second Person of the Trinity and the spread of the early churches. It covers what will be and how the history of the ages will come to its completion.

Thus far in these two volumes, the focus has been on the first world and the transition from Noah and his family to the development of the nations from the dispersion at Babel up through the time of Abraham. The preceding history is well documented both in Scripture and in secular annals. What is often not considered is the place these events occupy in the overall plan of God. His plan is ultimately the only one that is eternal. The nations may rage and plot many things, but "He who sits in the heavens shall laugh" (Psalm 2:4).

The Three Ages of Scripture

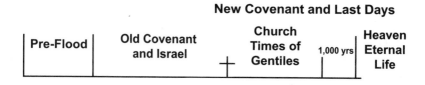

The Seven-Headed Beast

The prophetic insight given to the apostle John on the Isle of Patmos is both exciting and terrifying. In scene after scene, John was given access to the events of past, present, and future so that we who are still alive and awaiting the return of King Jesus might comfort one another. One terrifying passage presents a picture of a richly dressed harlot sitting astride the age-old beast who has, is, and will attempt to overthrow the Creator. The woman "rides" the beast throughout the ages and is portrayed thus:

> "Come, I will show you the judgment of the great harlot who sits on many waters, with whom the kings of the earth committed fornication, and the inhabitants of the earth were made drunk with the wine of her fornication."

> So he carried me away in the Spirit into the wilderness. And I saw a woman sitting on a scarlet beast which was full of names of blasphemy, having seven heads and ten horns. The woman was arrayed in purple and scarlet, and adorned with gold and precious stones and pearls, having in her hand a golden cup full of abominations and the filthiness of her fornication. And on her forehead a name was written:

> MYSTERY, BABYLON THE GREAT, THE MOTHER OF HARLOTS AND OF THE ABOMINATIONS OF THE EARTH. (Revelation 17:1-5)

In Genesis 3, we are introduced to "the serpent" that suborns Eve and entices Adam into a rebellion against the Creator. With just the information given in Genesis, we would have little idea of the entity involved if the book of Revelation didn't name "the great dragon... that serpent of old, called the Devil and Satan, who deceives the whole world" (Revelation 12:9). The book of Job gives us a unique picture of the apparent freedom that Lucifer exercises in his arrogant display before the throne and angelic courtiers of our gracious God and Creator.

Now, at the end of the Second Age, we hear from the mouth of the angelic host himself that Babylon has been riding the dragon from the beginning. More specifically, this evil beast rules through seven world empires from the beginning of the second world. Daniel saw visions of such a beast (Daniel 7) and was told then that this great empire would be the fourth kingdom to rise from the golden head of Nebuchadnezzar's great image (Daniel 2). The apostle John sets that information in perspective when he is told that the seven-headed beast of Revelation 13 is the ruling powers of "seven mountains on which the woman sits. There are also seven kings. Five have fallen, one is, and the other has not yet come" (Revelation 17:9-10).

From a historical perspective, five empires have fallen, one existed at the time of the apostle John, and one is yet to rise to power. Daniel identifies the three that preceded the one that "is" at the time of John. They are named in sequence as the Babylonian empire under Nebuchadnezzar (Daniel 2:36-38), followed by the empire of Media-Persia (Daniel 8:20), which is succeeded by the empire of Greece (Daniel 8:21). Then out of Greece rises "the fourth beast [which] shall be a fourth kingdom on earth, which shall be different from all other kingdoms, and shall devour the whole earth, trample it and break it in pieces" (Daniel 7:23).

Many, many books have been written on these great prophecies. It is not the purpose of this volume to do more than mention the obvious. The Second Age (our world) has been dominated by six great empires during the 2,000-plus years up through the life of Christ, with one empire still to come that will raise its head in open rebellion against all that is godly during the period preceding the destruction of the universe and the installation of the third world.

It is therefore possible to identify those empires by simply working backward from the one that existed at the time of the apostle John (Rome). Three others are named by Daniel. Prior to the Roman Empire, there was Greece. Prior to Greece, there was Media-Persia, and prior to Media-Persia, the Babylonian empire under Nebuchadnezzar. That sequence is clear from the statement in Revelation 17:10: "Five have fallen, one is, and the other has not yet come." Thus, the identities of empires three through six are known. The seventh is not yet on the scene.

The two yet unidentified empires (one and two) are not that hard to figure out. Although the Babel of Nimrod was a horrible influence (and may well have been the birth of the "harlot"), the nation of Babel, Nineveh, and Akkad did not develop into a worldwide or world-influencing empire until Egypt was conquered. Egypt became the empire that ruled the world through her riches, politics, and power. Egypt is the nation that figures so heavily in the early years of the formation of Israel—God's chosen nation. Egypt becomes the nemesis of the nation Israel from Exodus through Kings and Chronicles. Egypt is the first "head" or "empire" of the great dragon of Revelation.

Assyria began to poke its nose into the lives of Abram and Lot with the battle of the five kings headed by Chedorlaomer and Tidal (Genesis 14:1). Damascus is mentioned some 45 times in the records of the Kings and Chronicles, but it was the nation of Assyria that God used to destroy and take captive the revolting 10 northern tribes in 722 B.C. (2 Kings 17 and 2 Chronicles 15). Egypt had begun to fade after the execution of the ten plagues and the decimation of Pharaoh's army at the Red Sea. Though Egypt still exists today as a struggling nation, it has never regained the world status that it held in the days before Assyrian kings Tiglath-Pileser, Sargon, and Sennacherib, all of whom are mentioned in Scripture, rose to power.

The Assyrian empire began to be challenged in the late seventh century B.C. and was ultimately conquered by Babylon, which was consolidated under Nebuchadnezzar. As with Egypt, the Assyrian peoples continued to exist in various areas (Syria, Samaria, Jordan, and Persia), though much of its empire was destroyed and subsumed into Babylon under Nebuchadnezzar. Daniel writes from Babylon at its height, just before it was conquered by Darius the Mede (Daniel 5:30-31), who was himself conquered by Cyrus the Great. It was Cyrus who established the kingdom of Media-Persia, identified as the empire that Daniel 2 prophesied would succeed Babylon.

History has thus far easily identified the first six empires that dominated the world after the dispersion at Babel. Egypt was the first. Assyria was second. Babylon, Media-Persia, and Greece were specified and sequenced by the visions in Daniel 2, 7, and 8. Rome was the empire in power at the time of the apostle John—and Rome still continues in its scattered form in the European Union and the United States. We await Rome's final demise and the rise of the seventh empire as prophesied in Revelation.

The Long Career of the Beast

Revelation 17:10

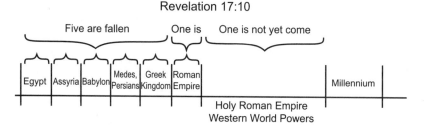

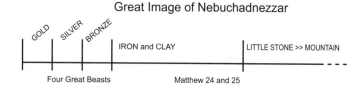

The Role of Babylon

Revelation 17 identifies the "great harlot" who sits astride the empires as "BABYLON THE GREAT, THE MOTHER OF HARLOTS AND OF THE ABOMINATIONS OF THE EARTH." This insidious Harlot, working her will and plundering the kings of earth, is nothing more than false worship of a false deity that delves into the philosophies and politics of the nations and drains their spiritual life and physical strength.

Abraham encountered her in Egypt, with its deified Pharaoh and pantheon of gods worshiped in temples and ceremonies throughout the land. Twice Abraham fell under her spell and was rescued by the one and only true God. The Hittites were smothered in the perfume of the Harlot's sensual appeal. The Canaanites were worshipers of Baal, who is perhaps none other than a deification of Nimrod. Israel encountered Baal, Molech, Ashtoreth, and many of the emanations from Babel during the days of Joshua and the Judges.

Each of the patriarchs, who will be studied in depth in the final volume of this series, was seduced or succored by Egypt—first to feed their starving families (God always uses the affairs of men to accomplish His will), and then to shelter the tender nation through 400 years of protective slavery. When Moses arrived on the scene, even he was ignorant of the name of the God of Israel (Exodus 3:13). Satan and his human acolyte, Nimrod, had done well. The Harlot of Babel proudly sat astride Egypt, "arrayed in purple and scarlet, and adorned with gold and precious stones and pearls, having in her hand a golden cup full of abominations and the filthiness of her fornication" (Revelation 17:4).

The Harlot of Babylon has had little to fear from the human nations, which are so easily seduced. Little remains but for her to grow stronger and more attractive to fallen man as the last days progress.

God's Plan for Babylon and the Beast

Most students of prophecy are familiar with the end of the story. But there may be some who read these pages who are not aware of what God has in store for the end of the ages. Many millennia have passed into the pages of history—and the Harlot still proudly sits astride the Beast, and "she says in her heart, 'I sit as queen, and am no widow, and will not see sorrow'" (Revelation 18:7). The world religions fight among themselves for power and renown, political leaders plot and manipulate to get ahead, but the Harlot and the Beast are the ones pulling the strings. The twice-born of God, however, have their minds set on God's Kingdom and should not be entangled in the worldly powers of this age.

As the book of Revelation closes, it is revealed to the reader that the Archenemy, Satan, works through the Beast, which is composed of empires run by human kings. The human agents are "ridden" by the Harlot over the ages of the seven empires. The Harlot is ultimately personified in "that great city which reigns over the kings of the earth" (Revelation 17:18). However, she (the city and all that she embraces) will be destroyed in one intense judgment so awful that the smoke from the destruction will be seen everywhere (Revelation 18:8-19).

Genesis records the "beginnings." This volume ends with the entrance of Abraham, the first of the great patriarchs of Israel. The First Age is no more. The Second Age is now underway. The Beast is enthroned in Egypt, and the Harlot is sitting in splendor among the demonic hordes that follow the Serpent's bidding.

May our Lord and Creator, Jesus Christ, give you eyes to see the eternal things so that you will not be swept up in the filth of the Harlot's fornication.

ABOUT THE AUTHOR

 Dr. Henry M. Morris III holds four earned degrees, including a D.Min. from Luther Rice Seminary and the Presidents and Key Executives MBA from Pepperdine University. A former college professor, administrator, business executive, and senior pastor, Dr. Morris is an articulate and passionate speaker frequently invited to address church congregations, college assemblies, and national conferences. The eldest son of ICR's founder, Dr. Morris has served for many years in conference and writing ministry. His love for the Word of God and passion for Christian maturity, coupled with God's gift of teaching, has given Dr. Morris a broad and effective ministry over the years. He has authored numerous articles and books, including *The Big Three: Major Events that Changed History Forever, Exploring the Evidence for Creation, 5 Reasons to Believe in Recent Creation, Pulling Down Strongholds: Achieving Spiritual Victory through Strategic Offense, A Firm Foundation: Devotional Insights to Help You Know, Believe, and Defend Truth,* and *The Book of Beginnings, Volume One: Creation, Fall, and the First Age.*

FOR MORE INFORMATION

Sign up for ICR's FREE publications!

Our monthly *Acts & Facts* magazine offers fascinating articles and current information on creation, evolution, and more. Our quarterly *Days of Praise* booklet provides daily devotionals—real biblical "meat"—to strengthen and encourage the Christian witness.

To subscribe, call 800.337.0375 or mail your address information to the address below. Or sign up online at www.icr.org.

Visit ICR online

ICR.org offers a wealth of resources and information on scientific creationism and biblical worldview issues.

✓ Read our news postings on today's hottest science topics

✓ Explore the Evidence for Creation

✓ Investigate our graduate and professional education programs

✓ Dive into our archive of 40 years of scientific articles

✓ Listen to current and past radio programs

✓ Watch our *That's a Fact* video show

✓ And more!

Visit our Online Store at www.icr.org/store for more great resources.

INSTITUTE FOR CREATION RESEARCH

P. O. Box 59029
Dallas, TX 75229
800.337.0375

S0-BSH-401

What Others Are Saying

"This is a must-read for anyone seeking new or different employment. Inside Dave's book you will find the sure-fire tips that will help you locate and secure the job of your dreams-and with a Christian outlook. Brilliant!"

Marsha Petrie Sue, MBA, award-winning author
of *The CEO of YOU* and international speaker

"David's book provides valuable insight and direction for those seeking God's will in their job search. He is a respected professional and his words are delivered to the reader from his heart."

Harvey Letcher, Partner
Sandhurst Group—Executive Search

"Rawles energizes job-seekers with the conviction that Almighty God has the right and perfect job for everyone. 'Ask and it shall be given to you.' Read, and find practical tools for your search. Believe, and you will find your perfect job."

Rose M. Hardenburger, President
RMH Strategic Marketing, LLC

"These pages offer practical and concise guidance. Drawing on three decades of experience and the straight edge of God's Word, David charts a clear course for those seeking to know the satisfaction of work done 'as unto the Lord.'"

Steven D. McMurtry, M.D.
Hilton Head Island, South Carolina

"David gives not only specific 'how to's' to get a job, more importantly, 'how to's' to keep your position. His 'trip tips' will help keep you on track . . . as you move forward, remember that today is 'one down with the BEST to go.'"

Patrick O'Dooley, C.S.P.
Author of *Flight Plan for Living*

"Dave Rawles knows business and employment. But most importantly, he knows God. And he knows the principles God gives for moving beyond or through tough employment experiences to a new and significant future. What Dave has done will help everyone in the workplace."

Claude Thomas, Ph.D., Senior Pastor
First Baptist Church, Euless, Texas

"*Finding a Job God's Way* captures the spiritual element that often is overlooked when people go through the search process. David's heartfelt message brings you closer to the One who really and truly can assist you."

Phil Resch, Captain USNR (Ret)
Author and motivational speaker

"For those going through the challenging and often painful journey of a job search, reading *Finding a Job God's Way* is like sitting with a trusted Christian friend. Practical, insightful, and seasoned with biblical and faith-based insights, this book will motivate, comfort, and guide those seeking God's will for the next chapter of their lives and careers."

Blair R. Monie, D.Min., Pastor/Head of Staff
Preston Hollow Presbyterian Church, Dallas, Texas

God has a plan for you! Jer. 29:11

FINDING A JOB GOD'S WAY

Moving into the HOV Lane of Your Career

DAVID RAWLES

HANNIBAL BOOKS
www.hannibalbooks.com

Published by
Hannibal Books
PO Box 461592
Garland, Texas 75046-1592
Copyright David Rawles 2005
All Rights Reserved
Printed by in the United States of America
by United Graphics, Inc., Mattoon, IL
Cover design by Greg Crull
Unless otherwise noted, all Scripture taken from the Holy Bible, *New
International Version*, copyright 1973, 1978, 1984
by International Bible Society
ISBN 0-929292-93-6
Library of Congress Control Number: 2004113008

TO ORDER ADDITIONAL COPIES, SEE PAGE 223

Table of Contents

Dedicated

to my parents, Jack and Phyllis Rawles, who, more than anyone, taught me how to work diligently. Most importantly, they made me believe that I could become whatever and whomever I desired to become. They instilled in me never to ask myself "if" I could do something or go somewhere but rather "how" I could get there, if that is what I chose to do.

My dad went home to be with our Lord and Savior a little more than four years ago. I miss him very much. I will have the privilege of sharing with my mom my great joy for the completion of this book. I have dedicated this book to both my parents. Mom will become the promoter here on earth; I'm sure Dad is smiling and telling everyone in heaven about his firstborn's first book.

Thanks for your loving encouragement.

Foreword

Moses wrote about God's call for craftsmen to build the wilderness Tabernacle, "*All who are skilled among you are to come and make everything the Lord has commanded*" (Ex. 35:10).

One marvelous benefit of following Christ is to find special purpose and joy in using the skill God has given you. Can you imagine the incredible satisfaction that the skilled craftsmen experienced when they worked on God's home, the Tabernacle? Satisfaction and pleasure are psychological paybacks that emerge with finding God's special place of employment, using talents He gave you.

That is why this book my friend, David Rawles, has produced is so valuable. It gives a proven and workable guide for finding God's best place of employment among the many confusing options and possibilities. That special place of employment and service then is accompanied by great delight and pleasure. The method David articulates is a proven and effective method for finding a position that is more than a job or occupation but a career and a calling.

David provides a wonderful method, a road map, for anyone looking for "the right job", who may be unemployed or unhappily employed and looking to make a job change. He speaks with great insight, clarity, and heart. The great insight springs from his experience, significant research, and conversations with many successful job-seekers. David's years of training and experience in human resources appear on every page. This man's comments are crystal clear with no ambiguity or question about what he is saying or the goal he is pursuing. Lastly, passion and concern for those who struggle with finding employment as well as the larger issues of self-esteem and respect show up continuously.

As I minister and counsel with former professional athletes who are adjusting to life after sport, this book will be a gift to help them find their way in one of life's most confusing and challenging situations.

Read and apply, study and digest *Finding a Job God's Way*. You'll benefit from the time you spend in this wonderful work. You, too, can find great joy in locating the work that God has planned for you. Thanks, David, for your labor of love.

John Weber
Chaplain, Dallas Cowboys
Director, Athletes in Action, Dallas-Fort Worth

Acknowledgments

I have many to thank, as much credit for this book goes to countless individuals.

I am grateful for my faithful wife and life partner, Fran. She, more than anyone, helps me see the roadblocks or dangerous curves ahead. She fills my fuel tank, tends to the maps, and always makes our journey fun. She helps me see what's important alongside the highway and makes each stop enjoyable.

Thanks to my accountability-group members, some of whom have been meeting together for almost 10 years: Eddie Price, Wil Theisen, and Bill Adams. They have kept me off the soft-shoulder.

Many thanks go to my publisher and new friend, Louis Moore, and my incredibly skilled editor, Kay Moore. Like two headlights, they have both kept me focused forward.

I extend thanks to Dick Matheson, my Sunday-school teacher, and John Weber, chaplain of the Dallas Cowboys and Dallas Desperados organizations, for pointing me toward life's true meaning. You each overlook my shortcomings—always allowing God to show me which turns I am to make as I approach each fork in the road.

And I extend a big thanks to the volunteers in our ministry, who give more than they get: Claude Smith, Steve Rose, Cindy Steen, Mike Richards, Brian Hess, Steve Dixon, Fred Gehring, Harrison Johnson, Frank Lugenheim, Andy Kozycz, Don Kriz, Brett Campbell, and Bill O'Donald. You make my job so easy, I feel as though as I'm on cruise control much of the time.

Thanks also to the Board of Directors of this ministry—friends and colleagues who have helped by volunteering, giving, leading, praying and encouraging: Bob Ohnstad, Eddie Price, Frank Rhodes, and Joseph Hopkins. You share the most challenging parts of the journey, helping me to change tires when I get a flat, or providing major directional changes when I forget my compass.

Finally, three men deserve special recognition. The first is John Davis, my idea man. You were that one person who first suggested two years ago that I write this book. What a vision you had! Next is my friend Patrick O'Dooley—a friend who sticks closer than a brother, a faithful encourager for many years, and the most positive force I have known in my adult life. Finally is my pastor, Dr. Claude Thomas. Thanks for lifting me up in your prayers, sharing my burdens, and living an example of love. When I am with you, I'm close to our Lord and Savior. And HE is so good!

God bless you, each and every one. By impacting my life you have surely played a major role in this book.

Prologue

This book began many years ago—back during the early stages of my human-resources career. Looking back, the journey for me began when I was recruiting and staffing professional sales and executive positions. I devoted time to learning the basics under the tutelage of leaders with great experience and excellent teaching techniques.

Weaving throughout this early training, I was able to ride with tremendous leaders such as Robert Wenzel and Ted Johnsen, who role-modeled positive examples, where good values were imparted daily. I was given a wide lane in which I could grow and learn. I was allowed to drive fast and make mistakes. I was encouraged to take off-road responsibilities outside my job description.

Part of my reward was greater responsibility, ultimately leading me to become vice-president of human resources and administration for one of the most successful business units of a Fortune 25 corporation. Our president and fantastic leader, Thomas Lysaught, gave me the greatest career opportunity of my life.

The pages of this book became more of a reality with other off-road opportunities that occurred along the way, allowing me to serve as adjunct professor for three scholastic institutions: University of South Florida, Tampa, Florida; Eckerd College, St. Petersburg, Florida; and University of Dallas, Irving, Texas.

As I look back, each challenge during the journey provided me with the necessary development, appropriate maturation, and personal growth I needed. Each victory was valuable—each defeat even more so. Each challenge increased my strength. Each opportunity helped me realize that the number of opportunities was endless if I made Jesus Christ my compass—my own personal guide during the career journey.

When I left the corporate realm to take on a ministry opportunity—to devote myself full time to **helping others achieve significance**—my Lord drew me closer than ever before to have me fulfill His purpose for my life. He had equipped me through three decades of experience. I thank God for the hundreds of individuals at Disney and GTE who had a part in preparing me to write the pages in this book.

Now as I devote my life to helping others find, secure, and flourish in careers, I wish to honor Jesus for the work He did in me. We conduct our workshops and seminars to help people learn practical applications to find their dream jobs and achieve their highest career ambitions. I unapologetically share biblical truths about God's plan and His promise for an abundant life.

We begin and end each of our seminars and workshops with a prayer. Beginning this book with a prayer also seems only appropriate.

Our Father in Heaven, we praise You as Holy. Sovereign in our lives; we lift up Your Holy Scriptures as lights to our path and offer ourselves as a sacrifice to You. Do with us, through the information in these pages, what You desire for our lives.

We thank you for all life's blessings—for making Your Word known to us and for providing Your Son as a doorway to eternity with You. We thank You for the trials, which strengthen us.

We also thank You for the array of choices before us and the guidance You provide to navigate among them. Thank You for each boss, each colleague, and each brother and sister who has stood alongside. Father, now I ask that the words in this book honor You. I humbly request that You open the heart of each person who reads these pages and that You provide the motivation and learning to enable each to put these principles in action. I give You all the honor and glory. In Jesus' wonderful name I pray, Amen.

David H. Rawles

Healing and Equipping

For most of you the loss of a job or the necessity of changing careers is far more stressful than you would care to admit. Often situations that precipitate career change are followed by feelings of anger, hurt, or bitterness that may then give way to self-doubt, worthlessness, or perhaps, depression.

Knowing that each trial has a purpose brings comfort. You will face various trials throughout life. How you choose to respond is often the key. God is with you in each circumstance. He will help you heal, help you move forward, and help you prepare for what He desires for your life.

*"Consider it pure joy, my brothers,
whenever you face trials of many kinds,
because you know that the testing of your faith
develops perseverance. Blessed is the man who
perseveres under trial, because when he has
stood the test, he will receive the crown of life
that God has promised to those who love him"*
James 1:2, 3, 12.

Put Your Behind in the Past

Why are you bitter and angry?

Let's begin this journey at the end—the end of your last job. If you were laid off, downsized, or fired, are you bitter or angry about what happened? Do you harbor negative thoughts about someone or something connected to your employment experience?

First, recognize and accept the fact those feelings are natural. Perhaps your dreams seem to have been obliterated. Or maybe this job loss appears to derail your plans for retirement. Without minimizing your feelings of loss, betrayal, bitterness, anger, and the like, I suggest that you find ways to move past these negative feelings. Get past them so you are completely free to conduct a truly effective job search.

Why are you talking about this psycho-babble, Dave? Let me assure you that you will be trapped, tripped, and tromped by these negative feelings. Whether you realize it right now or not, they may consume massive amounts of your time and energy. Inwardly, you will dwell on these feelings and may even create a compulsive need to waste your time and the time of others by repeating what happened.

The most important reason to put the event behind you is that it affects your networking contacts and employer contacts. Those contacts will detect your negativity in conversations whenever you attempt to explain your previous employment relationship. Your ability to talk about your past with sincere, positive confidence will translate into credibility with the person with whom you are sharing your story. Allow every encounter to be *upbeat, positive,* and *future focused.*

Look at your situation from their point of view. Would you want to hire someone who is hanging onto yesterday's smelly fish? Do you like being around people who are bitter and angry? Can you imagine how much more likely you would be to hire someone who is positive, enthusiastic, and eager to overcome challenges?

So, how do you *get over it* and *get on with your future*? Time will do it—so just wait around for a few months or a few years until the bitterness begins to fade. OR, with great dispatch, you can choose to put your past behind by following this simple, yet effective approach:

Step One: Sit down and compose letters to your ex-boss or that person's boss, peers, and whomever you begrudge. Don't be bitter or angry in this letter; rather focus on all the positive things you could have accomplished had you remained. **(But do not mail it!)** Conclude by *forgiving* these individuals.

Step Two: Next, write a letter to yourself from your boss. Yes, you are role playing. In this letter, have "your boss" write to you honestly and sincerely on why you were let go. Write it as if your boss knows everything about you. *Be honest with yourself;* only you will see the letter. The cathartic effect of this process can be awesome.

Step Three: Finally, schedule and carry out a personal sacrifice–"a ritual of burning" these letters in the yard, the barbecue grill, or the fireplace. Let this exercise signify putting the experience behind you. Now, commit to focusing on your *future*. As my friend, Patrick O'Dooley, says in his book, *Flight Plan for Living,* "You can be sure crises will occur, but you never know where they may lead. Given their certainty, your best response is to let their energy propel you to new horizons."

Remember the Genesis story of Joseph, son of Jacob (Israel). He was treated poorly by almost everyone he knew, even his 10 older brothers. Yet, Joseph never languished in self-pity or bitterness; he kept focusing on what was next in his life. His heart and faith moved him toward God's ultimate purpose. As he explained to his family after many trials, *"You intended to harm me, but God intended it for good to accomplish what is now being done, the saving of many lives"* (Gen. 50:20).

Stay focused on today and prepare for tomorrow. Love those who treat you poorly. Your faith and a positive outlook on the future will propel you *forward* on your journey.

God tells us to love one another unconditionally. You can do that in two ways, both prospectively and retrospectively. Love people without regard to how they may behave toward you. And, also love people in spite of how they may have treated you. The secret lies inside you. Forgive in the name of the Lord. Then you will be filled with grace to move beyond your past and in to your future. God is waiting for you there.

Tough Circumstances

How well are you doing during your season
of unemployment or unhappy employment?

In his New Testament epistle James wrote: *Consider it*
pure joy, my brothers, whenever you face trials of many kinds,
because you know that the testing of your faith develops
perseverance (Jas. 1:2, 3). We are asked to persevere in faith.
We are encouraged to consider our trials as positive,
growth/strengthening experiences. You may be tempted to
worry, blame, or even to withdraw and quit. Don't give into
that temptation, as easy as that may seem.

As you pursue God's plan for your life, focus on the
future. You will be more employable by interviewing powerfully, exhibiting your love, and showing self-discipline. Your
spirit will shine brightly once you can get over the feelings of
hurt and disappointment associated with being mistreated by
an employer.

On this journey, pray for those who have abused their
positions of authority at work. Forgiving those people whose
intentional and unintentional actions have caused you harm or
put you in the middle of unexpected trials is necessary.

Accept the fact our Lord is still in charge—that He
alone can change any circumstance. Begin to understand,

accept, and welcome the knowledge that He knows the reason(s) for our trials—even those caused by people.

Remember, when you're tempted to say "God, why me?" He wants only good for us. Remember, His ways are higher than our ways. Remember what is truly important to your future . . . eternally important.

"And we know that in all things God works for the good of those who love him, who have been called according to his purpose" (Rom. 8:28). Move forward, not backward. Learn what you can from your experience, yet do not become controlled by it, embittered, and trapped in temptation. Ask for His guidance, seek His strength, and knock on the door of future opportunity.

Rely upon our Lord for His spirit of power, of love, and of self-discipline (2 Tim. 1:7). To get some of His power, love, and self-discipline, spend some time in the Word of God—in your Holy Bible. He wrote it for you. Find time to be with other believers who can be encouragers and mighty prayer warriors for you. And spend time on your knees, seeking God's mercy and direction, as you look to the prize, which He has promised.

Great Comebacks

Have you failed recently?

Maybe you choose to call it something else, but all of us will stumble, fall, become victimized, or in some way have an undesirable consequence or circumstance affect us. Some of us will get fired, laid off, demoted, or passed over for that promotion we worked so diligently to get. The reality is that sometimes we are discouraged, disengaged, depressed, or demoralized by what happens.

If you have lost your desired employment and a door has been slammed in your face, take heart. First, be reminded that some of the greatest success stories in American history began mired in failure:

> **Abraham Lincoln** lost far more elections than he ever won. Confidence, faith, and perseverance kept him moving forward.

> **Thomas Edison** had more than 10,000 failures before he discovered a means to produce electric light bulbs. He was driven by the confidence that each failure eliminated one more incorrect attempt.

> **Walt Disney** endured financial failure multiple times before his new friend, Mickey Mouse, helped him find his way to success.

And earlier in history, the Bible provides evidence about the perseverance of God's leaders:

Moses, in spite of having committed murder, was used by God to lead the people of Israel out of slavery and into the land promised to his forefathers. Moses' faithful and obedient heart enabled God to use him for a great purpose.

Rahab, following a life of prostitution, was able to assist Joshua and the Israelites to a victorious battle. Because she acted on God's purpose for her life, Rahab was able to show kindness and faithfulness. In turn, she and her family were spared from God's wrath on Jericho.

Simon, whom Jesus renamed Peter, picked himself up. Jesus restored him to his calling after he denied his Lord and Savior three times.

Saul of Tarsus, who became the Apostle Paul, after being called to spread the gospel, faced every sort of trial and persecution and kept the faith until the end of his days.

Joseph, who went from the favored son of Israel with a coat of many colors to slavery, to being named second in command to Pharaoh of Egypt, kept moving always forward, relying on his God though foreigners and family members persecuted him.

Countless examples exist of individuals in more recent days making the right decisions and fighting the odds against them. You can learn from their experiences:

Colonel Harland Sanders of Kentucky Fried Chicken didn't find his big "success" in business until after the age most individuals retire. Age was not a barrier for him.

Mary Crowley, who created an empire with home interiors, faced many trials and difficulties in business during her lifetime. She didn't let opposition stop her.

Chuck Colson, a major figure in the Watergate scandal, found the most meaningful purpose for his life after disgrace and imprisonment. He didn't let wrong choices and failure deter him.

Cesar Chavez, noted organizer of the Hispanic migrant farm workers just a few decades ago, was reviled in the press, hated by many, and jailed. He never let the popular "majority opinion" derail the just ends he sought for the oppressed whose cross he carried.

Cassius Clay, who renamed himself Mohammed Ali, stood his ground amidst the onslaught of those who violently disagreed with his stand to refuse induction into the Army based on his faith. Later he was exonerated and regained the boxing title that had been taken from him.

These and many more individuals overcame dismal failures and major setbacks to achieve great success. Why didn't they give up or give in?

Speaker, author, and businessman John Maxwell may have the answer in a terrific book he wrote—*Failing Forward*. In the book, Maxwell states that everyone likely will encounter setbacks. If you can learn from those difficult times and get back on a solid foundation, you can move forward significantly, Maxwell says.

My personal definition of failure is "a temporary departure from one's success journey." In other words, failure does not have to be permanent or debilitating. Your choice is whether or not you let failure become a positive force in your life or let it tear you down.

Failure need not immobilize or discourage you. In fact, it can help you *learn*. It can activate your resolve to grow and press ever forward. It is a *choice* you make. In a book entitled *Conversations on Leadership*, Philip Resch tells us, "There's an old saying that if you haven't failed at something you're not really trying." How you respond to your temporary departures, in part, is affected by recognizing they are only temporary setbacks.

Stay on track. Use the greatest comebacks in history to inspire and prepare you for the unique success journey God has prepared for your life. Go ahead; fail forward! Repent, if any sin is present, and accept God's wonderful grace and mercy. He wants more for you. Know that if you stumble or fall, He is ever-present to help you up. Ask for His help. *"If you believe, you will receive whatever you ask for in prayer"* (Matt. 21:22).

Revealing Your Character

*How many times have you heard, it's not
'what' circumstances we face in life but
'how' we face them and 'how' we respond?*

Imagine for a moment having your parents deciding your life's career path before you were born. While you grow up, your parents spend every possible moment praying for you, teaching you, and exposing you to those individuals who could influence you about a future career. Then when you are a young adult, God personally confirms that the career your family chose is the one He desires for you, too. The position provides excitement while it demands courage and dedication. It is a career that requires integrity and strong leadership skills–and you rise to the occasion.

You grow well into your career and love your work. You wake each day motivated to do what is required; some times are difficult, other times are not. Your decisions are good ones, whether business includes a routine day of ceremonies or a month of dangerous encounters. Your boss is delighted with your work; you simply cannot imagine ever doing any other kind of job. You are emotionally connected and blessed with great wisdom. Even in the trials of your life, you are steadfast and at peace. You have a family of your own, a wonderful home, and a career many envy.

One person that lived this life in history was Samuel, son of Hannah and Elkanah in the Old Testament (1 Sam. 1-3). When Samuel was a baby, his mother dedicated his life to God and allowed the high priest, Eli, to rear him and tutor him. God called Samuel to become the *last* great judge and the *first* great prophet of the nation of Israel.

During the time when Israel was a theocracy, Samuel was the nation's leader, both spiritually and governmentally. God worked through Samuel to lead Israel and preside over the nation as judge. In many ways he held a "combination job" as both ruler and chief priest—similar to the dual roles Moses and his brother Aaron held earlier.

Samuel provided leadership for decades. But as he aged, the people began to reject God and Samuel. They asked for a king like all other nations had. They insisted Samuel take a "demotion" and for God to give them an earthly king.

Think of it—even though Samuel was hand-picked by God, the career for which he was groomed since birth was *being withdrawn or taken away*. Those whom Samuel had faithfully served for many years were truly ungrateful. The nation of Israel was **rejecting** its last and perhaps greatest judge.

Samuel was asked by the people of Israel to find a new king, so God provided Saul. Astonishingly, Samuel was charged with anointing Saul as king of all of Israel. But the rest of Samuel's story and his response to his circumstances are what really teach us about life.

Samuel held no ill feeling toward the people who asked for a new king to lead them. He gave all his attention to finding and training King Saul, even while he continued to pray for the people of Israel. What a positive response!

Also, Samuel became a close personal friend of King Saul. Samuel prayed for Saul and shared with him a deep love that originated from God Himself, even when Saul disobeyed

God. Samuel was given the wisdom to recognize that the change of command was part of God's purpose. He not only supported King Saul personally, he also preached among the various tribes so they would support God's chosen king. King Saul had the wonderful benefit of Samuel's experience and unquestioning loyalty.

And finally, Samuel continued to serve his people in a loving manner—praying for and counseling them. These are the same people who rejected him as their leader. Even when Saul eventually failed as king, Samuel never sank to the level of telling his people, "I told you so."

How do you respond when organizational politics turn against you, particularly after years of loyal service? Are you embittered and disheartened? Or do you seek God's direction that calls you to love others as yourself? Can you do this even in the midst of trials that others may have helped inflict?

Another character in King Saul's life worth remembering is his young successor, David. After David was chosen to succeed Saul, for more than 10 years Saul tried on several occasions to kill David. Never once did David retaliate or "get even" not even when he had the opportunity to do so. David continued to honor and love King Saul. His choice was to do so. With such humble behavior, David honored God.

So, what choices will you make as one of God's own? Angry and burdened by a heavy heart, will you justify retribution and revenge? Or instead will you seek peace through forgiveness? You have a choice. Consider that which honors our Lord and Savior and gives you the freedom to experience all that God has planned for the rest of your life. *What* Samuel or David endured was not what made them great, for they experienced significant trials and disappointments. *How* they responded to their situations is what made them great. They chose to respond out of love and obedience rather than out of bitterness and retaliation. Make it your choice, too.

Focus on the Destination

Someone once said to me, "If you don't know where you're going, any road will take you there." In the same vein, if you're starting a job or career change and are not sure what your ideal next job is or how to find it, will you blindly follow any old approach? Some strategies may or may not work out for you. But when you focus on a specific direction you want to head, your path becomes illuminated. When you truly know where God wants you to go and put your hand in His, following His lead, you will receive divine assistance. As you discover the steps necessary to obey God, He, in turn, gives you the ability and courage to follow a path He created especially for your life.

Just as God prepared Joseph, Moses, David, and many others, God is preparing you. He wants you to grab hold of a future He has uniquely planned for you. *Focus forward* on the goal God wants you to pursue in the weeks and months ahead.

> *"Brothers, I do not consider myself yet to have taken hold of it. But one thing I do: Forgetting what is behind and straining toward what is ahead, I press on toward the goal to win the prize for which God has called me heavenward in Christ Jesus"*
>
> (Phil. 3:13, 14).

Your Future Focus

If you're unsure what you want to do next since you've been laid off, how will you deal with the "fog of uncertainty"?

In a recent conversation with a friend and colleague, we began discussing the "fog of uncertainty"—an unusual period of limbo and confusion. It seems to be a time when you question your career choice and your capabilities. We agree that when you enter this "fog of uncertainty", turn on the **fog lights**.

To help job-seekers through the fog, *headlights* are available that can help you see more clearly; these are retractable fog lights that can give you visual acuity, enabling you see your future more clearly.

Before sharing the fog-light theory, first understand why you *need* to see your future better. Three reasons help you have a clear focus on your future—your target job:

    1. Employers generally prefer to hire people who know what they want to do and have a passion to do it.

    2. Network contacts and friends can help you be more productive in your job search, only when you make clear to them what job you want.

3. Your job search can be shortened significantly when your efforts are future focused.

Let's discuss these points. First, potential employers are encouraged when they meet a candidate who has a clear understanding of what he or she intends to do. These candidates appear more organized, more prepared, and more ready to do what needs to be done. They also appear very motivated. On the other hand, many job-seekers are in the "fog of uncertainty"—appearing lost and unmotivated.

For a moment put the shoe on the other foot—imagine you are the headhunter and you have a choice between two individuals with comparable skills and experience. One is unsure what he wants to do; the other specifically has targeted the work you have available. Which would you hire?

Second, your friends and other network contacts can offer you better roadside assistance when your target career is illuminated and easy to see. In simple language explain what work you want to do, so they can understand your future desires. When friends know what job you are looking for, they can have their antennae up, tuned-in, listening for the job you desire. By selecting and clarifying a future career focus, you now have additional help in finding that job you so want and deserve.

Next, many of us hope our job search ends sooner than later. Those with a clear *future focus* will most often land their next position sooner, primarily because they have fewer wasted efforts. You do not waste time considering or interviewing for jobs which you really are not prepared, motivated, or excited to perform. If you manage your time better, this will result in greater efficiency and effectiveness in your job-search efforts. With a clear *future focus*, fewer off-road rabbit trails are followed. You then can devote your valuable time to those tasks with the most likely payoff.

So, your main objective now is to get a *future focus*. Commit yourself to a specific career, job, and industry. Even select the type of company and kind of boss you want. Results prove that having a well-identified target will improve your job search more than will anything else you do.

Brian Tracy says in his book, *Focal Point,* "Among the most important personal choices you can make is to accept complete responsibility for everything you are and everything you will ever be." Perhaps a more enlightened perspective might be to *share responsibility* with God. But even this implies you must first accept responsibility and not blame it on other individuals, life circumstances, fate, or coincidence. The first part of your responsibility is to choose where you are going, while remembering to *"Commit to the Lord whatever you do, and your plans will succeed"* (Prov. 16:3).

Fog Lights

Here are seven *fog lights*—values which will illuminate your direction and guide you down life's highway when things get foggy. They will help you *see* your *future focus.*

• **Faith**—Be certain of things not yet seen. Know that God will guide your path. Believe He will fulfill His purpose for you. Allow the Lord to direct your steps by staying in His Word daily. Pay close attention to what God wants you to do. *"I will instruct you and teach you in the way you should go; I will counsel you and watch over you"* (Ps. 32:8).

• **Care**—Pay attention to what is important. Recognize worldly versus spiritual priorities. Know that many things you think are important are really things you ought not to worry about. Take time to learn and discern the difference.

• **Courage**—Be bold in your walk, even when you cannot see what is around the next corner. In spite of your fears, step out to do what is good and right.

• **Prayer**—Stay in constant contact with God. Allow your personal relationship with God to grow into one of significance so you can call on Him in every circumstance for every need and for guidance.

• **Power**—Tap into God's energy and wisdom to overcome fears and doubts. Receive the vast strength given by the Holy Spirit to take the high ground and to triumph over all that surrounds you. God will give you all the power you need.

• **Love**—Remember one of God's greatest commands for your life is that you love each other. Share the love of Christ with colleagues and strangers, with those who can help you in your career journey and with those who need your help.

• **Discipline**—Maintain self-control. Do good works, not just listen to the opportunities around you. Apply what you have learned. Now is the time to put into practice all that you know you ought to be doing.

These seven *fog lights* will help you see your way out of the "fog of uncertainty." Learn this little poem and you will keep all seven of these lights close at hand:

Proceed with *faith, care, courage,* and *prayer,*
Knowing at destinations' end God is there.
Proceed with *power, love,* and *discipline,*
For where you're going, He's already been.

Discovering God's Will

Do you desire employment in a career that will allow you to fulfill God's purpose for your life?

Most of us want to fulfill our God-given purpose in life, but we all struggle to discover God's unique purpose for us. The Lord has something very special for you! It is like falling into a cool, clear stream on a hot summer day. When you finally "get it", you are able to begin implementing steps to complete His purpose in your life in a refreshing, exuberant way.

You may have yet to find *how* to discover God's purpose. Establish and nurture three relationships in order to find the seemingly illusive, perfect path:

> • **With God**—Continually *develop a personal relationship with God*. You will be able to attain the insight and sensitivity to "hear" God's direction. This relationship is grown by studying His Word, the Bible, and by talking and listening to Him in prayer. *"You have made known to me the path of life; you will fill me with joy in your presence, with eternal pleasures at your right hand"* (Ps. 16:11).

• **With Ourselves**—Ironically, moving up Maslow's hierarchy pyramid toward "self-actualization" can be achieved by making yourself lesser while God is made greater in your life. By continually yielding your will to God's leading hand and searching for His application in your life, you can align yourself with God's master plan. Personal submission to God's instruction allows you to have a greater focus and energy to apply His teachings in your life.

• **With Others**–Also, you will continually grow in understanding, finding opportunities for application in your life through strong relationships with your brothers and sisters in Christ (Prov. 12:15; 11:25; 15:22).

As each of these three intertwining relationships mature, you will begin to fully discern your God-given talents, skills, interests, and passions. You have a unique personal blend of gifts. If you take time to write down and note what these gifts are, paying attention to your relationship with God, you will begin to see career opportunities that will give you a way to live, work, and enjoy all that God intends for you.

Pay attention to God's plan for your life by intentionally spending time in each relationship. In your prayers and by studying His Word, you will know Him. He reveals what you are supposed to be doing, with whom, and how. By spending time within yourself, you connect to who you really are—your true self. Aligning your "self" with the Father will give you power, love, and self-discipline (2 Tim. 1:7). It will help you fashion a life and career consistent with His leading through the Holy Spirit. For some this will occur early; for others this may take many years, but the Lord will show you His purpose for your life, just as he did for Moses, Hannah, Abraham, Joseph, David, Mary, Simon Peter, and so many others. The sooner you begin to seek God's purpose, the sooner you will find it. But always, it is revealed in God's time. *"Blessed are all who fear the Lord, who walk in his ways. You will eat the fruit of your labor; blessings and prosperity will be yours"* (Ps. 128:1, 2).

Some of my friends and colleagues have been searching for *meaning* in their lives for a long time. They are anxious about the *unknown* of their own futures, while others are faithfully following His steps, fully expecting positive results, knowing God will guide their careers. They have long since discovered how to be in God's will living a life of purpose and peace.

If you commit to establishing an ongoing relationship with God, with yourself, and with others in Christ, you will begin to see that unique, rewarding path God has prepared for you. As these intimate relationships grow and develop, your path becomes crystal clear and your direction becomes exactly what God has always had in mind for you.

What an invigorating way to live! *"Therefore do not be foolish, but understand what the Lord's will is"* (Eph. 5:17).

How wonderful when you connect your chosen profession to God's purpose for your life! While many different jobs truly can serve as the vehicles to our purposeful progress, once you know your purpose, you can do so much more with the career you have chosen. Therefore, seek God for your answers. Consider these valuable words from David, *"I cry out to God Most High, to God, who fulfills his purpose for me"* (Ps. 57:2).

Your Next Boss

*If you were given the opportunity to choose
your next boss, whom would you select?*

The truth is, you have as much opportunity to select
your next boss as your next boss has in selecting the next subordinate. This is not about wishing for a good boss. Nor is it
about getting lucky enough to find a boss that suits your work
style. This is actually about you choosing the person, or at
least, the kind of person with whom you desire to work.

When hiring, most bosses intend to choose the person
who best matches all the stated and unstated characteristics
they desire in a subordinate. They often expect to choose
someone from a broad spectrum of candidates, having a
choice from the "best of the best." Different firms may use
different methods but, in most cases, bosses intend to choose
who they believe will best fit. So, can the reverse be true?
Indeed it can, and most often, it's best to be!

One of the reasons you may not attempt to select your
next boss is that you simply have not taken the first step—
define what kind of a boss you desire. At best, you have a
vague idea of the ideal boss without defining any of the
specifics.

The first step then, is to define the best boss you could
work for—not in a broad, general sense but in decidedly spe-

cific terms. This step may not be easy for you, but it is well worth the effort to take out the yellow-lined tablet and begin writing. You have a significantly important stake in any boss/subordinate relationship. *"He who walks with the wise grows wise, but a companion of fools suffers harm"* (Prov. 13:20).

To begin, record all of the desired attributes of your next boss. Be specific. Brainstorm and create several lists— one describing **personality**, one for **values**, one for **skills**, one for **experience**, and one for **leadership/management style**. Try to exhaust the possibilities in each category.

For example, when listing "values," include ethics such as professional integrity, Christian beliefs, and individual initiative. For "personality," you may desire a sense of humor or a no-nonsense, serious person. Perhaps you want your future boss to possess excellent communication "skills" or in-depth knowledge of business finance and intermediate "skills" on a computer. You may want your boss' "experience" to be as broad as a general manager and as deep as a certified actuary. Regarding "leadership/management style", you may work best for someone who is hands-off and provides only broad direction, or you may work better for a boss who gives specific direction and seeks detailed, daily status reports on your progress.

Once you have exhausted your thinking on each list, reflect on prior interactions with previous bosses. Usually, you tend to remember the very positive and/or very negative experiences. Compare those personal experiences with your list to see if additional ideas spring to mind.

Next, make a list of the attributes of a boss under which you can best flourish. Bosses can represent many different things: authority, expert, judge, decision-maker, leader, counselor, encourager, collaborator, critic, teacher, mentor, roadblock, supporter, manager, taskmaster, and coach.

Then begin to prioritize each list using A, B, and C. The "A List" will be those characteristics in a boss which are *must-have*. The "B List" will represent those characteristics which are *highly desirable*. The "C List", your lowest priority of desired characteristics, includes those that would be beneficial but *not necessary*. Once you get each list prioritized, merge all the designated A's together from the various lists. Do the same for the B's and C's. You now will have on one page the critical, must-have characteristics (A's), on the next page the highly desirable traits (B's), and on the last page will be the like-to-have, but not absolutely necessary (C's) characteristics. This is your personal *yardstick* against which you will *measure* all potential bosses. You can title your prioritized list the *Boss Yardstick*.

One of the last steps in this process is to develop a series of potential questions which you will use to learn more about each potential boss. Carry these important questions with you to get answers whenever and wherever you can. For example, you might ask the boss's close friend, who just happens to be your good network contact, "What kind of boss is John regarding his management style?" or "What do you find to be John's most interesting personality characteristic?" Do not ask questions that will yield "Yes" or "No" answers. You need more insight. Well-constructed questions often will uncover several characteristics, which you can then compare to your *Boss Yardstick*.

Measure each potential boss just as you would if *you* were doing the hiring. The importance of the relationship is the same. You'll be doing yourself a favor. You'll be doing your next boss a favor as well. Select a good boss—a boss that is good for you: your learning, your growth, your performance, your motivation, and your future. Then, if you are extended a job offer, you will know with greater confidence whether to accept it.

Just as these fishermen were certain of their new boss, deciding to follow Jesus was an easy choice for Peter and Andrew. *"As Jesus was walking beside the Sea of Galilee, he saw two brothers, Simon called Peter and his brother Andrew. They were casting a net into the lake, for they were fishermen. 'Come, follow me,' Jesus said, 'and I will make you fishers of men'"* (Matt. 4:18, 19).

By getting focused on your destination with these career-search tools, you too can be certain when called to join your new boss.

Planning Your Search

God has allowed this major change in your life because He has something for you to learn. You may spend more time planning a two-week vacation than planning your life's work and the eternal consequences attached to it. Think about it; you also may spend many hours researching vacation-destination alternatives, available routes, and recreational sites to visit along the way.

Yet on the other hand, you may not consider the benefits of spending time to research various careers and daydream about your ultimate career goals. Have you recently taken the time to evaluate all of the possible routes to achieving your career goals? You are not alone; many looking for a career seldom *plan daily* for the immediate job search, which will lead to your desired job.

For the successful job-seeker, Job #1 now becomes relying on God to help learn the discipline and methodology used in a successful job search. Your obedience to God's Word will help you develop career plans according to His purpose for your life.

"Commit to the Lord whatever you do, and your plans will succeed"

(Prov. 16:3).

Planning Partner

When you are well-informed and confident
about your job search, what is the one thing
that can insure your success?

When Joshua went to the Lord in prayer, his victory
was certain! The same can be said for King Saul and his two
immediate successors, David and Solomon. Likewise in the
Bible, it was true for Hannah, Jonah, Ruth, and Noah. When
these same people decided to face challenges without prayerfully seeking God first, they inevitably stumbled and often
failed in their quest.

The *one thing* that can help us more than any other is
prayer. Prayer has literally parted seas, halted rains, defeated
superior armies, torn down city walls, returned lost kingdoms,
healed the sick, and raised the dead. Prayer can also ensure
that you find and secure the perfect work that God has for you
to do.

God wants you to rely on Him alone; approach Him
with your petitions. When you pray continually with joy and
thanksgiving, you will delight God (1 Thess. 5:16-18). He
desires that you reach out to Him to satisfy all your needs—
large and small even when you believe you can do it without
Him.

Are you due any reward from God? Yes, you are His child. When you pray with your focus singularly on God, He will reward you. *"Then your Father, who sees what is done in secret, will reward you"* (Matt. 6:6). God loves you so much He wants to help. He cares for you more than you will ever know. He desires a close, continual relationship with you. This is true in any endeavor, including your very own job search.

You can boldly expect God's best. You can confidently rely on answers to your prayers. When you pray as brothers and sisters in Christ, in His righteousness, you can count on God's power as He answers your prayers. *"The prayer of a righteous man is powerful and effective"* (Jas. 5:16b).

This brings us right back to where we began this chapter: what is the one thing that will insure your success? That one thing is the love of God. God will answer any request, large or small. He wants to help you with your jobs and careers, every step of the way.

Even through the many trials Joseph faced, he faithfully relied on God for each next step in his life. Also, during most of Moses' life, he went to God for direction, assistance, provision, confidence, forgiveness, intercession, and thanksgiving. And God gave each of his prayers attention.

Some of your needs may be large and some small. God wants you to present all of them to Him. The career decisions you need to make may be difficult ones or easy resolutions. God wants you to seek Him with all of your questions, needs, and desires. God wants you to realize that prayer (a close, personal conversation with God) delights Him and invariably benefits you.

Take a moment in prayer. Talk to God right now. Let Him know you value His love and that you love Him. Like any concerned parent, He will do what is right for you. You can count on Him!

Estimate Your Search Time

Now that you have started your search for a new career, can you estimate how long might be required to land your next job position?

For many years, a simple formula was used to generally estimate someone's length of job search. For every $10,000 of annual income, career counselors would estimate one month of searching. Therefore, if you were seeking a $65,000-a-year position, you would estimate a search lasting between six and seven months.

During a severe business downturn, such as we experienced during 2001-2004, this job-search timeframe may increase by 20 to 30 percent because of a higher ratio of job-seekers to positions available in the tight marketplace.

While only God knows for sure how long your search will last just as He knows the length of your days on earth, consider several factors which can impact your length of search. Said in another way, certain decisions you make can either increase or decrease the length of time you devote to finding your next position.

First let's deal with the factors affecting your search. In the short term, these factors cannot be changed: age, sex, race, and work experience. In today's marketplace, women and minorities still find locating work to be more difficult. Likewise, both younger workers (18-25) and older workers (50-plus) are facing great difficulties finding work. Also, if your work record to this point has been intermittent—up and down with short stays and without any clear direction—you will face greater difficulty finding work.

At the other end of the spectrum, if you are a white male, between the ages of 26 and 40, showing focus and steady growth in your work experience, you *probably* will experience a relatively shorter length of time in a job search. Notice the word *probably,* because several factors also lengthen or shorten the search by people in this category.

Outside Factors:

- Working people generally find work more quickly than do the unemployed. If you are contemplating leaving your current job to devote more time to your search, give serious consideration to the fact that *employed* job-seekers tend to be more desirable to potential employers. Though you may be able to devote more time to look for a job during an average week if you are unemployed, your search time may lengthen.
- Married-with-children is a positive status when seeking employment. As compared to being single, divorced, or a D.I.N.K. (dual income, no kids), married-with-children job-seekers often will find work sooner. This is because some employers believe that people in this category tend to be more stable and less likely to leave abruptly. It may not be true, but it is often the perception.
- Education can impact job search, although this asset depends very much on the profession being

sought. Generally speaking, those with a college education will secure jobs quicker than those without, particularly if the person has some work experience directly related to his educational background. In today's labor market, work experience has more impact than education, except in professions which are highly technical, scientific, or where employers choose to use education as a hurdle to minimize applicant flow.

- Career changes also impact search time. If you are pursuing a total change in profession, industry, and/or geography, you likely will increase your search time. Sometimes, changing career fields is desirable or necessary, but often it will add a few months to the search timetable. Though you see your skill set as transferable to a new profession, all employers may not agree.

- Health and physical presence often may affect one's employability. Those who are healthy, both physically and emotionally, make a good first impression. Those who are fit physically and have a positive, energetic attitude will spend less time seeking work than will those who are unfit, disheveled, emotionally weighted down, or who are carrying around a negative focus.

- Compensation desired can impact search length. As long as you are seeking a salary within 20 percent of your last income, you probably will not impact your search length. On the other hand, those individuals who are willing to work for half of their last income or seeking double their last salary will statistically incur a longer job search period. If you made $50,000/year in your previous job and you now are willing to accept $25,000-a-year (for several possible reasons), some interviewers may be concerned about the risk of your being lured away easily if another $50,000-a-year job comes along. And if you are expecting to double your last salary, many employers will view your optimism as unrealistic.

• Geographic limitations can negatively impact your search time, particularly if you seek middle- to senior-management positions. Those who are unwilling to relocate regionally or nationally will significantly reduce the number of opportunities they will receive for employment, hence adding to the search time. Think carefully before making a decision to not move geographically.

• Serving as a volunteer can shorten your search. Employers often are impressed with those who are actively engaged in helping others in their communities. Remember, you reap what you sow. Volunteer work is often equated to energy and enthusiasm to serve. It will represent to many a set of strong values.

• Longer Means Longer or LML is shorthand to say that the longer you remain unemployed, the longer you will need to find work. In other words, if you decide to "take a few months off to relax" after a layoff, you are certainly increasing the likelihood of a longer job search. Don't dally.

• Market agitation factor has influenced the business community in 2002, 2003, and 2004. Because the downturn in business created an increasing number of job-seekers relative to the number of available jobs, all job searches were lengthened. This is because during a recession employers become very cautious and literally slow the addition of new employees to their payrolls.

Here's what you can do to quickly push your job search to conclusion:

- Control the factors that you can control, e.g. if you're not volunteering somewhere, start now and find an organization that needs your help and skills.
- Do not worry about the past or the factors you cannot control. If you're a female over 50, work with the advantages that God provides you, such as wisdom and experience.
- Share with God the ownership of your search. Allow Him to do His part while you do yours.
- Take time to polish your personal skills, learn what's new in the workplace, and ask for career assistance in a positive program such as **CAREER**SOLUTIONS Workshop®, where you can seek support, network, and be accountable with a diverse group of business men and women.
- Choose your future career wisely and purposefully; align it with what God has planned for your life. Identify a target career, which will enable you to move forward more deliberately and with a synergy of resources.
- Accept full responsibility for the outcome. Realize that you are in charge of the fruit of your labor. Finding work is work; use the implements you're given.

• Persevere in faith, knowing the evil one would love for you to give in and give up. Don't quit; never give in to the temptations of self-pity, self-abuse, or the ease of failing. *"But as for you, be strong and do not give up, for your work will be rewarded"* (2 Chron. 15:7).

10

Speed the Search Process

*What are you doing now to shorten the
time you will invest in finding
your next position?*

This question assumes you are somewhat eager to get
a new job. I speak with men and women often who express a
deep need to find work . . . *fast!* If you are in this category,
you can accelerate the search process. Some tips are simple to
implement; others may require greater commitment and effort.
The choice is yours.

But first, a cautionary note: Besides finding work fast,
you also may have the objective of finding the *best position*
with the *best pay* in the *best company* in the *best industry*.
Often you may have to face trade-offs, including whether to
search for a job efficiently or spend time trying to be more
effective.

The search tips in this chapter are only going to deal
with the *efficiency* part of your objectives. Later, please give
consideration to your *effectiveness,* so you are not conducting
another job search six months down the road.

To shorten the length of a search:
- Pray (1 Thess. 4:16-18).
- Tighten your focus (Matt. 7:7-8).

- Gather greater knowledge and information (Prov. 1:29-31).
- Develop a plan and devote more time to work it each day (Prov. 14:23).
- Change variables that impact potential employers (2 Tim. 2:20-21).
- Briefly review each of these verses. Then copy them to an index card. Read and act on them each morning during your search. This will be your compass to a new career.

First, you *pray!* Pray for God's will in your life. Pray for his blessings on your career search and the gifts and talents He alone has provided you. Pray for faith to persevere— for knowledge to do the right things at the right time. Pray for energy and focus, for goodness, self-control, kindness, and love. Our Lord wants you to have these gifts in your life, whether you are working or diligently seeking work.

Next, keep your job search focused on your true calling. It will require less energy and cause less distraction. Even if you must accept lesser employment to pay the bills, do not give up your passion and your dreams for your unique calling. Perhaps it must become a long-term goal. Remain faithfully focused on what you desire. It can become reality.

Third, you can become "more employable" if you wisely spend your time gaining more knowledge and information. Start reading and don't stop. Keep on reading. Find and interview experts in your chosen career. Learn who the leaders in that field are. In Proverbs 12:15, Solomon counsels, *"The way of a fool is right to him, but a wise man listens to advice."* And in Proverbs 15:22, he reinforces it by stating, *"Plans fail for lack of counsel, but with many advisers they succeed."* Spend time in the library; attend free lectures. Even sign up to take an inexpensive course somewhere. Keep your mind sharp and challenged.

Fourth, develop a time-management plan to devote more hours and resources each day to looking for a job. The average job-seeker spends less than 10 hours per week seeking a new job. If you are serious, devote 30 or more hours each week. Develop a daily calendar that causes you to spend time in networking activities, responding to job postings, and doing research on industries and companies that are part of your target market.

If you don't have a target market, let your plan immediately include tasks to determine a target market. It goes without saying: a plan works best when it is *written down* and kept visibly *accessible*.

And in your plan, include a daily, disciplined approach to self-improvement, changing variables about yourself that will impact your appearance, attitude, education, and volunteer activities. If you've never made time to exercise, start exercising now. If you need to shed a few pounds, begin a diet. If you need a makeover, go get one. You have time. Also, use this season of unemployment to exercise *self-discipline*. You will gain more power and confidence. Your newfound confidence will have a greater positive effect on potential employers than the smaller waist you gain.

Self-discipline flows in to other areas of your life, too. If you are not already volunteering in your community or church, pull off the freeway at the next exit and do so. Volunteer, first and foremost, because it is the right thing to do. Most organizations really need your help. Understand that volunteering may also affect an interviewer's impression of you and how you spend your time.

My friend, Don K., devoted a year to his job search for an executive-level job. During this time he continued to volunteer for a local charity. He was skilled in fund-raising and provided considerable hours to that end for the charity. When a major civic organization was considering Don for a key position, his volunteer efforts were thought to be a key experience and strength by the team charged with filling the position. Don, in part, landed the job because of his commitment to volunteer and to give back to the community.

Have you finished your education? Do you need classes or degrees? Education is self-discipline, too. Return to school and take one or two classes. You'll likely learn something. And even if you don't finish a degree, just trying may improve the impact you make when interviewing.

Above all, do whatever is required to improve your attitude. Even in the midst of being unemployed or unhappily employed, be positive, energetic, and future-oriented during your job search. A great attitude will get you the attention of those wanting to hire the best candidate for the job. In Psalm 34:19, the lyricist reminds us, *"A righteous man may have many troubles, but the Lord delivers him from them all."*

If you commit to doing your part in finding work, God will provide the work at exactly the right time. It is a conditional promise. You have to do your part. You always can count on God to do His part.

Stretching Your Dollars

*Are you ready to do what is necessary to ensure
your financial survival during the job search?*

     "Stretching your dollars" is a bit easier if you have a
spouse who is still working, but many unemployed job-
seekers are without this kind of backup financial support. This
chapter primarily is designed to help those of you without
additional employment income. Nevertheless, many of the
principles discussed here apply to career seekers with or without a working spouse. For example, Paul instructs us in the
Bible to get out of debt and stay there. In Romans 13:8, Paul
advises, *"Let no debt remain outstanding, except the
continuing debt to love one another, for he who loves his
fellowman has fulfilled the law."*

     You will remember this formula from a previous chap-
ter: to find work you will devote an *average* of one month for
each $10,000 of annual income you require. Since the events
of September 11, 2001, the job-search time period has
increased the standard formula somewhat. Therefore, if you
are looking for a $70,000/year, middle-management position,
you will need to allow eight, nine, or 10 months, or more, to
secure a position to replace your last job.

     Here are some successful tactics that others have used
to *"strrreeetch"* their dollars:

- Cease impulse-buying by sticking to a grocery list when shopping.
- Clip and actually use coupons for groceries and household items.
- Stop purchasing pre-prepared foods.
- Eliminate or minimize eating out.
- Do your own laundry instead of taking it to the dry cleaners.
- Cancel your cable TV, DSL Internet, and/or satellite TV.
- Stop or minimize magazine subscriptions.
- Get rid of your credit cards unless you are able to pay them off every month.
- Re-finance your home, your car, and/or high-interest, revolving debt.
- Cancel all the optional features on your monthly phone service.
- Change your long-distance plan to a more cost-effective program.
- Eliminate cell phones except when needed for business.
- Try getting along with only one car if you have two or more.
- Sell a late-model car and purchase an older one.
- Visit the car wash less often or wash your own car.
- Adjust the thermostat. In the summer, turn it up; in the winter, turn it down and put on a sweater.
- Create a conservative budget and live at that level.

Many of these approaches need buy-in and participation by every family member. So rally the troops around you. Sit down and talk it over. If you have a family, make sure that all family members understand the importance of conserving dollars. If you live alone, talk with God. He will listen to your strategy.

Below are a few ideas the family can help implement this strategy to weather the financial storm:

- Include your family's financial and physical needs in your prayers. He has promised to meet our needs. You need only to ask.
- Seek *free* financial advice from knowledgeable friends or financial ministries. Our ministry offers a periodic Saturday Seminar entitled "Financial Freedom." Participants learn techniques to maximize cash flow, preserve capital, and negotiate lower interest rates with creditors during job transition. Each individual is offered a *free* private coaching session.
- Seek *free* professional credit counseling from Consumer Credit Counseling Service. You may call for your free appointment, 1-800-856-0257.
- Go to the library and find books and periodicals dealing with living on a tight budget. Read them for more good ideas.
- With your newly created, conservative budget on paper, pencil out again how long you can last during a lengthy job search.

Some of us may have saved as much as three- to six-months' worth of living expenses for such emergencies. You can prolong your ability to pay your obligations by finding creative ways to *"strrreeetch"* the dollars you have in the bank. Also, you may need to consider ways to generate some income to replace some of the lost salary, even if only temporarily:

- Sell assets. Consider selling things you don't really need. Remember it is just stuff. *". . . and he said, 'Go, sell the oil and pay your debts'. . .."* (2 Kings 4:7).

- Find temporary or part-time work to help slow down the drain on your resources. Here are a few ideas to stimulate your thinking. The list can be endless, if you really work at it:
  1. Helping friends with their business
  2. Working for a temporary agency
  3. Pet-sitting
  4. Working in your church part time
  5. Working evening shifts and all night shifts, which many companies have a difficult time filling
  6. Refereeing youth sports
  7. Volunteering, which sometimes leads to a paying staff position
  8. Renting out a spare room to a local college or seminary student

Once you do all you can to decrease your expenses and increase your income, you can devote your energies to finding that career position. My prayer is that you will trust in God as you weather this challenging season in your life and that you will faithfully do your part. I know the Lord will do His!

Planning Your Week

Reflecting on the past week, do you feel you've been busy but haven't accomplished much?

You normally will have times when you are very busy while simultaneously unproductive. As you compare those situations to times when you are productive, often the important variable is one of planning. If you plan well, you can frequently accomplish more, with better results. As with every successful business and with every successful individual, plans are developed and *written* down.

This is just as true for Microsoft Corporation's strategic plan as it is for the weekly schedule of any successful executive or professional. When developing short- or long-term strategies, whether highly complex or very simple, good planning is an important prerequisite for good execution of any goal.

Examine some of the elements of good planning listed below, so that the time you devote to your job search will be fruitful. Simply put, good planning involves:

1. *Analyzing* activities that need to be done
2. *Prioritizing* those activities
3. *Allowing* for contingencies
4. *Writing* out your plan

Activities to Be Done

You can take four approaches to find employment: cold-calling, responding to job postings, networking, and working with agencies or search firms.

1. *Cold-calling* involves contacting your target companies without any specific knowledge that a job exists. It can take the form of stopping by employers in your town, visiting their web site, or even telephoning a prospective employer to find out if any openings exist.

2. *Responding to job postings* often is the most familiar approach. Organizations frequently post job openings to attract applicants for those positions. Postings can be found in many places such as these in classified ads in newspapers and magazines, or online:
   - Positions available in professional journals
   - Retail bulletin boards
   - Industry organizational web sites and their job boards
   - Popular Internet job sites, e.g., Monster.com
   - Company signage in front of buildings
   - Networking groups
   - Billboards
   - Radio, television ads, and public-service announcements
   - Direct mail

3. *Networking*. This is probably the most successful of all the suggestions listed here. It is the process of connecting with people who, in turn, connect you to others and so on, until a position that matches your career goals is discovered or created. Networking is a reciprocal process, which involves meeting new individuals, dis-

cussing your search goals, and getting referrals to others in your field of interest and who may have knowledge of a job opportunity for you. That new contact may then refer you on to others he or she knows.

In a networking partnership, an unspoken desire exists to help the other individual—that you in turn, might also know someone who can help that person in his or her business endeavors—and you gladly share your information with that person first. The age-old process is called helping each other.

4. *Working with employment agencies or search firms* is an approach that uses an intermediary company representative, working solely for the purpose of finding available positions. A fee is involved, usually paid by the looking corporation, but not always. Search firms recruit candidates, the best of which are referred to employing organizations for consideration.

Each of these four approaches ultimately is used to put you in front of the hiring authorities. Each has strengths and weaknesses. Understanding how each approach works enables you to plan a productive, effective job search.

Prioritization of Activities

For most successful career-seekers, prioritizing your job search activities results in devoting 50 to 70 percent of their time in *networking* opportunities, 10 to 20 percent focusing on *job postings*, another 10 to 20 percent of their time spent *cold-calling*, and only 10 percent of search time dedicated to working with *agencies or search firms*, including "head-hunters."

With that prioritization in mind, as a successful job-seeker, you can plan your week in 10 increments of a half-day each. Divide each day into morning and afternoon segments. Then plan to spend:

1. one segment each week for agencies/search firms,
2. two segments each week for job postings,
3. two segments each week for cold-calling, and
4. five segments each week for networking.

Executive-level employees: consider increasing networking to seven segments, or 70 percent each week.

Allow for Contingencies

Occasionally, things may arise that require you to revise your plans. Unexpected interviews may cause you to delay other items, just as interview cancellations may provide you time you did not count on having.

Develop a plan that allows for these unseen, unexpected events. Leave open periods of time to be able to get to those unexpected emergencies or opportunities. Be ready to use time you gain by cancelled appointments. I have found carrying work with me every place I go to be very worthwhile.

If I am waiting for a coaching appointment to meet me at a coffee house and I arrive to find my appointment has called ahead to leave a message he will be 30 minutes late, I always have work to do—correspondence to write, reading to finish, and next week's plan to complete. Since I began this approach 10 years ago, I am never upset with someone who is late, or I am never disturbed by a cancellation, because I am prepared to make good use of my time when things change.

Write Down the Plan

Remember, a plan carried around in your mind is not a plan but just good intentions. Put your time-management plan on paper. Use a pencil to allow for contingencies. Writing down your plan for each week gives you a road map. It gives you *future focus* and directs each day. Specifically assign tasks to each day to enable you to achieve your priorities for the week.

I like to have one "main thing" on my calendar for each day that really helps me move toward the long-term objective. Today it might be to finish the final draft of this book; tomorrow, it may be to secure at least one corporate sponsor for our ministry. The next day it may be to ask three friends to contribute endorsements for my next book. I have other objectives written for each day, but accomplishing at least one "main thing" each day really helps.

Plan in Advance

Planning implies that you have made a conscious decision in advance on what you intend to accomplish, by putting your priorities in key time slots for the week. Experience has shown that planning-on-the-fly seldom results in productive, meaningful accomplishments. This is true on the job or in a job search.

Get Specific

When deciding on goals and activities you intend to accomplish, specify results in productivity. For example, in your networking segment, book contact referrals for interviews in advance, normally one to two weeks in advance—who, time, place, and purpose. If you intend to visit networking groups, use the same procedure. Settle way in advance the matter of which groups, where, and when. If you intend to contact three to five cold contacts, select specific, high-priority employers from your list of "targeted companies."

Work Your Plan

Here's one friendly reminder. The actual working of the plan, not the plan itself, is what counts. The work you then accomplish, which was planned in advance, is *where the rubber meets the road*. Get up and going each day. Diligently work to accomplish your intended priorities for the full day.

If you prioritize well, plan your week in advance, allow for things to change where necessary, and then work your plan diligently, you will be delighted with your productivity and ultimately with your results. *"The plans of the diligent lead to profit and surely as haste leads to poverty"* (Prov. 21:5).

Job Boards–Boom or Bust

Do you have time to respond to all jobs listed on Monster.com and CareerBuilders.com?

We know that fewer than four percent of all jobs are filled from postings on the Internet job boards, even with all the hype and attention they receive. Forrester Research reports that during the peak of the *dot-com* boom, the number of job positions filled never exceeded four percent.

Do you abandon the job boards? Absolutely not! But the best use of them is not to find specific jobs, it is to find out *who* is hiring and in *what* fields. The Internet is best used as a research tool.

The first approach is to determine your target companies—those you prefer to work for given their reputation, culture, values, potential, and management style. Then you can match those against firms hiring on the "big boards." Next conduct research on those businesses. Use the Internet to visit their home pages and visit your local library to do written research. If possible, speak with current and/or previous employees about how they view the company.

Because we know networking is the most effective career search tool, use the research results to point yourself toward contacts specifically appropriate for those firms, which are hiring and are on your *target* list. Online, sometimes you

64

can find appropriate contacts in "About Us" sections, or in reading corporate news releases by clicking "Press" buttons.

The Internet job boards do have a purpose. However, remember once companies post on the "big boards", the competition for a position can number in the thousands or tens of thousands. The idea is to use the job boards for your *personal research*. It sounds like work because it is work. Good research may be as important as anything you do, so spend your time and efforts in areas that may bear fruit. *"But as for you, be strong and do not give up, for your work will be rewarded"* (2 Chron. 15:7).

While hundreds of job-seekers are trying to find a match on the Internet job boards, remember your task is to find those jobs they don't know about. *"Do not conform any longer to the pattern of this world, but be transformed by the renewing of your mind. Then you will be able to test and approve what God's will is—his good, pleasing and perfect will"* (Rom. 12:2).

Do not allow yourself to become trapped into the "easy leisure" of surfing the Web, hour after hour, day after day. Time yourself. Use the Internet job boards for research and log off. Then, develop your plans around a priority of networking, focusing on the information you have gleaned from your online research. To find the best jobs, devote most of your time and energy to getting connected to people, face-to-face.

Building Momentum

Have you ever wondered why so many of us, once we reach adulthood, stop trying to learn? We seem to lose interest in becoming someone better—filling up our tanks, so to speak—with knowledge and wisdom.

In today's work climate, those who succeed are often those individuals who invest time and energy in improving themselves. They get sound advice from trusted mentors and then act on that advice as it applies to their lives. Adopting this mindset never occurs too late.

God certainly didn't plan a life in which you would stop growing mentally as you entered adulthood. He has continual plans to develop you and bless you with a role in prosperity: to work, to learn, to sow, to gather, to reap, and to grow. For you to achieve all that God has planned for your life, get actively engaged in learning and understanding the world around your career focus.

"Wisdom is supreme; therefore get wisdom. Though it cost you all you have, get understanding"

(Prov. 4:7).

Keep Getting Better

What Have You Done For Yourself Lately?

Perhaps by the time you read this, you have been unemployed for several weeks or months. Or perhaps you are languishing along doing work well beneath your skill level, your interests, and your true passion. You may be concerned that your current, less-than-challenging job or this rather lengthy period of unemployment will be considered a negative in your background. It certainly may. But I have a suggestion to minimize or even neutralize this negative period in your life: do something! Do something positive!

Do something to improve yourself. Make yourself more valuable to potential employers by increasing your own self worth. For years, you have wanted to lose weight, quit smoking, read more, take a class, pursue a hobby, and volunteer your service to a church ministry or to your community. Perhaps you rationalized that you never had time. Well, now you have time!

You might do these things because they need to be done, even when you are working. You might do these things because you can become more employable, more valuable, more skilled, more positive, more productive, and more energetic. Third, you might do these things because you will have a much better answer to interview questions such as these:

"What have you done since you were laid off last September?" or "Have you ever thought of finishing your education?" or "What have you done, or are you doing, to make yourself better prepared for pursuing that next career level you want?"

Keep learning and keep improving your skills throughout your life. You may not realize it, but increasing your skill base and knowledge level improves your confidence and your employability.

Some will seek wisdom as Solomon advised us to do in the following principles, *"Instruct a wise man and he will be wiser still; teach a righteous man and he will add to his learning"* (Prov. 9:9); and *"Whoever gives heed to instruction prospers, and blessed is he who trusts in the Lord"* (Prov. 16:20).

If you find yourself out of work, volunteer and help others. If you are unfulfilled by a meaningless (to you) job, return to school. If you are watching your peers pass you by, do something to improve yourself. If you feel unappreciated by those around you, find others who will give you positive feedback. If you lack a sense of direction, start reading about careers and successes of others.

Concerning each of us taking responsibility, my friend Marsha Petrie Sue wrote in her book, *The CEO of YOU*, "Set goals . . . Change, be flexible, move with courage, and be accepting of challenges. Take responsibility for you. Are you willing? Are you able? Are you response+able?"

By improving yourself, you will be saying to yourself and to others, "I care. I am motivated. I can and like to learn." You will be creating building blocks for your future! You cannot help but get better and better! *"May the Lord direct your hearts into God's love and Christ's perseverance"* (2 Thess. 3:5).

Back to School

*After contemplating your education credentials,
do you go back to school?*

Maybe furthering your education is **exactly** what you
need right now. Let us examine some good reasons to continue your education plan. If these following reasons apply to
your personal situation, then perhaps more schooling would
be helpful in your career search plan.

If you always have regretted not completing your col-
lege-level education, and you are confident that additional formal learning will help you reach that career you've always
dreamed about, then go for it. Study after study shows that
additional education often provides individuals more choices,
greater variety of alternatives to consider, and more career
avenues to pursue.

If you intend to make a career change which definitely
requires a degree you do not possess, and the education is one
obstacle that you know cannot be removed without the accomplishment of additional education, return to school. Ask yourself, "Is this the career or profession which I was created to
do?" If you answer in the affirmative, then begin your educational pursuits.

Most consider additional education a benefit because
of the potential financial payback. Studies continue to show,

for example, that individuals with a bachelor of arts or a bachelors of science degree will earn, on average, twice the annual income of an individual with only a high-school diploma. That earning cycle will continue throughout your working career. Furthermore, those who choose to earn advanced degrees proportionately increase their average earnings with each additional educational level achieved.

So decide: Are you ready to put your regrets behind you and finally decide on a career that requires more education? Or are you now determined to increase the financial rewards of your labors? Pray about your decision; discuss this with your loved ones.

Does this have a price tag? Yes. That's why you might consider it an investment. You may be required to invest money, time, and energy to attain that next educational level. Is the investment worth the return—freedom, more choices, fewer regrets, and greater earning potential? Only you can answer the question for yourself. Remember the decision you make is yours. Like every decision, it will have numerous consequences.

Many of those consequences will impact you; some will impact your family. Perhaps, some will include strangers in your life. Some consequences may have immediate impact for a short duration of time, such as having to live without some things while you save money for tuition. The consequences of other decisions may not be apparent for years, e.g., seeing the "fruit of your labor" or your income rise along with new job duties because of your college degree. Also, some potential consequences might have a long-lasting, multidimensional impact on your life. Perhaps, unfortunately, pursuing a higher degree could result in divorce. Seek family support before you invest in additional commitments such as going back to school.

If you are still undecided about your personal development, consider this command God gave to Joshua not long after his mentor, Moses, died. *"Do not let this Book of the Law depart from your mouth; meditate on it day and night, so that you may be careful to do everything written in it. Then you will be prosperous and successful"* (Josh. 1:8). God told Joshua his success was contingent upon reading, studying, meditating, and following God's direction as documented in His Word. Study God's Word to seek the answers you need. When you find them, do what they tell you.

Taken in a humorous vein, this *Yogi-ism* from New York Yankee Yogi Berra has a very poignant message: "When you come to a fork in the road, take it." Perhaps you are being blessed again with a choice—to return to school and follow your education plan or to follow another sign on the road.

Prayerfully consider all the costs, implications, commitments, rewards, and possible consequences those good and not so good. No doubt God has something wonderful planned for you. Perhaps finishing your education is a necessary, preparatory choice for you to make. If it is, then make it!

Mentoring and Accountability

Are you closely connected to a few individuals who will help you by holding you accountable, encouraging you, and praying for you?

If you have been fired or laid off, this can become a very lonely time. Your regular routine of going to work and your regular relationships at work will be turned upside down. If you do not have strong relationships outside your place of employment, you can often feel abandoned or cast aside. *"If one falls down, his friend can help him up. But pity the man who falls and has no one to help him up!"* (Eccles. 4:10).

Having a small group of individuals with whom you can discuss concerns, seek advice, and think aloud is important. I believe these small support groups are important, even when you are not in a crisis. But, in a crisis they are a real blessing. I have been a member of a small group of men that meets each week; we help each other with issues about family relationships, career crises, and the challenges of balancing life's tugs and pulls. We pray for each other. We counsel each other. We allow each other to ask the tough questions of accountability. We have honest discussions about our walk with the Lord, seeking God's will for each decision we face, our temptations, our human frailties, and more.

I encourage you to find at least two (but no more than four) other individuals who need and want such God-ordained relationships. In the Bible, Solomon encourages us to lean on others of like mind: *"As iron sharpens iron, so one man sharpens another"* (Prov. 27:17). You need a few people who will help you be accountable to these areas of your life, because one day the Lord will ask you to be accountable for your actions.

Though women seemed to be naturally wired for relationships and sharing, the first group I joined more than nine years ago consisted of four men who knew little about each other. Our ages ranged from early 30's to mid-50's. One was retired; the other three were in various stages of their careers. One was an empty-nester; one was in the process of accumulating six children. We all had different backgrounds. Circumstances were varied in just about every aspect of our lives, but we had one thing in common—a **desire to be held accountable to the standards established by Jesus Christ.**

During your job search, find a few individuals (besides your spouse) with whom you can share all your concerns. Meet at a regular time every week or two. Meet in a place away from home that provides privacy and an atmosphere conducive to candid dialogue. Share your spiritual journey with each other.

As you get to know each other, decide what areas of your life you want to be held accountable for and give others permission to hold you accountable to those things each week. Pray daily for each other between meetings.

If you are not exactly sure what small accountability groups are, I suggest you do a bit of reading on the subject. I found two authors who do a great job of fully explaining the process. For more information about forming small groups, read Chapter 23 in Patrick Morley's *The Man in the Mirror* and Chapter 6 in Steve Farrar's *Point Man.*

Whom do you invite to start an accountability group? Folks who have the same Christian heart as you do. Start with those in your Bible-study class, or a few people from a networking group, or with others you meet at church. If you get a few individuals who say they won't or can't, don't stop looking. Perhaps your pastor, minister, priest, or rabbi can help you find a few others who have the same desire to be held accountable. Though some may be hesitant, many know they need exactly what you are proposing. They need only a nudge. Pray for God's direction on this; He will send the right individuals to you.

If you're not connected to any support groups, I encourage you to get connected. This world can be a lonely place when you face huge challenges. God gave us each other to help get through every battle we face. *The prayer of a righteous man is powerful and effective* (Jas. 5:16b). Do you have others on whom you can rely for prayer and support? Don't face the months of unemployment and job search alone or the challenges of a career change without the loving encouragement from a close group of brothers and sisters.

Finally, remember what Paul said when discussing perseverance in your lifelong journey: *"And let us consider how we may spur one another on toward love and good deeds. Let us not give up meeting together, as some are in the habit of doing, but let us encourage one another—and all the more as you see the Day approaching"* (Heb. 10:24-25).

Networking: It's Not Whom You Know; It's Whom You Get To Know

How many times have you said, disillusioned, "Self, I just don't understand why someone else always seems to get those better jobs before I even hear about them." Or maybe you lament, "I don't seem to know the right people who can really help me."

The secret is *networking*. Those who succeed at networking will be the first to tell you that you, too, can learn to reap the benefits of *good* networking. You are *never too late* to learn to network *correctly*. The emphasis on *good* and *correctly* is important to note here, because many people in the business world do a very poor job of networking. They don't fully understand the mystery of properly connecting to others for mutual benefit, nor do they see the damage they do to themselves when they foolishly use politics throughout their careers.

Why you network and *how* you network will have distinct consequences throughout your life. Some may view networking as a means to gain employment. Those more astute will view networking as a lifelong opportunity. Many of the benefits you receive from your relationships are a direct result of what you put into them, not what you take out.

"Do not be deceived: God cannot be mocked. A man reaps what he sows . . ..
Therefore, as we have opportunity, let us do good to all people, especially to those who belong to the family of believers"

(Gal. 6:7, 10).

Why Network

So why bother to network when you already ask others for help when you need it?

Networking is the single best way to land that next career job. It is better than all other approaches put together. In fact, "networking has been proven to be *two to three times* more productive than all other employment sources *combined*, accounting for an estimated 64 percent to 75 percent of all jobs landed by the job-seeker," reported Richard Beatty in his book, *Job Search Networking*.

In a study conducted by the U.S. Department of Labor, which included more than 10.4-million job-seekers, almost two out of every three jobs (63.4 percent) were filled as a result of networking. Job postings accounted for filling about 14 percent of job openings, search firms followed in the list at 12 percent, while cold calls only netted jobs for 10.5 percent of the job-seekers.

Two similar studies—one by Harvard University professor and sociologist Mark Granovetter and the other by Brandywine Consulting Group—showed networking accounts for job landings in 74.5 percent and 68 percent of the cases, respectively. Clearly, more than two-thirds of successful job searches result from *networking*! By a large margin it works better than all other methods combined.

The Bible tells us another wonderful reason to net-work. God prefers that you network, connect with others, seek advice, ask for assistance, and find encouragement from your brothers and sisters.

1. *"Therefore, as we have opportunity, let us do good to all people, especially to those who belong to the family of believers"* (Gal. 6:10).

2. *"Let another praise you, and not your own mouth; someone else, and not your own lips"* (Prov. 27:2).

3. *"Listen to advice and accept instruction, and in the end you will be wise"* (Prov. 19:20).

4. *"Each of you should look not only to your own interests, but also to the interests of others"* (Phil. 2:4).

The Lord desires you to help others, working together like the different parts of the body, each for the benefit of the other. Networking connects you in a very positive way to the world around you.

In his book, *Connecting*, Larry Crabb discusses how valuable we all are to each other. He encourages us to serious-ly consider how much more we could gain from better con-nections. He says, "We haven't yet dreamed big enough dreams of what we could mean to one another. Maybe the time has arrived." Perhaps your time has arrived right now.

In the following chapters, you will discover how truly great networking will affect both your immediate and long-term concerns. Ultimately, it is very different from simply begging for help and pleading for favors. If networking is how a majority of jobs are found, and networking is what gives you favor with the Lord, why wouldn't you use networking with great joy and anticipation?

Good Networking

You've been told it's the key to a great job search, but what really is good networking?

First and foremost, networking is simply building relationships. It is about connecting with others in a fashion that may seem foreign to some people. As was written thousands of years ago, *"Plans fail for lack of counsel, but with many advisers they succeed"* (Prov. 15:22).

According to the Oxford American Dictionary, a network is a "chain of inter-connected people or operations." Simply put, your personal networks consist of people to whom you are connected through a mutual relationship. First, let's deal with the connection principle.

You may want to connect with everyone you can, not just those individuals or friends whom you know well in your personal life but to people you know throughout all arenas of your life. Take a few hours and make a list of network contact options. Write them down. Yes, think about all the avenues you have traveled that connect you to all sorts of people:

   a. Family

   b. Friends

   c. Acquaintances

   d. Church members

e. Neighbors

f. Former work colleagues

g. Ex-suppliers

h. Past customers

i. Ex-competitors

j. Ex-bosses

k. Social contacts

l. Suppliers

m. Contacts from your child's school

n. Sports contacts

o. Fellow hobbyists

p. Colleagues from **CAREER**SOLUTIONS
   Workshop®

The list goes on and on. Each of these categories consists of many individuals known as *primary contacts*. Any one of them might be able to refer you to one or more of their many associates, known as *secondary contacts*. It is all about connecting. And it is all about *whom* you get to know.

Another important aspect of good networking deals with the principle of **sowing and reaping**. The principle of *sowing first* always works. Paul, in his letter to the Philippians, said, *"Do nothing out of selfish ambition or vain conceit, but in humility consider others better than yourselves"* (Phil. 2:3).

Therefore, be careful when networking with others to make your primary objective discovering how you can help and refresh others. *"A generous man will prosper; he who refreshes others will himself be refreshed"* (Prov. 11:25). Networking is not about what you can get out of the meeting or relationship, but first and foremost, it's about what you can *give*.

To help further clarify what effective networking is, let's look at what networking is **not**:

1. It's **not** asking for job leads.
2. It's **not** looking for job postings.
3. It's **not** about pestering hiring managers.
4. It's **not** having others solve your unemployment situation.
5. It's **not** about "what I need."

Many people do not understand that networking is far more subtle. Good networking is about asking for advice and seeking suggestions. You need *never* ask for a job lead; rather, concentrate for a few moments on building a reciprocal relationship. Ask how you can *help* each other; or how you can *be a solution* to their problems; or listen to how you can *learn* from that person's experience and expertise; or finally, how you both can encourage one another.

Whether you are connecting with primary contacts, people you know, or secondary contacts, those brand new to you, *your first objective is to help them*. Challenge yourself to be the first giver. You can take with you information that may be of interest to them or help them in their position. Take résumés of candidates for jobs they currently have available, other than the ones you seek; or share a current article from a newspaper or magazine which may be of significant interest; or, on the other hand, make an offer to help with a particular need the individual previously mentioned, which simply could be a need for prayer, volunteer help, or for advice.

Out of all of this, one "little gem" is hidden in the idea of *not asking* for a job lead. Though you may be seeking advice for your job search, *avoid asking* for a job or job lead because it far too often puts your networking contact in a difficult, uncomfortable position. Here's the gem: if the networking contact knows of a job that is suited to you, the lead will be freely offered to you. Asking is unnecessary and ineffective. The lifelong connection principle we all need to learn is sowing, then reaping—not the reverse.

Most often, the value of the contact lies in the referral to someone else, who puts you much closer to your desired position. And as you move closer to your target position with that next contact, approach it the same way, seeking advice and counsel. If that person has suggestions to help move you forward, thank him or her, act on the suggestion, and move forward again, and again.

Networking is connecting by building relationships—long-term relationships. Jesus built relationships. Paul built relationships. King David built relationships. In the Bible read about their lives. See that you also have the opportunity to build relationships in much the same way. Seek wise counsel; give of yourself and your time; become a solution to others' problems. A successful job search and fruitful life absolutely depend on you making connections and networking the way God intended.

Early in my career, I connected to a colleague. Over the next few years, we developed a friendly relationship. Our common bonds included the study of human resources in college and a common employer—Disneyland. A few years after he left Disney, I called him for career advice, because I had moved on from Disney as well. At that time, he was a human-resources manager at a well-known competitor to Disneyland in Southern California.

I did not ask his help to employ me, but I did ask for his professional advice. I left a copy of my résumé with him afterwards. A few weeks later, and to my surprise, I was contacted by a person who had received a copy of my résumé from my colleague, who turned out to be his "old friend." Within a month I was working for the company. I stayed for a very successful, 26-year career.

The point I share is simply this: successful networking is not usually about the immediate circumstances of our lives. It is about forging long-lasting relationships with people of strong character. It's about helping others succeed. It's about connecting and then staying connected. If you only connect when you are needy and don't invest yourself in the relationship, it is hollow and empty. *Remember this: Whoever sows sparingly will also reap sparingly, and whoever sows generously will also reap generously* (2 Cor. 9:6).

On a final note, ask yourself this question, "In whose lives have I invested?" Some of us are *givers* and some are *takers*. Our Lord wants us all to be **givers**. Examples abound in God's Word, particularly in the sacrificial life of Jesus of Nazareth.

If you have been a *taker*, your network contacts may be few in number. You can still change. Start giving of yourself. Over time, you will be amazed how many people will count you on their list of valued connections. Keep sowing. *Each man should give what he has decided in his own heart to give, not reluctantly or under compulsion, for God loves a cheerful giver"* (2 Cor. 9:7).

19

When to Network

When is the best time in the job search process to network?

By now you probably appreciate the reasons *why* networking is so important. And you now understand what *good* networking is and is not. It makes answering the *when* question a bit easier. Let me take two different approaches to answering this question.

Approach One

First, you will want to approach *when* to network from the tactical, short-term view. You need to make contacts at the best possible times during your job search. Usually, the best possible time is *now*.

In other words, if your need is immediate, set priorities, establishing who your primary network contacts are from your list of options. Contact several each week. Ask for a brief time to meet with them, preferably face-to-face. These primary contacts may refer you to secondary contacts. This will require you to schedule new appointments each week, in order of priority. After each meeting send a brief, hand-written, thank-you note to each for taking the time to talk with you or refer you on to someone they know.

Looking again at your list of network options, now begin to work the primary contacts from a group or an association in which you have been involved or with which you would like to be involved in your ideal career. Some groups meet weekly or monthly; some are career- or profession-specific; some are salary-level specific; while others may have different commonalities which bring people together. Look online, ask around, or research options at the library. You quickly will discover dozens of such groups in your area.

In the meantime, join groups and attend events that will enable you to further network. Join local networking focus groups, which meet regularly for the purpose of advancing the interest of members and sharing contact information with each other. An easy, professional way to pass along your contact information is to print simple, computer business cards with your name, phone number, and email address. You may want to add a "tag line" that identifies your desired profession, e.g., financial analyst or home-repair specialist or caterer.

If you have allowed your membership in a strategic professional or social association to lapse, lunch with this group once or twice, then find the financial wherewithal and get reinstated and become active again. Great contacts are made weekly or monthly. Whether you are involved in one-on-one sessions or network with several members, both can be easily scheduled between the groups' regular gatherings.

And here is another idea that usually doesn't cost much. If you have attended career fairs in the past with disappointing results, reconsider your objectives. Re-establish the primary objective of the event to be networking. Remember you are looking for people to help. So down the road, they may in turn lead you to that perfect job.

When you attend career fairs, you can "fare quite well" (pun intended). Spend as much time connecting to the other fair attendees as you do speaking with the employer representatives. Take a deep breath, introduce yourself to strangers, exchange contact information, practice your "Two-Minute Drill" (The Two-Minute Drill is a very important technique discussed in Chapter 27), and offer to help others when a need is detected. Use this career-fair time to set up future networking one-on-ones when the opportunities arise.

Approach Two

Now, let's answer the *when* question from a strategic perspective. The best possible time to network is *forever*. What this means is: keep your relationships alive. Or, in other words, you will have to *work* at being connected to individuals who matter to you. The networking "experts" don't contact people *only* when they need something. They contact people to help the other person or to "check in" and say hello. But mostly, the good ones contact people solely for the purpose of nurturing the relationship.

One of my best friends, Patrick, takes the "long view" on his relationships—not just with me but with many of his contacts. Some are friends, some are business colleagues, a few are fellow Sunday-school members, and many are from other spheres in his life. Patrick is one of the best relationship-builders I know. He practices the biblical principle of having *"a friend who sticks closer than a brother"* (Prov. 18:24).

Patrick calls me regularly to "check in" and see if he can do anything for me. He's proactive in his desire to maintain our connection; our relationship is something in which he invests regularly. I value this connection and friendship almost as much as I value my family.

Recall the power of the principle of sowing and reaping. Successful networking involves sowing long before you can even expect to harvest. And remember, the harvest always occurs always!

Your Choice

When you connect with others is your choice. You can invest in relationships for the long-term or not at all. The Apostle Paul, in writing to Philemon and his friends, noted he needed their relationship and counted on them. Because of his personal investment in their relationship, Paul could then say, *Confident of your obedience, I write to you, knowing that you will do even more than I ask* (Philemon 21).

Your best relationships–with your spouse, your children, your parents, your closest friends, and our Lord Jesus Christ—all have one thing in common. They only exist because you are continuously investing time in maintaining the relationships. *Let us not give up meeting together, as some are in the habit of doing, but let us encourage one another— and all the more as you see the Day approaching* (Heb. 10:25).

In your job search, take to heart the great importance of networking. Work at it daily; keep at it. Make it the major task each week; don't back off. Great things are accomplished through diligent work and perseverance. God himself set the example, working through His mighty creation. Connect six days each week; then observe God's command to rest on the Sabbath. *By the seventh day God had finished the work he had been doing; so on the seventh day he rested from all his work* (Gen. 2:2).

20

The Networking Gold Card

Do I volunteer in order to build my networking contacts?

Good question. The answer may surprise you. But first, let me share a volunteering experience of my friend, Frank.

Some years ago, Frank and his wife, Terri, decided to volunteer at their church to help the tape ministry. So each week, they simply duplicated sermon tapes after the services and sold them on behalf of their pastor and church. The church grew and so the number of services grew, resulting in greater need for a growing tape ministry.

Frank's involvement broadened. Soon he was directing the efforts of several other volunteers, as well as the media library for the church. Eventually, even though Frank was employed elsewhere, he was offered part-time compensation for his growing and valued role in what grew to be the media ministry for the church.

Not much later, Frank lost his job and began a job search to replace it. This is when his years of "volunteering" bore fruit. His church offered to give him a full-time position, overseeing the media and library ministry, including directing many volunteers and staff members. His willingness to serve as a volunteer was rewarded, big time!

As you can see, Frank models the definition of a *volunteer*. According to Mr. Webster, to volunteer is "to offer oneself for service of one's free will." You may view volunteering as the act of giving your time and talents to those in need, particularly those who cannot afford to purchase your services. The key is that you give freely of yourself. Frank is still volunteering. He also gives to those looking for employment through the **CAREER**SOLUTIONS Workshop® held each week in Euless, Texas.

And here's another story. Several years ago the men's ministry at our church invited Coach Joe Gibbs of the Washington Redskins to speak and share his Christian testimony to several hundred men. Upon meeting Gibbs, I learned that he had volunteered his time to our church that morning, even though he, customarily, was very well-paid on the national speaking circuit. He told me he not only tithes from his income, but he also tithes his time—he gives 10 percent of his time to the Lord and tries to make a difference in the Lord's work. Wow! That day was the day I began asking myself, "How much of my time do I give?"

Now back to the first question about whether you volunteer to make networking contacts. The answer is a simple and emphatic "No!" You may not wish to volunteer, with your primary motivation being to "fill time", "find a job", or even "broaden your network."

Your motivation to volunteer may be to serve God by serving your neighbors, your brothers and sisters, and all of His children. True, those other things will be added. However, your primary motivation might best be to honor our Lord and Savior. Example after example is illuminated in Scripture, pointing us to a life of serving others. Jesus, the Good Samaritan, Nehemiah, Abraham, Paul and the other apostles, and even a few "reluctant volunteers", such as Moses and Jonah, all learned the value and virtue of volunteering.

First and foremost, you may desire to volunteer because it is the *right thing to do*. Pastor and author Rick Warren reminds us in his book, *The Purpose Driven Life*, "One day God will compare how much time and energy we spent on ourselves compared with what we invested in serving others." He also adds, "Whenever you serve others in any way, you are actually serving God." And the Apostle Paul reminds us, *"Each of you should look not only to your own interests, but also to the interests of others"* (Phil. 2:4).

In addition to giving your time to others, you can be motivated by other benefits of volunteering. You can provide energy for a worthy cause or learn some additional skills along the way. Often, you will meet new people, thus creating new relationships for future networking opportunities.

So, become a volunteer and make a significant contribution. Be encouraged as you follow these three steps:

- **Determine** what you have to offer–you have many talents and abilities that you could offer to organizations which need them. The Apostle Paul said it this way, *"We have different gifts, according to the grace given us"* (Rom. 12:6). It is worth recounting all the wonderful gifts and talents that God has given you that he wants you to use.

  List all the talents you might give away. Brainstorm a long list of what you have to offer. Then prioritize them based on which talents you would most like to share. Here are a few to stimulate your thinking:

  1. Greeting people
  2. Computers
  3. Phone work

4. Organizing files
5. Mechanical
6. Repair work
7. Creative talents
8. Cooking
9. Gardening
10. Cashiering
11. Writing
12. Fund raising
13. Audio visual
14. Animal care
15. Prayer
16. Public speaking
17. Child care
18. Training
19. Leadership
20. Research
21. Counseling
22. Menu planning
23. Web-site work
24. Carpentry
25. Painting
26. Event planning
27. Elder care
28. Furniture moving
29. Pick up/delivery

• **Find** an area or organization which needs your service—in most counties you can find lists of non-profit organizations, educational institutions, and government entities that need volunteer service. Online, visit *www.servenet.org* and look by zip code to see what's needed in your community. After you find what's available, begin to connect with organizations or individuals who can use what you want to give "freely." If you can't immediately find a group that needs the things you most desire to give, see whether organizations would benefit from some of your lesser talents. The point is to get connected.

- **Commit** to serving freely as unto the Lord. Jesus also instructs us to love one another. He wants you to remember that "love" is an *action verb!* The Lord commands us to serve each other with our talents, gifts and resources. In Romans 12:6-8, the apostle Paul tells us that Jesus has given us each unique abilities. Paul guides us by saying, *"Whatever you do, work at it with all your heart, as working for the Lord, not for men"* (Col. 3:23).

Be certain you can give what the organization needs and that you don't over-commit your time. Are you prepared to give five percent or maybe 10 percent of your time? And consider this: 10 percent of what time? Ten percent of your waking hours would be perhaps 11 hours per week, while 10 percent of a work week only might be four hours per week. You decide what abilities you have to give and how much you want to give; then give it with all your heart.

Rick Warren would add, "What matters most is not the *duration* of your life but the *donation* of it" (emphasis added). Enrich your life by enriching others. *Determine* what you have to offer, *find* a place to offer your service, and *commit* yourself as to the Lord.

Volunteering cannot be accomplished without receiving the fruit of successful networking. Networking is about relationships. Volunteering often is about relationships. But they are neither synonymous nor equal. Volunteering goes beyond networking even while it accrues many of the benefits of networking. It is volunteering–the offering of your service of your free will—which makes all the difference both now and forever. Volunteering is the *Networking Gold Card*, storing up treasures in heaven. *". . . whatever you do, do it all for the glory of God"* (1 Cor. 10:31).

21

Networking on Steroids

How can I use the basic tenets of networking to create a strong, effective, productive network?

In the previous chapters covering career-search tips on networking, we discussed why networking is so important to a productive job search. We also learned what networking is. We explored when to network.

But to be effective, all this networking stuff needs to be *systematically applied*. That's where my good friend and early workshop participant, Mike Richards, enters the picture. He's one who studied the what, when, where, and how of networking and then applied, developed, and honed a networking process which he dubbed, *"Networking on Steroids."* It gets its name because the process is **powerful**. If you apply it to your search efforts, it will propel you ahead of the pack. These principles put real muscle in your networking efforts. Mike teaches a Saturday Seminar for our ministry once each quarter. In it he shares the secrets he's discovered about great networking.

Networking on Steroids (NOS) is based on three principles: (1) Job searching is a marathon race. Job-seekers network and apply certain strategies for the long haul. You must be deliberate and well-paced to continue even when you are tempted to stop and give up; (2) People hire people; organizations don't hire people. Seekers must be willing to con-

93

nect personally with others, including those unknown referrals; and (3) First impression is the key. Success depends on proper preparation to make the best of each and every encounter.

The seven basic strategies of NOS are each separately and collectively important to achieve maximum effectiveness. They are listed in order of importance to the process:

- **Set clear weekly goals and targets.** To maximize your efforts, decide in advance how many hours you will devote each week to contacting and scheduling meetings with primary and secondary contacts. Richards recommends at least 20 hours per week. Then go one additional step and set targets for the number of meetings or informational interviews you will schedule— perhaps as many as six to eight each week.

- **Force yourself to make the calls.** Working from your prioritized list of primary contacts, make 15-25 calls each week. Schedule meetings with each person who will agree to meet for 30-40 minutes. If some people are unavailable, call others down your list. Continually request personal, face-to-face time to get some advice and counsel.

- **Keep great records.** By keeping records of calls made, meetings scheduled, meetings held, referrals received, etc., you not only keep track of who referred you to whom, you help guarantee your adherence to the goals you set. This improves your accountability and assists in your personal motivation. Attention to details is one of the keys to success.

- **Work one to three weeks ahead.** Many people are busy and not easily accessible; schedule your meetings one to three weeks in advance. Be ready and happy to respond to schedule changes. Schedule meetings when your contacts are most easily available.

• **Prioritize your time.** Often our goals are not accomplished because we do first things last and last things first. Devote a proportion of your time to all of the job-seeker tactics: make calls, attend informational meetings, attend one-on-one meetings, participate in networking sessions and job fairs, and surf the Internet for research. Prioritize what is important; spend your time proportionately on each task.

• **Carry your calendar.** Do not leave home without your DayTimer®, your Palm Pilot®, or a calendar! When you meet with a contact, you may be asked to schedule another appointment. When you travel between meetings, you may receive return phone calls from those with whom you are trying to connect. Take the call and schedule the meeting right then.

• **Remain diligent.** Thomas Edison once mused, "Everything comes to he who hustles while he waits." Stay after it; don't quit connecting with others. Truly, securing a job is only a matter of time. Review your goals; stay focused, and "keep-on-keepin'-on."

When preparing for these networking calls and/or meetings, consider these caveats to successful connections:

1. Pray first. Arrive focused and spiritually prepared.
2. Set clear objectives—to get advice and information.
3. Find common ground on some level other than job search, e.g., hobbies, children, education, etc.
4. Share any helps you have for the person—articles, information, contacts he or she needs, etc.
5. When asking questions, listen carefully and take notes.
6. Offer to send or leave your résumé, in the event the person thinks of something or someone later.

7. Identify the suggested referrals the person gives you, so you have the correct name, title, telephone number, and any other contact information you need before you leave the meeting.
8. Keep it brief—20-30 minutes, unless the person extends the conversation.
9. Say "Thank you." After the meeting, send a hand-written, thank-you note. On a few occasions, an email thank you may be appropriate.

Before every telephone conversation or meeting remember a few important points. *Networking on Steroids* rests on the networking principle of *not* asking for jobs or job leads. As you explain your circumstances and ask for advice, if your contact thinks of a job lead the person wishes to share, he or she will disclose it without you asking.

Remember, your networking contact's time is very valuable, so be respectful of it. Be early. Be prepared with your questions written out; know what you intend to ask. Conclude the meeting before or when you have used your allotted time.

By now, you are beginning to understand that effective networking, *Networking on Steroids,* takes considerable time. Do it right! Devote the time to develop a contact list, prepare for meetings and calls, pursue new contacts, keep good records, and conduct follow-up with everyone you meet. To suggest this can be done well in less than 20 hours per week is to suggest that Rome could be built in a day.

To devote your time to the right activities at the right time, *plan* what you hope to do each week. Someone once said, "Planning is very important; remember the ark was built years before the rain started." The prophet Isaiah wrote, *"But the noble man makes noble plans, and by noble deeds he stands"* (Isa. 32:8).

You as a job-seeker can decrease your search time, increase your effectiveness, and often find jobs better than those you've lost, by carefully planning your search approach weekly. Write your plans for the upcoming week. Devote time to each of the four job-search approaches. However, plan networking activities for at least 50 to 70 percent of your work week. Then divide the remainder of your time to job postings, search firms, and cold-calling.

Plan your time, taking a targeted approach. Make sure your appointments for networking contacts are made one to two weeks in advance. Avoid "chasing rabbits." Stay focused on your target jobs and target companies. Strive for effectiveness over efficiency and productivity over activity. You are better served to send five résumés out this week, which result in two interviews, than to send 500 résumés and get no response.

With a weekly, written plan you have something to follow each morning. If you plan one to two weeks in advance, you won't have time for aimless drifting, pointless Internet surfing, or hours of self-pity. You can plan your weeks with networking meetings, one-on-one meetings, free training, volunteer activities, meaningful job-fair visits, targeted cold-calling, while only responding to the most promising opportunities.

Yes, a lot needs to be considered; countless alternatives vie for your time. Remember the words of Solomon in Proverbs 16:3, *"Commit to the Lord whatever you do, and your plans will succeed."*

Résumés and Cover Letters

Here's a succinct description of a good résumé: "Marketing document causing telephone to ring, which briefly showcases core competencies and quantifiable accomplishments, while using active language, visual appeal, and error-free script." (It's less than 25 words, too!)

Most individuals are unaware of the importance of having **two résumés**. While the *oral résumé* is used to effectively network and to super-charge interviews, the *written résumé* can take many different forms to get you to that first interview.

All successful résumés have a few things in common. One common denominator is best explained by this quote from humorist Will Rogers, "The more you say, the less people remember." Brevity is truly one key. Résumés are not intended to tell your whole life story.

Along with your résumés, cover letters are another common denominator to separate you from the pack and are more valuable than you may realize. Good cover letters motivate interviewers to devote more than just a cursory look at your résumé. They immediately begin to reinforce how you can help the employer accomplish organizational objectives.

"As for the other events of Solomon's reign—all he did and the wisdom he displayed—are they not written in the book of the annals of Solomon?"

(1 Kings 11:41).

22

Great Résumés

Do you have a résumé with which you are really pleased?

One must take five major steps in order to develop a great résumé. First, understand that the primary purpose of a résumé is to get you *an interview*—not get you a job. Second, learn what makes a great résumé is both content and style. Third, draft a good one for starters. Fourth, have those whose opinions you value provide you with suggestions for improvement. Fifth, revise and rewrite your résumé until it contains the essence of **who you are** and **what you can do**. And don't stop revising it until you have a great résumé by *your* standards.

Remember, a résumé is a promotional vehicle. It is a living advertisement for your job search. Its purpose is to get you an interview. Some mistakenly believe their résumés are written to get them a job. That's a mistake.

A great résumé ultimately will be judged by its *effectiveness* in getting you interviews. In order to reach your goal of producing an effective résumé, consider the following items for its design and content:

1. Never let a résumé exceed two pages—ever!
   Use lots of white space and 1 1/2-inch margins
   all around, so the copy doesn't look crowded.

2. Use a 12-point font—Times New Roman or the serif equivalent. Limit the explanation of each accomplishment and each employment experience to a maximum of three lines. Be crisp and clear.

3. Display your name and contact information prominently at the top of the first page. Always put the most important items first—things such as name and your target future focus. Then bullet-point your most important achievements.

4. Communicate very clearly near the top of your first page the job or career you seek. Let this document reflect your *future focus*, but write it in the "present tense."

5. If you have accomplishments that don't support your future focus, consider leaving them off. You have only a few seconds to capture your audience and get placed in the "interview" stack.

6. Accomplishments are best stated in simple-to-understand measures, i.e., "decreased expenses 33 percent in two years."

7. Don't put the word "résumé" at the top of the page or "references available upon request" at the bottom. Both are assumed by those who screen and review résumés.

8. Write your résumé from the reader's perspective. What do you do that can solve the business challenges of the job and for the reader of your résumé?

9. Eliminate irrelevant items, which can confuse the reader. If you have credentials as a Certified Public Accountant, CPA, but are applying for a sales job, leave the CPA off the résumé as it can only create misunderstanding about your true focus.

10. Always use action verbs to create vivid word pictures—words such as "decreased", "eliminated", "improved", "streamlined", etc.

11. While many employers may want to see what you are capable of doing, most would rather see what you've actually accomplished. Show both. In the cover letter explain what you are capable of doing; in the résumé, show what you have accomplished.

12. Avoid unnecessary jargon, slang, and overly technical language. Be aware that many human-resource readers may not be familiar with the departmental language you're using. It may not communicate your desired intention.

13. Your résumé needs to be inviting to read and professional in appearance. Use good paper—92 brightness or greater and use a printer that does a quality job.

14. Write in short phrases and bullet-point style. This visual presentation enables most readers to grasp your strengths and accomplishments.

15. Avoid any reference to salary history or salary expectations. (This will be discussed in later chapters).

16. Include non-work experiences that support your future focus. This could include offices held in associations and your participation in volunteer and professional organizations.

17. Vary font sizes only to emphasize a statement and create interest. But don't overdo it. Use font variations only to add to the interest and understanding of what you are communicating.

18. Use spell check and your dictionary. Use the thesaurus so you don't use the same word over

and over again in the same paragraph. Have someone proofread your résumé. Then proofread it again. In many cases your résumé is like a work sample. Therefore you want it to look great without any flaws.

Once you have a draft that pleases you, get some valuable feedback from "experts." Get some outside counsel. Ask others if your focus is clear, if it reads easily, and if they would want to learn more about you after reading the résumé. Then ask for feedback on style and layout.

Finally, take the feedback you've received and decide which suggestions you'll incorporate into your next version. You may need more than one additional draft to develop the résumé that captivates readers. And you may need one more rewrite to encourage recruiters and hiring managers to say, "I need to speak with this candidate to learn more." Keep at it until it is just right. When you begin to get interviews, you will know you have a résumé that has effectively combined style and content in a fashion that motivates others to want to spend time learning more about you.

If you need help, ask for it. Putting together a great résumé is challenging work. If you just can't seem to get it together, consider obtaining professional help. Your résumé is just too important to settle for mediocrity. You deserve the best résumé you can assemble, so get to it! Your next job and future career may depend on it! Remember this encouragement: *But as for you, be strong and do not give up, for your work will be rewarded* (2 Chron. 15:7).

23

Résumés with Focus

Have you determined where you're headed?

Long-term, do you know your destination? Short-term, do you have a target position clearly identified?

When potential employers see your résumé, they want to know exactly where you are going. Network contacts can be of the most help in your search if they understand your target destination.

On your résumé, state your target position in a large, bold font, like a banner, and prominently display it. Your résumé can show anyone who even skims the document *exactly* what you do and who you are hoping to be. I like to suggest that you state your target *as if you are already in* that position. For example, if you are ready to become an advertising director, put "advertising director" right below your name and address. Begin thinking of yourself *as if you have that title.* Until you think of yourself that way, you are unlikely to convince others to hire you as their advertising director.

A résumé without focus is like a compass without a needle. A résumé with a clear focus communicates to potential employers that you know who you are, what you do well, where you are going, and what you are motivated to do for them. A future focus clearly states that decisions have been made, preparation is completed or under way, and that you do what you do in life "on purpose."

Your clear determination of a target position will enable you to speak confidently and specifically with your network contacts and potential employers. This will equip your contacts to become ambassadors for you when they hear about openings for your target position. When your focus is unclear, they are helpless to effectively become another set of eyes and ears for you.

So, take the necessary time to make some choices. If your target is not crystal clear, I highly recommend a résumé revision. That revision will help you move your job search along to the target destination.

24

Aiming at Several Targets

*Do I need several versions of my résumé
aimed at a variety of different jobs?*

Computers and word-processing software make custom designing résumés for various prospective employers and several different job types relatively *easy* and *economical.* One individual I know with a varied background had one résumé to become a finance director, one résumé to pursue a general manager position, and one résumé to respond to anyone who is recruiting a mergers-and-acquisitions specialist. He easily designed, redesigned, and printed varied versions of his résumé at will.

While a few have been successful with this approach, one word of *caution* is worth considering. While you may have a multifunctional background with varied interests and skills, *pursuing one position at a time usually is best.* Three good reasons suggest you funnel your efforts to one focus:

Value of Focus

If you focus on one job, your job search usually will be more successful. All of your resources enable you to devote concentrated time at one target rather than spreading yourself too thin. You can devote 40 to 50 hours per week toward one job rather than 10 hours each week toward four different jobs.

Likewise, potential employers often want to hire you based on where your passion is, "not for just any old thing you can do." Most employers will be more comfortable hiring you for a position they believe is currently *your one great desire.*

Networking Assistance

Your networking contacts can remember you more easily if you have one target destination. Contacts are then all focused in one direction to assist you. If you have multiple targets, they are less likely to remember what job it is you seek. Therefore your networking efforts can be either diluted or counter productive. Multiple targets usually mean multiple mistakes when your network contacts are trying to help you.

Simpler for You

As a job-seeker, you have lots of things to do and lots of tracks to cover each week. If you add the complexity of trying to remember to whom you sent various résumés and which network contacts are working on which of your varied targets, you are making the whole process much more complicated than you have to. Odds are, you will be less effective.

In your job search, you will need to do all you can to effectively muster your resources together to land *one* job, let alone two or three. The key is effectiveness, not efficiency. As job-seekers you will be more productive, shorten the job search, improve network relationships, and land the *job of your dreams* if you learn to get focused and devote your energies in a concentrated manner.

Great Cover Letters

***Do you struggle trying to write
effective cover letters for your résumé?***

Note the use of the plural "letters" above, because to
be effective, you will write more than one cover letter. Good
communication evokes the desired response. Direct a good letter specifically to the individual who will be reading it. Search
for and use the individual's name and address rather than
sending a cover letter to "whom it may concern."

A cover letter is used to motivate the reader to want to
know a little more about you and therefore to read your
résumé. The cover letter is like an appetizer to a meal. It gives
just a taste of who you are and what you can do.

Cover letters would be much more efficient if they
were mass-produced like the résumé. But our goal here is to
subordinate the efficient and *strive for effective* cover letters.
You want cover letters to effectively encourage the reader to
want to read your résumé. If the reader likes the résumé, you
then get an interview. Therefore, your effective cover letters:

- Are customized and personalized.
- Clearly align your strengths and accomplishments with the organization's needs.
- Are concise with enough specific information,
  but not too much.

- Connect you to the reader.
- Create curiosity about your abilities.

When you decide to send a résumé with an effective cover letter, consider the following tips.

- Try to get the name and position of the individual who has the hiring authority for the position you so desire.
- Research the company as best you can to discover the specific needs of the organization, so you can highlight how your strengths match company needs.
- If possible, find a "connection" to the hiring authority in your research and use it in the cover letter. (See the next chapter for more tips on this idea.)

In the concluding paragraphs in the cover letter, include questions to your reader on matters about the job you seek and about the next steps in the hiring process. Ask whether the company needs someone who can accomplish what you demonstrate in your attached résumé. These questions show corporate interest and likewise will generate an interest in you for the reader.

Again, effective cover letters are *customized* (tailored exactly to the person to whom it is sent), *clear* (direct and well-written), *concise* (get right to the point without including too much information), *connecting* (by creating a kinship with the reader), and *curious* (asks questions to attract the reader's interest). These types of cover letters are most likely to cause your résumé to be looked at (with interest—indeed, great interest!)

Not every good written communication evokes the desired response. The fault may not lie with the cover letter.

The problem may be with the one who receives it. Remember Deuteronomy 5:1-22, which says not everyone who reads God's Ten Commandments will be moved to action. Control what you can by writing powerfully effective cover letters to improve your chances of getting the interview. Many will respond because you went to the trouble to customize and personalize this important communication vehicle.

The Common Connection

How can you capture the attention of the reader when you write a cover letter?

Writing a cover letter which "connects well" with the reader is helpful. Your letters need to get the readers' immediate attention and answer the unspoken question, "Why keep reading and consider this person a serious candidate?"

A few great ways exist to build or create a connection in the opening lines of your cover letter. One of the best ways is to bring your life closer to the life of your reader by pointing out a shared connection. If you are associated with an organization, perhaps you both know the same person(s). If so, mention that connection in the opening of your cover letter. Before you send the letter, ask your network contact in that association about the person you desire to contact. Find out how they know each other or have worked together. Then use that in your first paragraph to create a quick, positive connection.

Here's an example:

Dear Mrs. Jones:

I have just finished speaking with an old friend of yours, Mr. Larry Johnson. Larry is a colleague of mine from Methodist Hospital.

He suggested I contact you because of your
continuing desire to take your organization to
the top of your industry . . ..

In your research, you have discovered that you and the
hiring authority have the same alma mater, the same fraternity
or sorority experience, the same hobby, or the same previous
employer. Use these common connections to help create a
bond. These common background experiences bring people
together and help us identify with one another. If the hiring
authority has 100 résumés on his or her desk, won't it be great
when that person finds he or she has a connection with you?

Maybe you've discovered other types of common connections or relationships you can use in your cover letter.
Perhaps you have similar successes or failures or a similar
career progression. These may be good connections that can
help motivate the hiring authority to read further.

Here's another example:

Dear Mr. Smith:

You and I share one common experience. We were both displaced by the dot.com
downturn a few years ago when many successful individuals found themselves without a
home.

One caution before we move on: do not invent, guess,
or exaggerate common ground. That can be very risky. You
risk offending or disappointing the reader if you try to create
something out of nothing. However, when you can truthfully
find something in common, this approach works really well.

You may ask yourself, "Why does this approach
work?" Whether we want to admit it or not, most of us are
more comfortable relating to *those who are like us* . . . at least
in part. Remember, common values, experiences, languages,

and appearances create entire cultures and nations. When people find common bonds, they are more comfortable. So discover and use the common connections. You'll like the results.

Your next question might be, "Okay, I'd like to use this approach to open my cover letter, but how do I discover someone else's background, friends, interests, and all that other stuff?" That "stuff" just may be all around you out in the open once you start looking in the right places and asking the right questions of the right people.

If the hiring authority is a senior executive of a publicly traded company, some information may be online in the organization's annual report. In some instances, you can order a free copy of the annual report online from the "Investors" link. Try the library for additional information about the firm. Or call the company and ask to speak with an assistant; then ask questions about the hiring authority with the intention of learning about the firm and the "boss."

If you can network within the company, find out how to contact other subordinates; then contact them to gather information. The information you gather also will be invaluable when you get to the interview stage. Perhaps your inside network contact knows enough to point out common connections. Other possible sources might be suppliers and customers of the company—perhaps even competitors. If you have connections in any of these organizations, they may prove helpful.

You won't always be able to find common connections for every cover letter you submit, but if you work at it, your batting average will improve significantly. And with improvements to your cover letter, you will be viewed in a much better light, leading the pathway to more interviews and more opportunities to sell yourself.

Here's wishing you good writing.

27

Two-Minute Drill

Can you explain, clearly and concisely, your past, present, and future employment journey?

In interview situations, face-to-face with hiring authorities, you will be asked, "Tell me a little about yourself." This question, or one of several variations, requires you to give a quick summary of *"You."* This is a *wonderful opportunity* for those who have prepared themselves.

The preparation task is the often-misunderstood, oral résumé–called the Two-Minute Drill (TMD), or Two-Minute Commercial, or the Two-Minute Oral Résumé. The apostle Peter instructed the early church to *"Therefore, prepare your minds for action; be self-controlled; set your hope fully on the grace to be given you when Jesus Christ is revealed"* (1 Pet. 1:13). I, too, encourage you to prepare your minds and become self-controlled as you hope for productive outcomes from your job interviews.

Prepared job-seekers are able to craftily describe their history within the acceptable two-minute span of time (concise) and leave a memorable (clear) impression with the interviewer or network contact. On the other hand, without a prepared, consistent message, you may leave conflicting impressions with different people. Also, you may answer questions with less assurance and often miss the opportunity to focus discussions where *you* want them to go. You may ramble incoherently.

In many companies, you may be required to interview with two or more individuals. Will they hear the same story about who you are or where you're going? The TMD can consistently help you deliver the same message. Much like the repetition of a successful commercial advertisement, which reinforces what a product or service can do to satisfy your needs, your TMD will help others remember just what you have to offer.

Sample Two-Minute Drill

"I grew up in Lincoln, Nebraska, where my father and grandfather served as law-enforcement officers. At an early age I learned the benefits of diligent work. I put myself through the University of Nebraska, where I worked two to three part-time jobs simultaneously and graduated in four years with a bachelor's degree in criminology. I was the first in my family to receive a college education.

"Upon graduation, I accepted a commission as a 2nd lieutenant in the United States Army, where I was assigned to a military police command. During my five-year hitch in the MP's, I completed my graduate degree in criminal justice at University of North Carolina, where I was an honors student.

"My first civilian job was as a police officer with the Rocky Mount, NC, police department, where I served for six years. I received three commendations and advanced to the rank of detective.

"I am currently a lieutenant of detectives for the Charlotte, NC, police department, where I have served with distinction for four years. Last year I was assigned to the Governor's Task Force on Organized Crime and have been on special assignment for the last 18 months.

"I have a gift and passion for law enforcement and service for my community. I am an action-oriented, purpose-driven criminologist. I am looking for a leadership position as deputy or precinct captain, where I can develop young law-enforcement professionals.

"What are some of your key challenges?"

Without advance preparation though, your answer to that often-asked, opening question will not come across with confidence, comfort, and clarity. The hours spent rehearsing your Two-Minute Drill will give you confidence to begin your interview with a "calm sense of command." You will be more relaxed; that will speak volumes to your interviewer.

If you are not rehearsed and confident in your TMD, you most likely will miss the best opportunity to present yourself in the interview process. You have an opportune time to position yourself in the organization's "big picture" and substantially impact the direction of the interviewer's questions during the rest of the interview. Your well-created, broad-brush answer can directly influence how, why, and what subjects are pursued in the remaining balance of the interview.

Finally, without a prepared TMD, most job-seekers simply will appear to be rambling, unfocused candidates and will leave a questionable first impression. These, "Tell me a little about yourself," exchanges are usually the first, down-to-business questions used by interviewers to "break the ice" and "set the stage."

So what are TMD's? They are primarily an oral representation of your written résumé but better. Before they become oral, first write them down on paper in a prescribed format. The Two-Minute Drill contains the following elements: a 90-second synopsis of your personal and work history, followed by a 30-second explanation of your future focus. It concludes with an open-ended question. This is easy, because it's all about you.

First, the 90-second history deals with your pre-career stuff such as where you were reared, your education, early family values, etc. Then you very briefly discuss all of your employment history. Leave the largest chunk of time to discuss your last employment and your most significant accomplishments. Now use a short transition statement that enables you to change the focus from past to future by saying, "That brings us up to the present and why I am here today," or "That's a summary of where I came from; now here's where I'm headed." Then take no more than 15 to 30 seconds to summarize your future focal point, which answers the question, "Where *exactly* are you headed in your next career assignment?" Give this *future focus* something to do with the open job position. Then end the TMD with an open-ended question.

To conclude the TMD with a pre-planned, open-ended question, you might ask about the job opening, the needs of the company, or department or even the skills being sought for this position. Asking this kind of question does several positive things:

1. It gives you a chance to catch your breath.
2. If it's a good probing question, the answer provides confirmation.
3. It lets you know if you need to further sell your attributes.

4. It helps you maintain control over direction the interview takes.
5. It creates dialogue.
6. It builds a stronger relationship between you and the interviewer.
7. It definitely demonstrates interest and thoughtfulness.

Lots of great reasons to prepare a Two-Minute Drill exist. Begin today; write it down; and read it repeatedly until you can comfortably and conversationally share your history and *future focus* in two minutes. Say it in front of the mirror to practice emphasis on certain points. Smile. Say it in the car while you run errands. Smile again. Let it roll off your tongue from memory. Your interviewers will be impressed that you are complete, concise, prepared, and focused. So will you!

28

Salary History

When a job posting asks for résumé submissions, do I include salary history?

A prospective employer who posts a job opening on the Internet or elsewhere may request your salary history, but don't give that information up immediately. That would be too soon in the process. This employer hasn't even met you. The hiring person doesn't have much information about you; you have very little information about him or her. You also aren't even sure how the person will use this very personal information anyway.

In addition to not yet having any relationship with the company, some good reasons exist for not submitting the salary history this early. First, you probably don't know what the position is paying yet, or what range of pay is possible for the position. If you supply a salary history that is much higher or much lower than the target compensation for the posted job, you run the risk of being prematurely disqualified without the proper consideration of an interview.

Another reason to defer discussing salary information concerns your potential salary negotiation later. If this employer were to like you enough to eventually extend a job offer, your salary history might paint you into a corner. If your latest salary was lower than the market average, some prospective employers might be inclined to "low-ball" their offer to you—particularly if you've been unemployed for a while.

It's true, salary history is used as a measure of qualification—but that is often inappropriate. What you made with a previous employer is a reflection of *your duties there* and not what that individual employer is willing to pay for those duties. Seldom will both the responsibility and compensation plans match exactly. If you give a prospective employer your salary history, unfortunately, that person misjudges your capabilities due to his or her own standards. You may be prematurely viewed as over-qualified or under-qualified based on nothing more than your last salary. Your last salary may have little bearing on your current value in the labor market.

Your true market worth in this free-market economy is exactly equal to what someone is willing to pay for all the skills and talents you possess and all the responsibilities you are able to discharge. Until a potential employer knows what you can do to contribute to the organization's needs, talking about compensation is somewhat premature. Likewise, until you fully understand what the expected performance levels will be, amidst the tools and challenges that go with a job, determining what an acceptable salary would be is perhaps too early.

If possible, always defer salary disclosures and discussions until much later in the interview process. Consider setting a personal objective to always defer such matters until a job offer is extended. For now, if you can, *defer, defer, defer.*

Some corporations and most executive search recruiters will require your salary history before they can effectively consider you as a bona-fide candidate. In those cases, of course, definitely supply your salary history if you are to be a candidate. But even in this situation, try to defer any discussion on salary expectation for your next job. If the recruiter insists, give him or her a *broad range* that is acceptable to you.

Remember, early discussions of salary expectations are often (not always) nothing more than an additional screening device used to eliminate candidates that are outside of certain parameters. Why else would potential employers ask the question of salary so early in the process?

Here's one example of deferring:

"I know you would like to have a sense of what I am willing to work for, but now is a bit early to narrow that down. I don't know enough about the job you need to have performed. You probably don't yet know what I am capable of contributing. Like you, my expectation will probably rise or fall based on what you want me to do, how challenging the objectives are, and what help and resources you supply. Do you have a range for this position?"

29

References with Clout

Do you include your references on the
résumé or as an attachment to the résumé?

Included on the résumé? No. Attached to the résumé?
No. In almost every situation handing out reference lists at
this point is premature. Unless a prospective employer specifically asks for references along with your résumé, no benefit
exists to providing them until *after* an interview.

However, during your résumé preparation is a good
time to consider who from your work experience would be a
good reference to list. As you review your work history, make
notes of bosses, peers, subordinates, customers, and others
who would likely substantiate your skills, values, and accomplishments. Also make note of those who would be articulate
and credible when making their comments about you.

Once you have a list of 10 to 20 possible references,
prioritize them. Then call each in turn. First, ask each for permission to give his or her name and contact information as a
reference. A few reasons exist for this. First, it is the courteous
thing to do. It also "warns" this person to begin thinking about
that previous relationship with you. The reference also immediately becomes another networking contact once you've
made the person aware of your circumstance.

Second, if they agree to become a reference, ask each individual you contact to tell you *the positive* things they would be inclined to share with your prospective employer. This process lets you know what things they each remember. It gets them thinking about the "positives." It also allows you to make notes about what each might discuss. If one contact is particularly positive about your "great teamwork" and you eventually interview with a hiring manager who seems to really value teamwork above all else, you can use this particular reference, knowing he or she will stress what the manager is looking for in his next hire. Using references that are most articulate about the strengths desired by any particular hiring manager is important.

Finally, always thank your references and keep them informed by email or a quick telephone call each time you use their name with a specific employer. They will appreciate the notice. Your courtesy and organization will reinforce their positive thinking about you.

After you've contacted and *received permission* from between 10 and 15 references, you are now ready to provide the best three to five references each time references are required. Each list will be specifically customized for each employer. You can feel secure that these references are the best references for this specific employer.

Once you gain employment, notify each of those people who gave you permission to use their names as references. Especially thank those who have helped you land a great position. If you ever need their assistance in the future, they usually will be happy to help.

Preparing for Interviews

In the past when I vacationed, I used an automobile club package that had all of the driving directions I needed. With my destination mapped out ahead of time, I always arrived without trouble. When you are courting a potential employer, you may want to consider doing the same thing. Prepare yourself ahead of time by following the steps necessary to help you obtain a favorable interview.

Today, people still devote more time to preparing for their annual vacation than they do preparing for a successful employment interview. Successful job-seekers testify time and again that much of their success is directly attributed to interview preparation. Mastering this one area is guaranteed to put you in front of the competition.

By dedicating your time and resources to prepare for each interview, you geometrically increase your effectiveness. A focused preparation helps create maximum return on your effort—greater confidence in yourself and better odds of favorably impressing the interviewer. Like others before, you will be delighted in the positive results.

The Lord said to him, "Who gave man his mouth? . . . Is it not I, the Lord? Now go; I will help you speak and will teach you what to say"
(Ex. 4:11-12).

30

Interview Prep

***Do you know what steps to take
to prepare for each interview?***

     Like any worthwhile endeavor, you want to do it well; so it is with interviewing. Your future, your income, and your career depend upon it. To do anything well, planning ahead is important. Just as NASCAR drivers train and prepare both physically and mentally to succeed, do the same as you prepare for each and every interview.

     Here's another example. If you were preparing to take a family vacation, you would want to ensure that everyone has a great time. So you would plan the destination, save the necessary money, fix the car, research fun things to do, plan for contingencies, and help your family members prepare and look forward to the adventure.

     The same is true when preparing for an interview. The time and effort you devote in preparation will impact the outcome. The Bible says, *The plans of the diligent lead to profit as surely as haste leads to poverty* (Prov. 21:5).

     As a rule of thumb, I often suggest that for every 60- to 90-minute interview, devote two to three hours preparing for it. For best results, follow these 10 steps:

Ten Steps to a Successful Interview
1. Pray. Recognize God gave you your job skills, job opportunities, and all job assignments.
2. Get to know the company. Learn all you can.
3. Learn more about the interviewer.
4. Prepare answers for the questions you will be asked.
5. Prepare thoughtful questions to ask your interviewer.
6. Prepare physically and mentally.
7. On an index card establish your interview objectives.
8. Prepare thank-you notes and follow-up correspondence.
9. Confirm the time, place, and directions the day before the interview.
10. Arrive 10 to 15 minutes early.

The fact that the first step of the Ten Steps is **prayer** is important. Only through prayer will you have the right foundation for lasting success on the job. Recognizing God's power and position in your life is imperative *before* you go on the interview. If the interview leads to an offer of employment, you can rejoice with thanksgiving, believing that God's hand was involved from the very beginning.

The other steps are not always accomplished in the exact sequence listed above. Researching the company and learning about your interviewer are also key preparation tactics. Order is not significant, but each step is important. Make it part of your preparation for each interview. The other steps will be explored in future chapters.

31

Prepare Your Answers

*Are you prepared to answer the questions
you likely will be asked at your next interview?*

By *prepared*, I mean having your answers written on
paper and rehearsed orally. Experience has proven repeatedly
that individuals who prepare their answers ahead of time perform better in the interview than those who just show up and
give it their best shot. Remember, *direct, clear,* and *positive*
answers will have a greater impact on virtually all interviewers.

First of all, in the interview, direct answers speak to
the question. Good answers are neither rambling nor evasive.
Clear answers communicate your intended purpose—to draw
a connection between the company's needs and your capabilities, accomplishments, and motivations. Optimistic answers
impact interviewers positively and are evidence of your *can-
do* and *will-do* attitude.

Next, after preparing your answers in advance, you
will be more confident throughout the interviewing process.
This effort *before* the interview allows you to concentrate on
matching the requirements of the position with your ability to
fulfill them. Also, it will allow you to remain relaxed enough
in the interview to listen empathetically as well as observe the
non-verbal communication of the interviewer.

At this point you might ask, "How do I know what questions I will be asked?" You never will know *exactly* what the questions will be, but here is a list to help you prepare for the most commonly asked ones:

Be Prepared to:
1. Answer the *most often-asked* question, "Can you tell me a little about yourself?" The reply is often referred to as your Two-Minute Résumé or Two-Minute Drill.
2. Explain any gaps in your employment.
3. Tell how you can solve current problems in the organization.
4. Address reasons why you left previous employers.
5. Explain things you do well and a few you do not do so well.
6. Articulate your career goals.
7. Answer questions about unusual circumstances, positions held, accomplishments, and responsibilities that may be evident on your résumé.
8. Communicate what is really important to you concerning relationships, values, job tasks, bosses, and outside interests.

Literally hundreds of ways to answer these questions that may be asked exist. But if you take the time to write down each question and follow it with your own answer, you will be more prepared than 80 percent of the other candidates who just show up for an interview. *From the fruit of his lips a man is filled with good things as surely as the work of his hands rewards him* (Prov. 12:14).

32

Prepare Your Questions

*In what ways would you like
to impress the interviewer?*

Write down several questions that you can ask your interviewers. Here are four important reasons to do so: 1) it demonstrates your genuine interest; 2) it gives you an opportunity to learn more about the job, the organization, the boss, and the long-term potential of a career with the company; 3) it's a survival tactic; and 4) it gives you an opportunity to learn more about whether working there is best for you.

First, it *demonstrates genuine interest*. By writing down specific questions you'd like to ask and arriving well-prepared, your efforts show the interviewer that you place value in the interview and the job. When asked if you have questions, you can open your pad, binder, or notebook and refer to these questions.

Second, having researched, prepared, and written questions out in advance gives you an *opportunity to learn* vital information about the organization, the job, the boss, and your career potential. This information will serve you well in answering future questions from the interviewer. Take the opportunity to probe with some of your questions at the beginning of the interview, and then later, use them in follow-up interviews.

Third, asking questions of the interviewer at the end of the interview is a *survival tactic*. Having no questions is a killer. It conveys an arrogant attitude that you already know everything about the job and company. You are off the island.

Finally, being prepared to ask important questions *helps you make your decision*. The information you gather will enable you to confidently say "yes" or "no," if and when a job offer is given. As I have often said when interviewing potential staff members, "I want you to know as much about me, the company, and the position as I want to know about your background, skills, talents, and interests." It's a two-way street. Both the hiring authority and the applicant need to be well informed about each other before making good decisions.

So, before you leave your house for the interview, one of your preparation steps is to write out the questions that need to be answered. Perhaps they would include questions such as these:

1. What kind of a boss are you? What is your leadership style?
2. What accomplishments do you expect of the person in this position?
3. What are the long-term career opportunities with this organization?
4. What are the real challenges here to help someone grow?
5. Why is this position vacant?
6. Would you tell me just a little about your boss?
7. How is performance measured and rewarded?
8. What is the most important thing you want to know about me?

Of course, many others exist. Ask them if you get the opportunity. Most importantly, *listen carefully* to the answers you receive. *Listen to advice and accept instruction, and in the end you will be wise* (Prov. 19:20).

129

Gathering Research

*After scheduling an interview, are you ready
to do your homework, creating maximum
impact with this potential employer?*

Many job-seekers know they need to be fully prepared,
but the majority still do little or no preparation before that all-
important employment interview. One neglected area of preparation involves researching the company and the interviewer.
This seems to be neglected many times, because job-seekers
simply do not know how to go about it.

The interview can be and is a time of getting and giving information. However, to become more effective in your
interview, take time to properly prepare. Assuming you have a
few days or as much as a few weeks before the big event to
prepare, you can effectively accomplish several of the following objectives during the actual interview:

Maintain control so you influence what is discussed.
- Share attributes and achievements that you
  understand the interviewer will value in the
  available position.
- Make the best possible first impression,
  becoming the logical candidate for the next
  step in the interviewing process.

- Gather appropriate organizational information to enable you to make a correct decision when you receive a job offer.

Assembling good information in advance is one way to improve your chances of accomplishing your objectives. Here are some helps in pulling together *what* information you need and *how* to gather it so you can create that maximum impact on the interviewer.

What to look for*:*

1. Specifics about the company—the culture, values, reward systems, challenges, mission, and long-term vision.
2. Specifics about the boss or the interviewer—temperament, management styles, personality traits, personal values, job responsibilities, and time in that position.
3. Specifics about the open position—why it's open, duties, objectives, challenges, skill set needed, and external or internal customer expectations. Compare the job posting you have with the organization's online posting to get the best overall picture of what the company desires.

How to research*:*

1. Talk with ex-employees of the company.
2. Talk with current employees of the company.
3. Talk with customers.
4. Talk with suppliers.
5. Call and speak with the interviewer's assistant or the company receptionist.
6. Read the company's web site.

7. Visit the library and find annual reports or articles in business, trade, or professional journals.
8. Network inside the organization. Speak with peers or subordinates of the interviewer.
9. Visit Chambers of Commerce for information about the company.
10. Contact professional associations to which your interviewer belongs.

These sources above may, in turn, lead you to other, good avenues of information. Collect data carefully and methodically. Use this intelligence-gathering to focus on areas of importance from the *interviewer's point of view* when you prepare meaningful questions. It will impact significantly your understanding of what questions the interviewer may ask you. And, it will enable you to respond with focused and relevant answers that impact the interviewer. In short, you will impress the interviewer with your knowledge and your preparation. This well may move you to the top list of candidates for the job.

God gives time-outs. Remember, as you think about your interview that is scheduled in the near future, *There is a time for everything, and a season for every activity under heaven: . . .* (Eccl. 3:1). Wisely use this downtime to research your future employers.

34

Dress the Part

Are you confident about how to dress for your interview?

You have heard the term "dress for success." This applies to interviews just as certainly as it applies to your career success once you land a job. In fact, clothing is only one aspect of your physical presentation that is very important while you interview.

Just as you prepare internally—emotionally, mentally, and spiritually—you can improve your chances for a successful interview by getting ready physically. Your *outward appearance* has a very significant role in the all-important, first impression you hope to make. Someone once said, "The first impression is the one impression you can only make once."

In selecting your clothing for an interview, remember to *dress the part*. Dressing for the part involves two separate aspects. First, dress for the position for which you are interviewing. If you are applying to work in the mailroom, you will dress differently than if your interview is for a senior-executive role in the company.

The number-one rule is to dress conservatively. Wear clean, sharp, ironed clothes. Dress for the role in neutral, color-coordinated styles, unless you know for certain that flash and provocative style is favored at the company—i.e., a recording studio or a cutting-edge advertising agency.

For example, if you're interviewing for a chief financial officer position, research how other corporate officers dress. Whether the atmosphere is formal business suits or the corporate casual look, reflect the dress of the organization. You want to look as if you would immediately "fit in." You are usually safe to consider over-dressing rather than jeopardizing your first impression by under-dressing. *Then Pharaoh took his signet ring from his finger and put it on Joseph's finger. He dressed him in robes of fine linen and put a gold chain around his neck* (Gen. 41:42).

The second aspect of dressing for success deals with the quality of threads you choose. It's not necessarily how much one spends, but all garments are not equal. Remember, you are attempting to show your interviewer how you "fit in" with the rest of the organization. Avoid wearing clothing that is out-of-date, out-of-style, or out-of-sync. A plaid jacket or a pair of unpolished shoes may actually distract from your polished interview skills. If you need some fashion help, get it. Ask a close friend to help you select an interview outfit from the best you have. Do your best to dress the part.

In addition, remember to wear clothing in good repair—no missing buttons, loose threads, tears, or holes in stockings. Wearing something that is "worn-out" isn't a great idea, either. If you are not sure what the correct dress would be in a particular company, call someone in that company and ask. Most often a staff assistant will graciously advise you on what is considered appropriate in his or her organization. But remember, when in doubt, dress conservatively.

Here is a final, noteworthy caution on interview appearance concerning your grooming. Even little things will impact your first impression, so clean your fingernails, get your hair cut, styled, colored, and washed. Brush and gargle.

Then, top it off with *a big smile* in the middle of your face—a smile that is relaxed, not too big, slightly open, and sincere. That smile may be the most important thing you can add to your appearance. Practice in the mirror.

Like it or not, how you appear affects the first impression you leave with others. Career consultants say that you make that *initial impression in the first 10 to 20 seconds.* Some things such as height, facial features, and skin color are genetically determined. But many other aspects of putting your best foot forward are under your control and contribute to landing a great job. How God built you is not the most important thing. What you do with what you have can make the difference.

One other choice impacts your looks more than does any other thing: it is your *attitude.* So put on the attitude that says to others, "I am one of God's wonderful children. He has given me great gifts to use." Put on the attitude that says, "I am a contributor; I am a loyal employee. I am here to help your organization. I am here because this is where I choose to work." Put on confidence without cockiness. Put on friendliness without familiarity. Put on that *best-pressed attitude*; do the best you can to show who you really are to the interviewer. You can only be your best by spending valuable time preparing your presentation, your appearance, and your attitude. God will do the rest. *Put on the full armor of God so that you can take your stand against the devil's schemes* (Eph. 6:11). Then, you will be successful.

Interview: Purposeful Conversation

Questioning, answering, gesturing, seeing, listening, gathering, selling, emphasizing, probing, thinking, smiling, and praying . . . interviews contain all of these elements and more.

Through interviews, learning occurs. During interviews, relationships are developed. As a result of interviews, conclusions are drawn. Throughout interviews, futures may be established and careers launched.

Effective interviewing involves the combination of several skills. If you can combine these skills to illustrate how you are the answer to an employer's problems, you improve your chance of being hired. When you help the interviewer visualize your *fit* with the job, you create opportunity for *membership* in the organization.

By preparing for interviews beforehand, you can often influence what is discussed and ensure you have the opportunity to sell your strengths and accomplishments meeting the employer's needs.

The king said to me, "What is it you want?" Then I prayed to the God of heaven, and I answered the king, "If it please the king and if your servant has found favor in his sight, let him send me to the city in Judah where my fathers are buried so that I can rebuild it"

(Neh. 2:4-5).

35

Phantastic Phone

Are you ready to dazzle the prospective employer as you speak over the telephone?

Sometimes prospective employers will contact job-seekers directly. At other times, you initiate telephone contact with them. You will have questions. They will have questions. In many cases, this first contact may be crucial because it may be your *only* contact if you don't make a really good impression.

Doing well on the telephone is about being prepared. Know your objective, what you will say (selection of words you use), and how you will say it.

But giving "phantastic phone" is more than you think. Telephone etiquette and technique is uniquely important because the connection made with potential employers is so critical. Let's review several important considerations for telephone use during a job search:

1. Attitude
2. Using notes
3. Answering machine
4. Children taking messages
5. Call-waiting

Attitude

Have you ever spoken with someone on the telephone who was depressed or disinterested in talking? On the other hand, can you remember when you spoke with someone who was positive and enthusiastic? Most of us would much rather speak with those who are upbeat, interested, energetic, happy, and positive. The same is true for interviewers.

Attitude comes across the telephone like 3-D pictures jump off the movie screen. Think about how your attitude shows when you turn your automobile into the church parking lot with a scowl on your face, unwilling to yield to pedestrians walking into the worship service, nervously honking at anyone who is in your way, and allowing your mind to stay fixed on that problem you were having 20 minutes ago at home . . . your attitude is showing "big time!" You will impact others with that negative attitude whether you intend to or not.

This is also true over the telephone. Your positive attitude over the telephone will make a great impression and will impact the interviewer. It is one very significant attribute most employers desire in an employee. A good attitude often is more important than are technical skills, experience, or education. You've heard people say, "Attitude is caught, not taught." Many employers believe that if you have the right attitude, you are on the inside track.

The best way to demonstrate a good attitude is to be *warm and friendly*. One often-used method is to place a *mirror* in front of your phone. During your conversation, *smile*! The smile travels right over the telephone lines. It can be heard in your voice. The person on the other end begins to actually visualize your smiling face and warm demeanor. And the best way to adopt this good attitude is to smile more often. All around your work area, place some strategically located reminders on sticky notes that read, **"Smile!"** Put them on the telephone, on the mirror, on the desk, on your résumé, etc. And keep smiling!

Another attitude indicator is your energy and enthusiasm. Be *positive, full of life and energy*, but don't go overboard, nervously babbling and appearing hyper. Give yourself reminders to remain interested and enthusiastic about the interview conversation. And be confident, expressing your eagerness to be included in the next steps of the employment process.

Using Notes

One of the advantages to telephone interviews is being able to rely on notes. Keep your résumé, Two-Minute Drill, company research, your questions, your stories, and your accomplishments strategically located next to your telephone. Have the information laid out in an orderly fashion, so you do not shuffle through papers, making noise while answering and asking important questions.

Often times, telephone interviews are scheduled in advance, but not always. So be prepared by having your notes "at the ready"—in a folder, on a yellow-lined tablet, or on large index cards—whatever works for you. You then can offer good, well-prepared answers and can ask the questions without fumbling around. Feel free to rely on your notes during these tense times, while you continually remind yourself about your new telephone attitude—*smile*!

Answer Machines

Every impression counts, so carefully craft the message on your telephone-answering machine. During the job-search process, make your personal message brief and professional. Now is not the time to share baby Jane's first words nor to use your funny singing message. If you are one who takes great pride in your unique, off-the-wall phone messages, save them until after you've landed your job. Believe me. Your telephone message will leave an impression with a potential employer. Well-script your message. Pay close attention to the tone in your voice, so that it is upbeat, friendly, and positive. This is the lasting impression you want to leave in the interviewer's mind.

Children Taking Messages

One area, often overlooked, is the training of family members on telephone-answering etiquette. A teen-ager or child answering the telephone with little more than a grunt can be devastating. Also a red flag goes up when another family member is unable to answer simple questions concerning your whereabouts and doesn't offer to take a message or otherwise seems unable or unwilling to respond in a helpful manner.

Discuss the importance of message-taking during your absence by asking your family for help. Explain the importance and the need for proper telephone etiquette, particularly during this job-search time.

If older children answer the telephone, teach them to answer it with a clear, energetic voice. Practice with them. Give them a card with the proper words to say such as, "I'm sorry my father/mother isn't available right now. May I take a message? I will make sure he/she gets your message as soon as he/she returns."

Put message pads and pencils by the telephone so family members can use them when they take a message. Ask them to repeat the message to the caller to confirm that the information was copied correctly. You and your family are in this together. The assistance they provide can help significantly. You will get the message you need; the employer often will be impressed with the way your family works together and the assistance given—everyone wins.

Call-Waiting

Here's my brief opinion on call-waiting. While you are in your job search, consider canceling this service. If an employer calls while you are on the telephone, he or she will get a busy signal or a voice mail, depending on your service. If you are talking to an employer, you do not want to put the interviewer on hold or allow the annoying beeping sound to continue while you answer important questions. Don't think twice about *canceling* call-waiting. Do it immediately!

"Phantastic phone" is equal parts of common sense, preparation, courtesy, and proper use of today's technology. During your job search, the telephone can put you miles ahead of the competition. Remember these few verses as you meditate on how to effectively use your telephone:

A happy heart makes the face cheerful, but heartache crushes the spirit (Prov. 15:13).
Pleasant words are a honeycomb, sweet to the soul and healing to the bones (Prov. 16:24).
A man finds joy in giving an apt reply and how good is a timely word! (Prov. 15:23).

36

Honesty, the Only Policy

Do you often wonder how you can deal positively with the negatives in your background?

Perhaps you made some poor choices in the past or have been victimized by employers' poor choices. This may cause your employment record to include one or more jobs of very short duration. Or, perhaps your last boss fired you. Or, maybe the last job created such pressure, anxiety, or negative circumstances that you left without giving any notice, or you left "under a cloud" of poor relationships. Or, perhaps you never finished your education. Perhaps you worked yourself into a level that normally requires a degree, but you just don't have one. Or, you may have other, not-so-good circumstances in your background. Some negatives may be small, while others may loom large.

You may wonder if you can omit this information. Have you been tempted to "fib" a little so you do not draw attention to the career negatives that may disqualify you? You know you need to present yourself in the best possible light if you are to have a chance to get this job.

God's Word provides the best advice, as in these few examples:

1. *The Lord's curse is on the house of the wicked, but he blesses the home of righteous* (Prov. 3:33).

2. *The Lord hates . . . a lying tongue . . .* (Prov. 6:16-17).
3. *Whoever is dishonest with very little will also be dishonest with much* (Luke 16:10).

Of all you possess—your skills, talents, strengths, personality, achievements, attributes, and training—nothing will be valued more by virtually all employers than your **honesty**.

Yes, some of your career negatives will preclude you from being a bona-fide candidate. You will reap the consequences of past decisions and circumstances. But honesty is the best policy; in fact, it is the only way to go if you want a long-term, rewarding career position. The Lord will honor your honesty. And, He will see to it that you land the correct job at the correct time. Any position gained by any degree of dishonesty will be dishonored, uncomfortable, and probably short-lived.

Therefore, on your résumé, do not falsify information. During interviews, give truthful answers. You have strengths and flaws. Attempt to honestly match your strengths to the needs of prospective employers. When necessary, *come clean* about those few parts of your work history that are not very admirable. You can relate how they helped you learn more about life. Turn a negative into a positive.

For example, when an interviewer asks me about a flaw in my history, I often will offer something such as this:

"Early in my career I often was impatient with others. I set very high goals for myself and became frustrated when others seemed to just drift along. As a young trainer, I learned that we all work with different motivations and different strides. I learned that everyone was not fast-paced like me. Perhaps some were more 'thinkers' and solved problems by methodically analyzing a problem, while others perhaps had a slower, deliberate pace and never had any re-work or never had to be told what to do next. Clearly, I learned how we each may contribute in different ways."

If you ever hope to establish a meaningful relationship with a valued employer, come clean. You will receive your rewards for your honesty. Isaiah 33:15-16 confirms it: *He who walks righteously and speaks what is right, who rejects gain from extortion and keeps his hand from accepting bribes, who stops his ears against plots of murder and shuts his eyes against contemplating evil—this is the man who will dwell on the heights, whose refuge will be the mountain fortress. His bread will be supplied, and water will not fail him.* That's a guarantee!

37

Controlling the Interview

*What must you do to be in control and
relaxed during your interview when you
are anxious and un-nerved?*

Simply stated, job-seekers can maintain significant
control by:
Being prepared,
Relying on God's presence, and
Listening well.

I believe in a 90-Percent Rule—actually it's the
"90/90/90-Percent Rule." You can be in control of 90 percent
of your interviews during 90 percent of the interview conversation with 90 percent of the interviewers. When you master
this kind of *control,* you are using the best sense of the word.
You can learn what you need to learn and at the same time
make sure the most important things you wish to share with
the interviewer are covered in some detail.

Many interviewers are un-prepared or ill-prepared to
control where the interview goes or what is discussed. Some
of this occurs because they are so busy staffing many depart-
ments while being under-staffed themselves; at other times
this occurs because interviewers are not well-trained in their
responsibilities. This is true of many HR professionals and
most hiring managers.

Often interviewers do not plan their questions but rather rely on their skills as experienced *extemporaneous, question-asking professionals*. Many interviewers have not combed through your résumé in advance. And some interviewers are just primarily interested in how well job-seekers respond to random questions; therefore, they ask questions based on what occurs to them during the moment. That is precisely why candidates who are not prepared will not be able to steer where the conversation goes 90 percent of the time.

In the previous section, we talked about the value of preparation. Your well-developed and well-rehearsed Two-Minute Drill (TMD) almost always will dictate the direction of the interview. Your preparation will arm you with good questions to ask. This will enable you to create dialogue and gather the information you need.

The *interest* demonstrated by your preparation will, in turn, encourage many interviewers to pursue your expressed areas of interest. Finally, your preparation will give you confidence to think clearly during the conversation and to pray continually during the interview process.

If you've done your homework and have a well-developed, intriguing Two-Minute Drill, many follow-up questions will spring to the interviewer's mind based on your introductory response. If you mention in your TMD significant results in past assignments, many interviewers will want to follow that lead. They will gather more information on your achievements that relate to the pending job opening.

Your well-developed questions planned for the interviewer will direct conversation to important needs, which connect you to the company. If you ask about why certain needs or problems exist or what precipitated the issues, you can often discover information that will help you to answer future questions. Listen carefully, as the interviewers' answers may better prepare you for a second or third interview within the organization. These answers will even help you to decide if this is the right organization or position for you, if the company offers you a job.

If good dialogue is created with this approach, you will have time to send momentary prayers between answers. You will seek God's immediate intervention with each question. *To man belong the plans of the heart, but from the Lord comes the reply of the tongue* (Prov. 16:1).

Pray for God's leading during the interview. Seek His peace and quiet confidence. Ask for His enthusiasm and loving spirit during your interview. Prevail upon God to show you how to behave, what to say, and what not say. Ask Him to give you the ability to discern the answers you receive from your interviewer.

Listen to each question—both the words and the motivation (spirit) of the question. When Samuel was a young boy, he did not hear God immediately. Finally, *The Lord came and stood there, calling as at the other times, "Samuel! Samuel"* *Then Samuel said, "Speak, for your servant is (finally) listening"* (1 Sam. 3:10). If you thoughtfully listen to your interviewers and to God, you will hear what you are supposed to hear. With God's help you can apply the 90/90/90-Percent Rule.

Successful, skilled interviewees confirm the wonderful results time and again. By being prepared, God will lead you step-by-step. Recall how Nehemiah responded to the king of Persia. As Nehemiah longed to return to Jerusalem to rebuild the city and its walls, he said, *The king said to me, "What is it you want?" Then I prayed to the God of Heaven, and I answered the king, "If it pleases the king and if your servant has found favor in his sight, let him send me to the city in Judah where my fathers are buried so that I can rebuild it"* (Neh. 2:4, 5). The king not only gave him the assignment, he also provided protection and personal assurance of assistance.

Your chances of success will be greatly improved through sincere preparation, prayer, and listening. The result will be a very fruitful interview. *In his heart a man plans his course, but the Lord determines his steps* (Prov. 16:9).

38

Storytelling

***Do you know storytelling involves more
than childish fibs and fabricated fairy tales?***

Good storytelling need not include untruths. As a matter of fact, just the opposite is true. Good storytelling will portray an accurate account of an *event* or a life *circumstance*. During an interview, good storytelling can *grab the attention* of an interviewer better than almost anything can. If you *plan* your stories with intent and purposefully *craft* them, a good story will connect the interviewer to the point you're making.

Have you ever heard someone tell a story in which the person stammered, hesitated, backed up, and started again all the while unsure of where he or she was going? No one likes to experience someone droning on and on.

Picture this. You are sitting in an interview, a bit nervous, knowing you really want this job. The interviewer is behind the desk, pen in hand, confidently looking over your résumé. Making a few notes on your work history, the interviewer says "Here at XYZ, Inc., we value teamwork. How well do you work as a member of a team?"

Not withstanding the poorly planned question, you have done your research and discovered "teamwork" is an important value at XYZ, Inc. So you have mentally prepared your thoughts and reply, "I really like teamwork because it lets everyone be responsible, accountable, and contribute to the success of the group."

While that answer is a well-planned response with some good *buzz words*, it misses a wonderful opportunity to tell a compelling story. Here is an example of the power of good storytelling, thanks to my friend Carol:

"One day at a previous job, our manager presented a challenge to our group to improve our core work processes. Then he left the room. All five of us at first were puzzled; then I said, 'Well, he wants us to accept this challenge and fix these processes. Let's get to it.'

"We divided up the areas to be addressed, planned who would be responsible for scheduling our weekly improvement meetings, and accepted accountability for our respective contributions. We worked daily on our areas and met weekly in team meetings. If questions arose, we visited each other's offices without hesitation.

"Within six weeks we presented an assessment to our boss. Our presentation included the current process disconnects, the major and minor improvement areas, the alternatives evaluated for each disconnect, and our group consensus as to the final, re-engineered process. He was delighted and asked us to implement the recommendations according to the plan we presented. The team effort ultimately saved the company $2 million."

Don't just talk about teamwork. *Illustrate it.* Draw a word picture with **you** in it. Let the interviewer easily visualize you as a *team player* as you illuminate that trait important

150

to the job description. If it is about *teamwork*, tell a story about how successful a team was that you served on a sports team, work team, or community improvement team. If it is about *commitment*, tell a story about how a bit of extra work and attention gave you a victorious conclusion. Include quantitative results.

Recall the great, effective stories Jesus told in the few years of his ministry. His stories and the stories told about Him captivated hundreds, then thousands, and then millions. From carpenter, he became the Savior of the world. His story included miracles, then false accusations, imprisonment, death on the cross, and then resurrection. Each successive story captivates the listener.

Each interview response that you choose to answer in the form of a story contains the following elements. I suggest a response that is:

- Prepared carefully in advance,
- Delivered succinctly,
- Focused clearly on the point or moral of the story,
- Demonstrating something *you do* that is valued by the organization,
- Memorable,
- Delivered with some humility, and
- A truthful version of the events that happened.

Somewhere between the strengths and accomplishments emphasized in your résumé and the company needs that you uncovered in your research, craft several meaningful stories. These are not the kind one tells as a child, bending the truth, but career circumstances which, in a compelling way, paint a picture of what you can accomplish for the new employer. If the interviewer can visualize you demonstrating a desired characteristic in a previous situation, then the interviewer only need take a small amount of time to picture you providing the same for this new employer.

39

Powerful Hidden Language

*Besides writing an admirable résumé,
mastering interview skills, and preparing
background information, what else do I need?*

Your carefully prepared words will carry you a long
way in the interview. Also, having a powerful Two-Minute
Drill and other well-prepared questions are necessary for successful interviews. But *more is also needed*!

Any good speech coach, interview coach, or seasoned
public speaker will tell you about one other very important
part of powerful language—that piece is the *non-verbal* component of any communication. They are both the conscious
and unconscious body language signals you share during conversation.

It has been said that in any communication, the words
(verbal) account for approximately seven percent of its effectiveness, while body language (non-verbal) accounts for the
other 93 percent. Therefore, if you are to be successful, you
must not only be prepared with the *right words* to use, you
also will want to consciously use the *proper body language*
when communicating. Several books have been written on this
characteristic of communication. You probably have heard the
old adage, "Actions speak louder than words." How true that

your non-verbal gestures can both confirm and reinforce what you say, just as conflicting body language can negate every word out of your mouth.

In Exodus 4, Moses is being prepared by God to go to Pharaoh and ask to lead the nation of Israel out of Egypt, where it has been in slavery. Moses asks God, *What if they do not believe me or listen to me and say, "The Lord did not appear to you?"* God immediately answers, *"What is that in your hand?"* He was referring to the staff God had given him. Moses was to use the staff to punctuate and reinforce his communication by throwing it on the ground and lifting it high into the air.

God taught Moses to use his hands. Finally, God told Moses, *"Now go; I will help you speak . . . I will help both of you (Moses and Aaron) speak and will teach you what to do"* (Ex. 4:1-15). God knows the benefit of well-delivered, non-verbal communications and used the following examples in the Bible to help us learn from them:

- Jesus communicated by washing the feet of his disciples.
- Paul communicated by mastering his tent-making skills.
- King David, with his dancing.
- Daniel, by getting on his knees daily.
- Abraham, by building an altar.
- A blind man, by washing the mud from his eyes.
- Peter, by stepping out of the boat onto the water.
- Mary Magdalene, by washing Jesus' feet with her hair, using expensive perfume.
- A leper, by throwing himself at the feet of Jesus.

- Men guarding Jesus, by beating and mocking him.
- King Saul, by hurling a spear at his son, Jonathan.
- Hannah, by presenting her son, Samuel, to the Lord.
- Joseph, by fleeing from Potiphar's wife.
- The Magi, by bowing down and worshiping a baby in Bethlehem.
- Simon Peter and Andrew, by abandoning their nets to follow Jesus.
- Jonah, by finally going to Nineveh.
- Noah, by devoting decades of his life to building an ark.
- Jesus, by stepping out of the tomb and into Glory.

Many examples exist in which body language says more than words can ever say. In your interviews, think about the positive effects you can have with *eye contact, smiles* and *enthusiastic hand gestures.* These simple actions will reinforce your words, communicate interest, and add energy to the conversation.

Also consider the value of voice tone, leaning into the conversation, and sitting erect, especially when discussing your background as it applies to helping your employers succeed. You can create tremendous impact by nodding your head to affirm something the interviewer is expressing. Remember the value in facial expressions when emphasizing an important point, such as momentarily raising an eyebrow to suggest a question or concern about a comment made.

Powerful language is full of appropriately delivered words combined with, and supported by, well-executed *body language.* This powerful combination will leave your interviewer secure in who you are and what you believe.

Practice non-verbal gestures and moves just as you would the verbal portion. First, practice will help you know the words you intend to use. Once you've mastered the words, you can work on the delivery so it becomes natural. Next, stand in front of a mirror and practice delivery. When you have the content *down cold,* you can concentrate on the best gestures, posture, eye contact, expressions, and enthusiasm.

Work at it; practice until you are comfortable. Get feedback from others. Practicing will result in a gift of quiet confidence that God is with you during each interview and will guide every step. If you do your part, God will do His part just like he did for Abraham, Moses, Jesus, and the rest. Right now I am smiling, knowing that you, too, will be blessed.

40

Self-Incriminating Questions

*Do you worry so much about probable
interview questions that you'd do
anything not to answer them?*

How do you answer questions that deal with negatives
in your background? You may be inclined to claim the privilege of the Fifth Amendment when a hiring authority asks you
about major gaps in employment. Or you may want to change
the subject when you are asked about that last layoff which
cost you your job or that college education you never quite
finished.

You know you can't avoid those questions and remain
a viable candidate. But you fear the detrimental effects of
exposing your career negatives. Here are a few suggestions
which may ease your mind and help keep you in the driver's
seat for your next position.

God, speaking to those in Jerusalem said, *"These are
the things you are to do: Speak the truth to each other . . . do
not love to swear falsely. I hate all this,"* declares the Lord
(Zech. 8:16, 17). Also, in Proverbs we are reminded dozens of
times about integrity and honesty in dealing with each other.
God does not equivocate concerning honesty and integrity. He
says acceptable degrees of honesty do not exist. You either are
or you are not an honest individual.

As a leader I believe no more important virtue exists in employees than honesty. Consequently I recommend that you answer all questions honestly. Your integrity will be far more important than anything gained by misrepresenting the facts.

But, you can do some things to help offset the negative effects of certain aspects of your background. For example, if you're unemployed for a lengthy period of time, showing you have done things to help others or yourself can be *less negative*—things such as resuming your education; volunteering regularly for a ministry or community need; or using your skill set to help someone you know with his or her business.

If you were fired or otherwise released in an unpleasant fashion, deal with any questions honestly. Discuss the positive aspects of your employment there. Talk about things you liked about the company and your boss. Remember, this potential employer will be far more impressed with honestly and a positive frame of reference than he or she will with an attitude full of negatives, excuses, rationalizations, and blaming.

Answer questions honestly and positively. If you made a mistake, acknowledge it. Discuss the positive impact of personal growth it had on your life and move on. Your interviewers will admire your refreshing, straightforward response.

Here's an example my friend, Jonas, offered a would-be employer. Jonas had been fired because he just didn't accomplish what his boss had hired him to do.

"Yes, I was fired for a good reason—my boss told me that I just was not delivering what he had hoped for. I simply did not discover in advance what my boss really wanted from me. This was a good lesson on how I need to ask plenty of questions and to get clarification about expectations.

"I really liked the company and my boss. He gave me much freedom to perform. I didn't even realize I had set my priorities incorrectly. He suggested that I needed a more structured environment. I agree. I am really looking forward to my next position so I can really contribute the right stuff."

If you do not get selected for the position, this will not be solely because of the negative aspect in your background. Seldom do you get selected or rejected for a job because of one thing—particularly, if you can deal with it showing integrity, growth, and positive focus on your future.

Discriminating Employers

What do I do as a job-seeker if employers ask questions or make comments which are inappropriate, offensive, and/or illegal?

This is an area surrounded by quicksand and booby traps. As you enter this ground, navigating without taking a wrong turn is somewhat difficult. Proceed carefully and purposefully, as if under the caution flag.

First, recognize that every time a hiring decision is made, discrimination is at work. You are discriminated against because of your education level, your work background, your interviewing skills, your résumé-writing skills, your natural gifts and talents, your dress and appearance, your perceived attitudes, and many other things which are perfectly appropriate based on the requirements of the job. Discrimination is only *bad* when illegal and inappropriate discrimination occurs. When you are selected or excluded based on skin color, race, national origin, age, and other inappropriate factors, this often is illegal and is a disservice to our culture and all of humanity.

Consider a few facts. Many job-seekers and interviewers often misunderstand *Title VII of the Civil Rights Act of 1964*, a federal law prohibiting job discrimination, as well as other non-discrimination legislation and executive orders. Many initiatives became law during the 1960's and 1970's.

These were followed by various revisions and modifications during the next 20 years.

Often untruths and half-truths are "bantered" around by employees, corporations, and even well-intentioned attorneys, who earn a living from such alleged discrimination illegalities. If you want a good legal opinion, don't guess; go ask a Board Certified attorney specializing in employment law. Things get complicated really fast. If your employer is a government contractor or sub-contractor, different rules apply than if the employer is not a contractor.

Then on top of all the federal legislation, many states have their own regulations. Also, during the last 40 years federal and state court systems independently have established much case law on discrimination.

Some general answers on discrimination are never as good as specific ones, when confronted with specific circumstances. For your purposes here, however, the generalizations are necessary and may provide some measure of guidance.

Now let's get back to the original question—"What do you as a job-seeker do if you believe you are being discriminated against?" First, pray for a loving spirit and discerning heart. Then, confront the interviewer in a manner that preserves the dignity for both of you.

Be direct and kind. Share your concerns about what you perceive, all the while hoping the employer can benefit from your *kind confrontation*. You can ask your interviewer *for permission* to seek clarification about the question just asked. If permission is granted, in a non-threatening voice and demeanor, ask the interviewer whether that information is a requirement for the job.

For example, if the interviewer asks about your marital status, you say, "Before I answer your question, may I ask for some clarification?" When the interviewer agrees, you may then state, "I wasn't aware that marital status was critical to performing this job or working for this company. Would you clarify that for me?"

You will have to analyze the situation quickly. This is where the skill of discernment comes into play. Sometimes seeking clarification *after* you answer the question may be more appropriate.

When innocent but irrelevant questions are asked, this sometimes occurs because an interviewer is attempting to generate conversation. Your answer is really unimportant in his or her decision-making. Other times, the interviewer is merely a poorly trained interviewer and has misguided intentions. Keep your radar up.

Unfortunately on occasion, interviewers do seek inappropriate information to make unlawful decisions regarding race, gender, handicap, etc. If you believe unlawful decisions are being made concerning your employment, your only recourse is to seek legal counsel or contact a field office of the U.S. Equal Employment Opportunity Commission (*www.eeoc.gov*), which may then take your case and act as your counsel.

Seldom does a job-seeker do any good by arguing with the interviewer.

If this happens to you, strongly consider withdrawing your candidacy with this employer. If inappropriate and illegal discrimination appears to run deeper that just one individual interviewer, would you really want to work there?

Though some of you may be outraged and demand justice, most often the justice you seek does little to further your career search objective. While this tip is not intended as a substitute for good legal advice, most cases are difficult to prove. Seldom does a remedy exist. The Lord will take care of the judgment. *The man of integrity walks securely, but he who takes crooked paths will be found out* (Prov. 10:9).

42

Ask for the Job

*Now that you are concluding
the interview for a great position,
how do you leave the interview?*

Close the deal! Take a stand! Let your desires be known! In other words, tell the interviewer you want the job. Say it with *determination, enthusiasm, and confidence.*

Of the thousands of individuals I have interviewed, a large portion of them *never* asked for the job—most to their own detriment.

Many interviewers misinterpret the absence of someone asking for the job. First, if you fail to ask, the interviewer may assume you just *don't want the position* and are reluctant to express your low interest level.

Another assumption by the interviewer may be that you didn't ask for the job because you are *unenthusiastic.* You don't appear to be motivated by much that occurs in your life. In fact, you don't seem to be one to suggest new approaches or improvements, which makes you that kind of person who performs at the minimum-level of acceptable requirements of the job.

Third, if you don't ask for the position, the interviewer might assume you *feel unworthy* of the job. The interviewer may think you'd accept the job, even if you were to be sur-

162

prised by the offer. But in reality you know, deep within yourself, that filling the position and performing well is beyond your current capabilities.

An interviewer making these three assumptions may eliminate many otherwise qualified candidates who just simply did not ask for the job. If your interviewer, either a screening interviewer in HR or the actual hiring manager, misjudges you, you may be eliminated as a candidate.

For those who might say, "Well, the job wasn't all that good anyway," consider this idea. If you are not interested in the job or want to self-disqualify, you act in your best interest by openly expressing those doubts or decisions. If you no longer want the position, tell the interviewer, because you may later be considered for something else—something more suitable to your background or interests. Or, you may be referred on to another department or even another company who has a more appropriate position. This may occur just because you expressed yourself confidently (not arrogantly) and honestly (not in a disinterested manner).

By disclosing at the end of the interview where you stand, the interviewer may become a very valuable network contact and may help you further in your search. Jesus assures, *For everyone who asks receives; he who seeks finds; and to him who knocks, the door will be opened* (Luke 11:10).

Now back to those of you who really want the job but usually just hope for the best, figuring you'll get an offer if you interview well. Hope is great. Interviewing well is a valuable asset. But like stepping on the gas pedal propels you forward, so does the statement, "I really am excited about this job. I want to contribute to the organization and become a valuable member of the team. Will you give me this position?" Again, you have influenced the course of the interview.

Use your own words that are appropriate to the interview conclusion. Lean forward as you say it. Say it with a

163

smile and enthusiasm in your voice. Say it with confidence, knowing you are ready for the position. Say it so the interviewer has no doubt in his or her mind. And say it so the interviewer is easily encouraged to respond to your question. Sometimes, asking for the job can be that one small difference between two well-qualified candidates. Many times, *asking for the job* may put you over the top.

I want to share a valuable gem here, though it easily could be included in chapters 20, 30, 32, or 49. This information deals with volunteering, preparation, and rejection. It's what I call the "Rudy Factor." I'm offering it because I have seen it work successfully twice already this year.

In the 1993 movie, *Rudy*, the main character dreams of someday playing football at the University of Notre Dame. One afternoon he strolls onto the football field while the groundskeepers are tending to their work. Rudy asks the supervisor for a job and is quickly rejected. After being rebuffed, Rudy offers to work there for free. He tells the supervisor of his dream and his desire just to be present in this famed stadium. He wants it so much, he volunteers to work there for no pay.

If you find yourself rebuffed, even tentatively, and you really, really want the job, offer to work there for one month for no pay just to prove your motivation, desire, and capabilities. It worked for Rudy; it has worked for two job-seekers I know. And in all three cases the free offer turned into a regular paying position because of the attitude and the heartfelt motivation.

Try the "Rudy Factor" when you really want the opportunity to prove yourself. You may or may not be paid—but you may get in the door.

Post-Interview Gems

Much of the job-search process is based on common sense, proper business etiquette, and Scriptural advice. Once the interview has been completed, successful job-seekers can impact the interview process by doing several positive tasks. By having *a follow-up system* in place, you will positively influence the decision process.

You may stay in touch with the interviewers in several ways without being considered a *pest*. Knowing which references to share and, importantly, when to send them are key ingredients to a good follow-up plan.

Also, thank-you notes to interviewers can be powerful. Giving thanks is illustrated countless times in Scripture. In 1 Thessalonians 5:16, Paul writes, *Be joyful always; pray continually; give thanks in all circumstances, for this is God's will for you in Christ Jesus.*

And of course, one can always benefit from investing a few moments doing some self-evaluation after each interview. Use each meeting as an opportunity to learn and improve.

Sow your seed in the morning, and at evening let not your hands be idle, for you do not know which will succeed, whether this or that, or whether both will do equally well

(Eccles. 11:6).

43

Don't Be a Pest; Be Persistent

When you have just left the interview and are hopeful about the position, how often do you re-contact your interviewer?

Many job-seekers are ill-informed about how to appropriately follow-up after their interviews. Some become *pests* because of their approach, while many make the common mistake of never re-contacting their interviewers.

An effective follow-up approach might be summarized as having good reasons to regularly put your name in front of the interviewer without being considered a pest. Avoid calling and asking, "Am I still in consideration?" or "Hi, I'm just calling to see what's going on." To be a strong candidate, make the follow-up call with more punch, creating a positive impact.

Let's examine a positive scenario. You completed an interview with one of your target companies. You did a good job. You are very interested in the position. You asked the interviewer what the *next step* was and were informed that, if you were selected, you would be notified within two weeks.

When you finished the interview, you immediately began to develop a tentative follow-up plan that included the following steps:

•Thank-you note,
•Submission of references,
•Informational note of personal interest to interviewer,
•Follow-up contact telephone call, and
•After-the-deadline telephone call.

The thank-you note is best written and mailed the day of the interview so it is received the following day. If the interviewer's mailing address is not listed on the web site, be certain to ask for a personal business card before you leave. Then within a few days, you can submit your customized reference list to the interviewer by mail or email.

Finally, because this scenario allows for several days to pass, you can contact the interviewer or send an email, following up on any specific item you recall from the interview conversation. Begin this piece of correspondence or conversation with a *common link*.

Perhaps your common connection was that both of you have children playing high-school football. You might first mention some current item about your high-school football player before you share the specific information. Or perhaps the interviewer revealed a major business challenge the company faces concerning poor employee relations. You found an article from a recent magazine dealing specifically with that challenge. Use this time *only* as a contact opportunity, saying, "Here's hoping you find this information enlightening and helpful."

By developing a persistent follow-up plan, you will create contact opportunities for the benefit of the interviewer. Send the interviewer references, related business news, personal-interest articles, or items of mutual interest. This, in turn, will cause the interviewer to appreciate you as a network contact rather than think of you as a needy pest. *Nobody should seek his own good, but the good of others* (1 Cor. 10:24).

No Reference Before Its Time

Do you present your list of references before the interviewer requests them?

No! Some job-seekers, in an effort aimed at impressing their interviewers, may not realize that one seldom is to send references along with the résumé before an interview is scheduled. This practice of early submission is not the best approach for looking professional.

So, how does the subject of references best arise during the interview itself? At the close of the interview, if they have not been asked for, feel free to ask the interviewer if references would be desirable. If so, tell the interviewer you will be happy to provide them via telephone, mail, or email. Ask for the interviewer's preference.

Then, once you arrive home, create a customized list of names, home addresses, emails, and telephone numbers for this particular job. Once you have contacted each of your selected references, simply send your customized reference list to the interviewer in the prescribed manner.

Most of the time, provide your references during a short period following the interview perhaps within a few days to a week. Three very good reasons exist to adopt this approach. First and most importantly, sending or giving your references after the interview enables you to develop a *customized reference list.* Your targeted list will consist of individuals you will select after the interview because, having asked several questions, you'll have a much better idea what important qualities the interviewer is seeking. You can then submit names of those whom you believe will support your candidacy and will tout those particular qualities. Confused? Don't be. Chapter 45 will help you define your best reference list.

The second reason to wait is almost as important as the first. By waiting until after the interview, you have another good reason to contact the interviewer. As part of your persistent follow-up plan, you have one more very legitimate reason to connect with the interviewer to keep your name foremost in his or her mind. Name recognition and repetition marketing work wonders for Coca-Cola® and Disney®; they will work for you, too.

One additional reason exists for waiting to supply references. You need a little time to notify the references in advance, telling them that you would like to use them for this particular potential employer. You can telephone them, briefing them on your candidacy, what the employer seeks, and letting them know they may be contacted soon.

Later, you may want to check back with them to see if the interviewer ever made any contact. If this did occur, ask your reference whether the interviewer wanted to know anything in particular. You may be able to glean information that will help you be successful in your next interview.

45

Your Best References

How many and what persons do you include on your reference list?

Some people believe previous bosses are best on your reference list. Some prefer customers and subordinates. A few even like personal references. Your best list may include all of these acquaintances.

What's most important is how you develop the *best list* and then how well you use it. A good vehicle to use is called a *reference matrix*. It contains as few as 10 and as many as 15 to 18 individuals.

Think of a *reference matrix* like a map. When planning a trip, you may have 20 ways to get you to your final destination. You may want to take the Interstate highway and get there fast, take the backcountry roads and enjoy the scenery, or drive a combination of both. Though each road on the map will get you where you want to go, some offer a more positive traveling experience.

Similarly, your reference matrix may contain 10 to 18 people, but seldom will you ever need more than three to five references for each interviewer. Like a map, this matrix gives you a quick, visual choice of whom to use as a reference after each interview. In a moment we will return to how to do the choosing.

After you develop a list of 10 to18 people, then develop a list of all the positive traits, accomplishments, and qualities you hope to offer about yourself. List those across the top of your matrix: teamwork, leadership, computer skills, problem-solving, written communication, persistence, analytical, strategic, detail oriented, etc.

Now you're prepared to call each person on your reference *roster* or *matrix*. First, tell the person about your job-search campaign. Second, ask permission to list the person as a reference. If he or she is agreeable to supporting you in your job-search efforts, then ask the person to think of a few positive things he or she is likely to say about you. Without any prompting from you, allow the individual to share his or her thoughts while you quietly make note of any trait mentioned.

Also, you may want to send the reference a brief thank-you note for his or her support, including a copy of your latest résumé. You never know whom they know or who may need your skills and talents.

After you telephone each person on the roster, then you will know someone who automatically will speak about your *leadership skills*, someone who will speak about you in regard to *teamwork*, someone who will think of your *willingness to do whatever is needed*, someone who will mention that you are *financially responsible*, someone who remembers your *kindness,* while others will mention your *technical capabilities*. You get the idea.

Now, back up to choosing those three to five references for employer "X." During the interview when you asked great questions, you discovered qualifications and characteristics the interviewer desired for this position. If you clearly sense that "leadership" is wanted, select those individuals from your matrix who remember your leadership skills. If "technical skills" are required for the position, then choose one or more of your references that likely will offer that trait as one of your strengths.

You simply pre-select a specialized reference group that will recall your best strengths to match the interviewer's needs. Recall the story of Joseph, the son of Jacob, who had been falsely imprisoned in Egypt yet who did a kindness for the cupbearer to the Pharaoh. At the appropriate time, when the Pharaoh had a need that Joseph could fill, the cupbearer proved to be a sterling reference by telling the Pharaoh about Joseph's particular skills. From there, Joseph was given an interview, his freedom, and an extremely wonderful leadership position in the Pharaoh's employ (Gen. 41:8-40).

46

Thank-You Notes

Are thank-you notes really necessary?

Thank-you notes are necessary; they are more helpful than anything you can do after the interview. In fact, most professional interviewers will tell you less than two percent of all candidates bother to send a thank you note. So, if you want to stand above the crowd, send one.

Here are a few words about good thank-you notes. In almost all cases, send a handwritten note, unless your penmanship is impossible to decipher. Make your note short; let it express sincere gratitude for the interview. If multiple interviewers were involved, send a separate note to each person.

A thank-you note *is not* to be used to share something about yourself that you forgot to mention during your interview. Remember, the thank-you note is not about you; it is all about the interviewer expressing appreciation for the interviewer's time, kindness, courtesy, and professionalism given to you during the interview.

Also, your thank-you note is another wonderful opportunity to have your name in front of the interviewer. Mail your thank-you note the moment you leave the interview. No matter what distance you travel for your interview across town or across country, take your thank-you notes and your stamps with you. After the interview is over and while the conversation is fresh in your mind, handwrite a note and drop it in the nearest mail box. The objective is to have the note arrive on the interviewer's desk the next day.

Many people ask about the viability and effectiveness of email thank-you notes. In a survey reported by *USA Today*, April 22, 2004, 78 percent of executives said email thank-you notes are okay. Depending on circumstances or the particular corporate climate, a quick email thank-you is fine, but it is seldom a substitute for a handwritten thank-you note. Rather, today emails are used for additional contact purposes or to confirm any other follow-up actions which you committed to do. Remember, often an email is deleted immediately after it is read and sometimes before. But a sincere, thoughtful, old-fashioned thank-you note may be kept for days, or longer.

Even if you determined that you don't want the job, or the interviewer disqualified you during the interview, *send a thank-you note anyway*! First, do it because it is common courtesy. Second, your interviewer has the potential to become one of your best networking resources. Many instances exist when courtesy shown in a thank-you note has influenced the interviewer to refer an individual to an associate in another company. This resulted in a job offer for a hidden position.

Here's an example of a good thank-you note:

December 19, 2004
Dear Mr. Sandstone:

Thank you for the time we spent together. I greatly appreciate you for taking a moment from your busy schedule. The information you shared about working for the government was both comprehensive and enlightening.

Of the many topics we discussed, your concerns regarding implementing a Team Concept and Customer Focus between your functional work groups were very interesting. As we discussed, consulting and modeling other industry leaders could effectively shorten your implementation time.

During our next meeting, we can explore further how your agency could benefit from my passion and experience.

As you had mentioned, if I have not heard from you in the next two weeks, I will contact you via your mobile number at 817-555-4567.

Best regards,
Cynthia Candidate

You reap what you sow. A few minutes invested in writing and sending a thank-you note may pay off in huge dividends. Then, thank the Lord for His assistance and love. *But thanks be to God! He gives us the victory through our Lord Jesus Christ* (1 Cor. 15:57).

Self-Evaluation

What else is a good idea for an applicant to do after the interview?

Take an immediate look backward at how well you did. As soon as you can after each interview, take time to evaluate yourself and your performance.

To make this evaluation effective, try to do it within an hour or two after you leave the interview. *See if there is any offensive way in me, and lead me in the way everlasting* (Ps. 139:24). Some experts suggest that you go to your car and do this even before you drive home. Spend 10 to 15 minutes alone and evaluate the following:

- Your preparation,
- Your performance, and
- Your potential impact.

Preparation

Consider all those things you did well and not so well. Be very honest with yourself. *But the noble man makes noble plans, and by noble deeds he stands* (Isa. 32:8). Ask yourself these questions:

- Did my preparation alleviate any of my anxiety?
- Was my Two-Minute Drill delivered effectively?
- Did I do enough research before the interview?

- Did I rehearse my answers to the questions that I believed would be asked?
- Did I need to talk with others before this interview?
- Did I have my questions written out in advance that I wanted to ask the interviewer?
- Did I discover in advance any common connections with the interviewer?
- Did I prepare my attitude before the interview?

Performance

Concentrate next on the actual interview. Reflect back on how you performed and answer these questions about yourself:

- Was I in prayer continually during the interview?
- Was I at ease and did I connect with the interviewer?
- Did I effectively deliver my Two-Minute Drill with a relevant, open-ended question?
- Did I balance the conversation by providing answers and asking questions?
- Was I in control by directing much of what was discussed?
- Were my answers honest, thorough, and relevant?
- Did I paraphrase the interviewer's comments for better understanding?
- Was I consciously aware of my non-verbal communication?
- Was I using good eye-contact, a friendly smile, proper hand gestures, and good posture?
- Did my positive attitude show throughout?
- Did my energy and enthusiasm shine?

- Did I forget to mention any strengths?
- Did I forget to share any accomplishments?

Potential Impact

Finish your self-evaluation by dealing with an honest assessment of the impact you left on the interviewer:

- Do you know if you are still in the game?
- Did the interviewer respond favorably to your close?
- Did you learn what the next step is?
- What is your overall assessment of this interview on a scale of 1 to 10, with 10 being the most positive side?

Consider doing a written evaluation of yourself. Print up your own evaluation form with some of the above questions. Close your eyes and recall the whole meeting. Carefully replay the interview in your mind to see where you need to improve your performance. By committing your immediate thoughts to paper after the interview, you can use your evaluations to better prepare for future meetings. An honest, thorough self-evaluation is one of the best *free* vehicles you can use to improve your interviewing skills.

As you reflect on your interview, open yourself to God's correction. Pray to receive further guidance from the Lord as you prepare for your next interview. *Blessed is the man whom God corrects; so do not despise the discipline of the Almighty* (Job 5:17).

Follow-Up Systems

After you've sent countless résumés,
spoken with dozens of network contacts,
and participated in several interviews,
how do you keep track of everything?

The simple answer is to develop and use your own personal, dynamic follow-up system. It can be the easy paper-and-pencil approach, a computer contact-management system, an Excel program, or one of those already programmed into a hand-held device.

The key element in developing a good follow-up system is to devote time tracking *every* one of your contacts. You will write down what was important to remember after each meeting, especially those tasks you committed to do for the person. Several successful job-seekers I know use an index-card system. On each card they list the contact's name, address, email, and telephone information. You can file these cards alphabetically for easy retrieval. Always remember to keep the card file with you for immediate use.

Whether conversations are held by means of a tele-phone, meeting, interview, or email, make a brief entry on your card or system. Note things such as actions you need to take, items discussed, or referrals made. Also note the date when you plan further contact with this person.

If not daily, at least weekly review your contact cards to make certain you are attending to details that you committed yourself to do. If you have references to submit or follow-up calls to make, put those items on your weekly planning calendar. Note on the cards the date when completed.

As weeks and months pass by and you are getting all the activity you anticipated, you'll need this follow-up system to keep track of everything that is supposed to occur in a timely manner. You'll be glad you set up such a system.

Good follow-up systems are written down, easy to maintain, easy to access, and will be *kept up-to-date.* You always will know with whom you spoke last, what was discussed, and what needs to occur next. Dynamic follow-up systems will enable you to stay connected and track progress with every interviewer at each potential employer. These personal follow-up systems function as a reminder like a string tied around your finger.

Our Lord, who knows the value of the written word, reminds us of those things that are important to our lives. He gave Moses the Law to write down for generations to reference. He gave us the entire Bible, so we could have His truths close at hand to remember. In Joshua 1:8, God reminds Joshua, *Do not let this Book of the Law depart from your mouth; meditate on it day and night, so that you may be careful to do everything written in it. Then you will be prosperous and successful.* Use a written system to follow-up on everything thoroughly—it pays dividends.

Job Offers or Not

Many job-seekers experience one or more rejections before employment offers are finally received. How you respond to these rejections later will impact how you approach potential offers.

Also, you might be surprised to learn that many job-seekers receive multiple job offers at the same time. If you pursue numerous employers, this may result in two or more employers desiring your services. How wonderful to be given a choice of where to work!

When the job offers are presented prepare yourself to deal with them in a thoughtful, professional, and pre-determined manner. While money is usually the center focus of the offer, don't let it be the total essence of your consideration.

Put money in proper perspective. Make it your primary objective to receive the job that God has for you so His purpose will prevail in your life. Rejections can be answers to prayer, just as job offers may not be accompanied by God's blessing. Be wise and prepared to discern the difference.

What good is it for a man to gain the whole world, yet forfeit his soul?

(Mark 8:36).

49

Rejections May Be a Blessing

*Is being rejected once again
a prayer gone unanswered?*

Have you ever considered that, while rejection can hurt, it can also be for your benefit? Look at this statement in the light of your job search. For instance, have you ever thought that being rejected for a job is a blessing in the long run? Perhaps the recent layoff you went through was God helping you move forward. Actually, God may have something better planned for you.

Have you considered that maybe a job opportunity that didn't materialize was God helping you pull into another lane to avoid another potential career accident? As Proverbs says, *A man's steps are directed by the Lord. How then can anyone understand his own way?* (Prov. 20:24).

Though rejection seldom feels good, you can take comfort in knowing that God has your best, long-term interests factored into His plans for your life. *In his heart a man plans his course, but the Lord determines his steps* (Prov. 16:9). You can be encouraged in knowing that *The plans of the diligent lead to profit as surely as haste leads to poverty* (Prov. 21:5).

To prove the point, look at how the Bible describes several individuals who overcame rejection in their own lives.

182

First, consider Moses, who was rejected by Egypt and then later by his own people on several occasions.

And remember how Ruth was rejected in her mother-in-law's native land, gleaning barley fields for food. David was rejected by both King Saul, the king he loved and served, and by Absalom, his own son, whom he also loved very much. Esther lived in a foreign land but not beyond God's care. Also, think about the rejection experienced by Samuel, Eli, Job, Mary, John the Baptist, Mary Magdalene, Stephen, Paul, and the near-death traveler who was finally rescued by the Good Samaritan.

Most importantly, Jesus endured painful rejection from the Pharisees, the Sadducees, the Romans, his brothers, and even Peter. While these individuals endured different kinds of rejection, God used these various situations to create great opportunities in each life. He will do the same in your life.

In comparison, many of the rejections you face today can be as hurtful and as mean-spirited as some of those I've already mentioned. But remember that each individual mentioned in the Bible had a *purpose* that could only be fulfilled as a result of experiencing rejection.

For instance, if Jesus had not been rejected and crucified, the greater purpose of His resurrection could not have occurred. Had Joseph, the son of Jacob, not been rejected by his brothers and sold to nomadic Ishmaelite merchants who took him to Egypt, he would not have been in the position to serve his family and his nation many years later.

Sometimes *after* you experience rejection, you can look back and understand the reasons why God allowed the situation to occur in your life. At other times, you may never completely understand some difficult situations. You may never know why the rejection or defeat occurred.

Many times during a job search you can identify with the words of Job, *So I have been allotted months of futility, and nights of misery have been assigned to me* (Job 7:3). The rejection of a layoff, coupled with the multiple rejections during a job search, can for some, become emotionally disturbing and spiritually challenging. Sometimes it may be severe. In those times, petition God to hear your cry for mercy (Psalms 142, 143, 144) and seek help.

Take comfort in knowing that God knows best which jobs are right for you. In your career pursuits you may have made hasty decisions that were poor choices. Clearly, our God in Heaven, who is a loving father, wants the best career and the best long-term future for you. So embrace the idea that the rejection you experience may be nothing more than the loving hands of God, gently nudging you to pursue something better on down the road.

So take this precept to heart. Remember, while rejection can hurt, it can be for your benefit. Ultimately the job you get is the *blessing* that would not have occurred had you not experienced the prior rejection. Identify with the rejection our Savior experienced.

Take courage from the knowledge that you need not worry about tomorrow, for God is already there. *He will never reject you.* He will, however, use the rejection you experienced to bring you to a better, higher place, *for it is God who works in you to will and to act according to his good purpose* (Phil. 2:13).

50

The Right Job vs. The Right Job

If you've been searching for months and just received an offer for the job you've been looking for, do you grab it?

Perhaps. But not so fast! It may be the right job; or it may only appear to be the right job. Let's take a closer look at the situation.

Many might describe your *right job* in terms of job duties and responsibilities, challenges, objectives, assignments, pay, and other rewards. In other words, if they offer you a job to accomplish "X" and you will be well-paid, then you may think that this is the *right job*. Well, maybe.

You may be so eager to get back to work—and that's a good thing—that you fail to complete due diligence. That's a bad thing. You have a responsibility to yourself not to rush into the unknown. On the surface you possibly think that this is the right job, but underneath your excitement, you know it may be wrong for you because it's in the *wrong company*, in the *wrong location*, with the *wrong boss*, or part of the *wrong culture*.

If you discover a great job with great pay but find out it's an organization that financially is not sound or technologically is desolate—is this really the right job for you? It could prove to be a very short period of employment—thus, it may be the *wrong company*.

If you find that great job with great pay, but you fail to uncover information that your personal boss is a tyrant, you may be stepping from the frying pan into the fire. Perhaps worse, you may discover that the entire corporate culture is one where tyranny and dictatorial practices abound. Your initiative, creativity, and need to contribute will not be accepted. Discovering these facts six days or six months into employment is too late.

If you take a *great job* solely on the basis of the job itself, you probably are making a big mistake. The entirety of the job, including the boss, company, culture, industry, and geography, needs to be understood before saying yes. You still may not realize the real reason why this is important to you, so read on.

Even if you are a perfect match for the job, but for some reason, the job does not last because of your boss, the culture, the company, the industry, or the location—**you** will be held accountable down the road for the situation. Whether you leave of your own accord, or you are released, future employers often see it as a bad job match between you and the job duties and responsibilities. Though your short-term failure here may have nothing to do with your abilities to do the work you love, it sends a flashing light out to future interviewers regarding your judgment.

Therefore, be diligent in searching and finding out all you can about potential jobs, bosses, companies, industries, cultures, and locations. Certainly you do not want a short-term position. Even more, you don't need future employers questioning your judgment about your chosen line of work.

Before you say yes to the right job, make sure it is the *right job* for you; both for the short- as well as for the long-term. Every decision has consequences. Therefore, pray for guidance, listen to good advice from God's people, and then, faithfully follow whatever the Lord is telling you to do.

What is Negotiable?

*Now that you have an offer for a job on the table,
what can you consider negotiable?*

Almost every item concerning your pending employment may be considered negotiable—compensation, benefits, and working conditions. In fact, far more is negotiable than most people realize.

In the area of compensation, in many instances, *the salary may be negotiable.* Also, possible incentives, at-risk pay, or how your first raise is determined may be other negotiating points. Recognize that how much you get paid is not the most important factor; determining beforehand *how* and *when* future pay changes may occur is highly crucial. Both are possible areas of negotiation, too.

In the benefits arena, you can find much to discuss. Especially in today's economy whether or not certain benefits exist is one of the main questions. Some ways exist to enhance the benefits you are offered. You can ask to consider changing waiting periods imposed before benefit eligibility. For example, some firms may impose a 90-day period before your group insurance is effective. Negotiate for a shorter waiting period or no wait at all. Also, consider negotiating areas that are important to you, such as time off with pay, including vacations, holidays, and sick time, as well as time off *without* pay, i.e., excused days off, a leave of absence, and family emergencies.

The third broad category that is open to negotiation is working conditions. You may find several items important enough to ask your new employer to change for you. Consider the following:

- Hours of work—per day, per week, lunch breaks, and flextime,
- Location of work—on site or telecommute from a home office,
- Start times, end times, and lunch breaks,
- Dress-code requirements,
- Work-space environment—chairs, cubicle, décor, and personal items,
- Use of telephones, cell phones, and computers,
- Training and development during work hours,
- Freedom to interface with others—supervisors, customers, and suppliers,
- Job duties and responsibilities—current and future,
- Performance evaluations—formal and informal, and
- Opportunities for improving work processes.

Rarely is negotiating *everything* necessary or appropriate. Rather, learn what the company is offering as your total package—salary, benefits, and working conditions—and then be up-front with your questions. Negotiate those areas that are not acceptable before saying, "I'll take the job."

In the parable of the *Workers in the Vineyard*, Jesus illustrates the importance of understanding the conditions under which you accept employment and then agree to live happily with those arrangements (Matt. 20:1-16). Far too often you agree to a job offer without fully understanding all of the details. Then you decide to negotiate changes after you've begun working. This approach is seldom effective. Do any necessary negotiations *before* you agree to the total offer.

Negotiation is a learned skill. Consider all the elements of the job offer before you agree to any piece. Wait until all of the pieces of the puzzle are fully uncovered and your questions are answered before you decide "yes" or "no." For example, if the salary is okay, but certain benefits are unacceptable, do not agree to the salary and think later you will negotiate the other areas. If the employer is unable to bump up the benefits you need or accommodate any of the working conditions you'd like changed, perhaps a higher salary will be necessary to offset those areas that you find lacking. If you rush in to agreement on the salary amount, you may be limiting your negotiation leverage in other areas which are important.

Negotiations Etiquette

Since you've been out of work for weeks
or months, do you accept a job offer,
no matter what the pay?

Let's recall the words spoken by John the Baptist to some Roman soldiers who asked him how they were to live. He answered, *Don't extort money and don't accuse people falsely—be content with your pay* (Luke 3:14b). He was telling them to do a job for the salary that had been established and to be content with that income, rather than dishonestly seeking additional gain.

In the parable of the *Workers in the Vineyard* (Matt. 20:1-16), Jesus illustrates that you have a responsibility to commit to what is agreed *up front*. If the salary offer is too low, the benefits incomplete or the working conditions unsatisfactory, you have at least two other alternative negotiation paths to take.

You can say no, or you can attempt to change any unacceptable terms *before you accept* the offer. If you really want the job, then negotiate a conclusion that is a win/win situation for both you and your new employer. Here are 10 basic principles you may want to adopt to improve your negotiation capabilities and help you achieve a win/win result:

Defer salary negotiations. *Always* try to defer any salary discussions until it is in the context of a firm job offer.

Consider the whole package. Salary negotiations are part of a larger process called job-offer negotiations. The salary offer usually is accompanied by defined job responsibilities, benefits, and working conditions. Look at the entire package; all is negotiable.

Know your bottom line. Decide what your minimums are— minimum salary requirements, minimum benefits, and minimum job responsibilities.

Understand the company's expectations. A compensation package is only considered good or bad in relation to what it is being exchanged for—what hours, duties, commitments, and deliverables are expected from you in exchange for the salary the company offers.

Review an offer before accepting it. Ask for time to consider the offer in total, to discuss it with loved ones, and to pray about it.

Hold out for a complete offer. If you receive a salary offer with things such as benefits and working conditions to be determined *after* you start work, politely decline the offer. You will lose almost all of your negotiating leverage once you begin work (recall the *Workers in the Vineyard* parable and read Matt. 20:16 again).

Value your contributions. Negotiating is about fair compensation in exchange for your contributions, skills, and talents. In reality, this is about fair-market rates, which can vary widely, so don't be greedy.

Realize your market price. Your market salary usually is a range of dollars. Learn this *before* you get to the point of having to agree to an offer. Many online sources provide labor-market rates for many positions in many professions. The local librarian can help you find this information, too.

Remain positive and thankful. The person extending the offer is saying, "I have chosen you to work here." If the offer is too low, remain courteous and thank the person who extends the offer, indicating that you are interested in negotiating a positive change.

Deal with concerns now. Ask about or discuss areas that concern you before you say *yes* to the offer. If not, you most likely will regret it later. Even if negotiations change nothing about the job offer, you will be glad you were able to better understand each facet of the employment offer *before* you begin your new job. In part, it's all about minimizing distressing surprises later.

Though the right salary plays an important part in taking a job when you have been out of work for a period of time, it's not the main focus of accepting a job offer. I have witnessed many new employees become disenchanted or disappointed because expectations during the interview process never materialized. In almost every case, the individuals being interviewed didn't do something:

- They didn't discuss important issues before agreeing to the offer.
- They didn't verbalize their employment expectations in advance.
- They didn't do their homework to know if they were receiving a fair-market offer.
- They didn't get commitments or job responsibilities fully explained.

Your responsibility is to do a thorough job of understanding what compensation you are getting and what talents and skills you are expected to give in return. The employment relationship will be far more positive when both parties understand each other's goals and objectives and expectations.

Trouble-shooting Your Job Search

Some people cruise through their job search and arrive at a job in a few weeks or months. Others struggle, work diligently, and keep struggling; they have problems really identifying why they just can't land a job.

Some people seek and receive good advice from friends and networking contacts during their search. Though they have above-average employment backgrounds, they too, cannot land a job.

While many variables—some controllable and some not—impact each individual search, two tactics deserve consideration above the others. In the following chapters, learn how both trouble-shooting approaches just might help job-seekers get back on track.

A man of many companions may come to ruin, but there is a friend who sticks closer than a brother

(Prov. 18:24).

53

A Friend Closer than a Brother

What do you do when your job search just isn't going the way the experts said it would go?

For many years I have advised friends, family, and casual acquaintances about how to conduct a successful job search. Having been behind the interview desk for more than 25 years, I am encouraged to share what I have learned about the process. Good suggestions have been given, job-hunting means explained, and emotional support were provided to hundreds of individuals amidst the trials of a job search or a career change.

Throughout my coaching experience, two major reasons seem to sum up why people get bogged down, discouraged, and otherwise run into the proverbial brick wall. Day after day, they often are surprised by their lack of success. One of the main reasons is they haven't found *a friend that sticks closer than a brother* (Prov. 18:24).

You might respond, "But yes, I have several friends who are encouraging me, praying for me, and who genuinely try to help me during these difficult times. They are sympathetic, empathetic, and offer regular encouragements to keep me going. They truly want to *be there* for me."

Yet, for all my "friends and acquaintances", I have *only* three friends who fit the definition of one who sticks closer than a brother. Bob, Steve, and Patrick all know what it is to give of themselves so unselfishly and completely. I hope God will place friends such as this in your path, too.

Here's a story about another "friend"—Stan. Some time ago, he was somewhat discouraged during his job search. He was using most of the right means of conducting a good search. He very methodically prepared a good résumé; he learned the art of good letter-writing; he mastered the tools of effective networking; and he took care of all the meticulous details to mount a successful job search—from proper telephone techniques to timely thank-you notes.

He kept detailed records of each contact made and interview conducted. Stan had a good work background, a likeable personality, and was a warm, generous, faithful Christian. But with all of this in his favor, he was not succeeding in his job search.

After several conversations with Stan, I discovered the obstacle in his pathway to success, which another of Stan's closest confidants confirmed. Stan had one blind spot; yet, he didn't have a friend close enough to confront him with the flaw. Similar to the king in Hans Christian Andersen's tale, *The Emperor's New Clothes*, Stan was not being told by anyone about the one thing that stood between him and success in his job search.

Do you have someone in your life who will tell you *anything* about yourself for your own good? Do you have a friend who is willing to *hurt your feelings* or *step on your toes* because he or she loves you so much that the friend will risk the relationship for your welfare?

In the book of Proverbs, Solomon urges you to find a true friend. *As iron sharpens iron, so one man sharpens another* (Prov. 27:17). Think about that verse for a moment. Kid gloves don't sharpen iron. Iron does! Apply pressure to sharpen the blade. Similarly, tough, truthful answers sharpen a person. Like iron against iron, close contact and some pressure are required to make a needed change. Don't forget occasionally this will cause sparks to fly!

Do you also have friend who will hold you accountable to be who God wants you to be? Some individuals, like the central character in *The Emperor's New Clothes*, have set the tone in their personal relationships so those people around them never will tell them the cold, naked truth.

Have you created a barrier, even among your closest friends, so no one intimately will tell you, "You are naked!" Just as in the classic tale, where the emperor wanted a new suit of clothes and was duped into thinking he was wearing a wonderfully new regalia of gold, no one would be honest and tell the emperor the truth because they feared his response.

Consider allowing yourself to be open and vulnerable with one or two close friends. Give them freedom to tell you *anything*. Create a relationship that gives those particular individuals permission to level with you and tell you about yourself to tell you what most people won't tell you. Yes, at first you will find hearing what they have to say to be difficult, but realize they have your best interest at heart.

I often ask individuals if they can possibly visualize any aspect of their job search in which they may be *naked*. Is it possible that you, too, are doing something poorly without knowing it? Go to your closest confidants and ask them to be *brutally honest* with you. If one will become that kind of close friend, don't get defensive or try to rationalize away the suggestions they offer. Rather, thank the person for being truthful and risking your friendship. Then privately, give careful and sincere consideration to the critique being offered.

In Stan's case, it was his *attitude*. Because he was a good prospect for employers and using all the job-search techniques the right way, he had adopted a *know-it-all* attitude. To some he appeared arrogant; to others he appeared aloof and

196

uninterested. This was a subtle thing, but it almost always was present. And it didn't appear anyone was willing to risk a confrontation with Stan to inform him. Unfortunately, Stan was not consciously aware of how he was affecting others—potential employers and his good network contacts alike.

After several months, Stan finally found the friend he needed. He was lovingly informed about his attitude and how he was being perceived. Humbly accepting the information, he changed his manner almost immediately. Predictably, he landed his dream career position not long after his friend confided in him.

Though it costs many conscientious job-seekers additional months in their job search, those without *friends closer than a brother* soon will discover they need something more. You need a friend who will love you so much that that person will risk losing you. The friend will tell you things you may not always want to hear, but you will listen to him or her. If you *have* a friend such as that, thank God. If you *are* a friend such as that, God is smiling!

54

Measures That Never Fail

On a special occasion, have you ever received a practical gift that was really something you needed?

Perhaps on your birthday, you received the latest cordless drill, or an energy-efficient laundry machine, or possibly, an iPod®. Each of these gifts has a distinctive function or purpose. Each can make your life easier saving you time and helping you accomplish certain tasks that you could not do otherwise. Notably, each has been carefully designed and constructed by competent individuals who understand the purpose for which they will be used.

Each of these gifts has been warranty-tested and is more effective and more efficient than those used by previous generations. Cordless, battery-powered screwdrivers perform faster, with less effort, and are more effective than hand-turned screwdrivers your grandfathers used. The newest, high-tech, no-hassle washing machines clean, rinse, and spin clothes faster, easier, and more efficiently than your mother's did. And today, you can download music from your computer or a satellite without using a turntable. Amazing!

Gifts for special occasions are given with love and joy, knowing you will benefit from their use. Through the years, though, the designer, the builder, and the giver cannot control one critical factor—its use! If you don't use the cordless drill, then the computer stand won't be put together so you can have a place to write your résumé. If you don't use the clothes washer, your jeans will remain dirty. And you can't whistle while you work if you don't hear the music.

So it is with this book. If you don't learn to use the suggestions provided throughout the book, they are worthless. The design concepts of a two-page résumé, the development of your Two-Minute Drill, the use of pre-planned questions for your interview, and the implementation of good networking techniques are given to you for a reason—to help you obtain the career God has planned for you. To get the maximum benefit, use the ideas, tactics, and Scriptural truths from this book in your own career search.

Many years ago, I received a radial arm saw just at the time I was planning to build a gazebo in my back yard. For the first few days I looked at my new saw and wondered whether or not it would really help me build that gazebo. I read the manual. I practiced using the saw on scrap lumber. I practiced on a few small projects until my proficiency improved. Then I built my first gazebo! Years later, I built another gazebo; this one was larger, stronger and even more beautiful than the first.

Over the years, I have received many woodworking implements. I've learned that no matter how good the device, only my mastery of it would determine the outcome of the project. *Laziness brings on deep sleep, and the shiftless man goes hungry* (Prov. 19:15).

You who have received and read this book about the means to locate and secure a great career position are only halfway there. Now, learn how to use each suggestion, practice until you're proficient, and then build a successful job search that ultimately will result in securing the future God has planned for you. *You will eat the fruit of your labor; blessings and prosperity will be yours* (Ps. 128:2).

To build a successful job search, practice each of the suggestions you've been given in this book. Keep practicing until you are good at using each one. They are some of the best tactics available today. Each was designed and tested for effectiveness. Each was given with love. Now you can decide to what degree you will use each. If you do, you'll be pleased with your results.

Off to a Great Start

You got the job! Hooray! Is the challenge finally over? Well, not really.

Are you ready to move from one challenge to the next? After you find the right job, the real work is just beginning. As you transition from one pathway to another, faithfully begin the next career stage doing the work God has provided, working hard to survive, and believing in your success.

I am convinced that the years of preparation Moses endured in Midian were easy compared to the work God had planned for him to do—leading his people out of slavery and into the Promised Land. Preparing for a new job fills your mind with many questions and great anxiety; the work ahead also will have its challenges to be faced and properly addressed. Moses, with God's help, accomplished the mission set before him. You will, too.

I hope you have started to look at your career as a part of the journey God has prepared for your life. You can stay squarely on the highway. God will guide you better than anyone can. He'll remove barricades or provide alternate routes when needed. He'll keep your radiator from overheating and your fuel tank full. When traffic slows to a crawl, God will enable you to move right into the HOV lane.

For God did not give us a spirit of timidity (fear), but a spirit of power, of love and of self-discipline.

(2 Tim. 1:7).

55

Succeeding by Serving

*After you've arrived at your "dream job",
how can you ensure you will start strong
and make a great lasting impression?*

Different people will offer numerous suggestions on
how to begin a new job well. Many ideas will spring to mind
as you ponder this question. I recommend taking a long-term
point-of-view, adopting 10 Key Strategies, which if implemented, will reward you well. Consider each, with a new spirit and the heartfelt objective of *serving* your employer, customers, and fellow workers.

1. Embrace honesty . . . 100 percent.
Of all the assets you bring to your new job, nothing
will be of greater value than honesty. Your boss counts on
your integrity. Your customers value honest relationships.
Fellow employees need to trust you with reliable information,
commitments, and truthful relationships.

Though you may have a great attitude, a breadth of
experience and valued skills, this is meaningless without a full
measure of integrity. God used King David to pen, *No one
who practices deceit will dwell in my house; no one who
speaks falsely will stand in my presence* (Ps. 101:7). The
words of Solomon, David's son, may encourage you, *The man*

of integrity walks securely, but he who takes crooked paths will be found out (Prov. 10:9).

2. Develop a one-and-only focus.

Whether you are serving your boss or a customer, go *beyond* treating the person as though he or she is very important to you. Rather, during the moments you work with that person, treat that individual as though he or she is the *only person* you have to serve. Give people your undivided attention; show each you really value those moments you have with him or her.

3. Exceed your promises.

Several years ago, auto dealer and author Carl Sewell suggested that one of the greatest ways to make a positive, lasting impression is to "under-promise and over-deliver." In essence, if you deliver *above and beyond* what is expected, you will delight a boss, subordinate, customer, or colleague. If you promise it by Friday, deliver it on Thursday. If you promise to deliver a 100-percent improvement, deliver a 150-percent improvement. Give them more value, more attention, more courtesy, and more follow-up than expected.

4. Relax; enjoy humor.

You can't joke around all the time, but avoid taking everything too seriously. A prominent corporate leader and previous boss of mine once said, "Take the job seriously, but never take yourself seriously."

It's good advice. Show those around you that you do have a lighter side to your personality. You don't need to perfect the art of joke-telling, but enjoy a good laugh now and then. *Roll with the punches.*

5. Practice 1-2-3's of good listening.

Listen with your *ears*,
Listen with your *heart*, and then
Think about what the speaker's objective is.

Oftentimes you take conversations too literally; other times you are preoccupied with other thoughts; while occasionally, you just don't put much importance in what other say. To succeed in business long-term, build a reputation of being a good listener. It is a valued skill in all relationships. Listen to discern the heart of the messenger. God always will help you "read between the lines" to understand what the other person intended to say. Then, engage your thinking mechanism for a few moments to formulate a positive response.

6. Put others' needs above your own.

Many find this action unnecessary. Some find this impossible to do. That is precisely why it is valued in the work place. It is the right thing to do because, if you're satisfying someone else's need, your service will be valued.

7. Give friendly greetings.

When you offer others a warm, cordial greeting to acknowledge their presence, your stock value automatically goes up with most people. Then you quickly become approachable and often trigger a level of friendliness in others, which they may have forgotten exists in a business climate. A warm word can melt almost anyone.

8. Stick to your principles.

Your core values are *too important* to compromise. Don't ever compromise your values to be accepted in the new business culture. Whether responding to inappropriate jokes, gossip, unkindness, or language, remain true to yourself.

Likewise, treat everyone with respect. Charles Thornton, in his book, *Headed Home*, tells us, "Aretha Franklin got it right when she sang about respect . . .. It shouldn't come as a surprise to know that's what most people want." Though you may not agree with your colleagues' behavior, you still can remain courteous and respectful without condemning them.

9. Demonstrate confidence

Some people can *talk* a great game. But what's truly important is that confidence is *demonstrated* in your life, instead of just boasting about it. You can demonstrate personal confidence by your carriage, eye-contact, and ease in meeting others. You can demonstrate confidence in your professional abilities by volunteering for assignments and setting stretch objectives. You can demonstrate strategic confidence by showing a willingness to learn, grow, and accept new challenges. Each can be demonstrated without arrogance, horn-blowing, or cockiness.

10. Love to serve

Even when those you serve are unaware or unwilling to accept your talents, inwardly and quietly, you can love and care about what you're doing to serve them (Matt. 20:26, 1 Pet. 4:10, Luke 6:38, John 13:34, Col. 3:23). This is a command by our Lord and Savior. He knows just how important loving others as He loved us is. Unconditional love will take you places in your career and in your life you never dreamed were possible. You can succeed by serving. Serving others often is a very *high priority* of successful men and women whose lives are meaningful, especially because their purposes in life are eternally driven. Though the business world may not always reward such service, believe in your heart that your Father in heaven will honor you and will reward your efforts.

56

Clean Up the Mess

Can your work record be fixed if it is a mess from job-hopping, little stability, and few successes?

Yes! Yes! Yes! "Put your behind in the past." These are the wise words used by Pumba in the movie, *The Lion King*. Pumba was trying to comfort the young lion prince, who was suffering from guilt, believing he had made a huge mistake which cost his father's life. Pumba was a true friend. He tried to help Simba realize he needed to move on and not get discouraged by his past.

The first thing to cleaning up the mess you've created in your work history (or any part of your life) is accepting the fact you can put your mistakes behind you. Seek forgiveness; then accept the consequences for your actions and decisions, and move on!

A man after God's own heart, King David, made a big mistake. He accepted the bitter consequences of committing adultery, deceit, and murder. He asked and received God's forgiveness. Then David moved on. You, too, can repent, receiving God's mercy and grace. Then move on!

No reason exists to punish yourself—no reason you can't get up, clean yourself off, and move on down the road from where you are this minute. You can move forward, secure in the knowledge that you, too, can turn a messy work history into a positive step.

King David wrote, *I cry out to God Most High, to God, who fulfills his purpose for me* (Ps. 57:2). Seek God's forgiveness and put your past behind you. If you have been a job-hopper, stay on your next job long enough to show a *stick-to-it* commitment. If you continually have been a victim of layoffs, find employment where layoffs are less likely.

If you've had relationship problems with previous bosses, you can minimize conflict by selecting a different kind of boss this time around. Also scrutinize yourself and uncover that thing about yourself which contributed to your previous job relationship problems. Or again, ask a close friend to help you identify the problem. Then change it. *Listen to advice and accept instruction, and in the end you will be wise* (Prov. 19:20).

Most importantly, get out of the *victim mode* and into the driver's seat with a mindset that propels you to victory. You are given opportunities each new day to walk forward in confidence, guided and disciplined by the Holy Spirit, and to do what God has planned for you.

If your *poor* work record took a few years to create, it may take that same length of time to create a good slate. It can be done. Start today and do it confidently, knowing that over time you will clean up the mess and God will reward your efforts. *Wealth and honor come from you; you are the ruler of all things. In your hands are strength and power to exalt and give strength to all. Now, our God, we give you thanks, and praise your glorious name* (1 Chron. 29:12-13).

Go forward with God in the front seat and create a new pathway for career success. Will this be easy? Not likely. God, though, is willing to help you personally because He loves you more than you can imagine. It will take time; God will give you all that you need.

Land Mines

After an agonizing search, how can you be certain that you won't be without work again?

You may not want to hear this, but you have *no guarantees*. The possibility exists that you will be without work again. The average American worker today can look forward to changing jobs 11 times during his or her career. You will experience seasons of plenty and seasons of want. You have good choices on how to prepare for each season, using God's road map to help you.

If you have worked diligently to discern what God has planned for your life, you can learn a few ways to avoid the destructive land mines along your path. While you can do many things to maximize your possibilities for success, you can guard against these potential stumbling blocks:

1. Arrogance
2. Blaming
3. Distractions
4. Family problems
5. Fear
6. Imagined barriers
7. Lack of focus
8. Laziness

9. Lying to self
10. Poor decisions
11. Procrastination
12. Selfishness
13. Spiritual bondage
14. Spitefulness
15. Unwillingness to pay the price
16. Victimization
17. Wrong focus

Each of these personality imperfections represents a potential land mine along your journey. Each is a *real threat* and may be extremely hazardous to your success. Some are disguised, some are ignored, some are rationalized, and some even may be considered inherited traits. But they are all costly diversions that you will confront; they will be used *to run you off the road* to success.

The first line of defense is to recognize that these land mines do exist. Then, be ready to deal with each as it appears in your pathway. Next, how you deal with each one becomes very personal, and for some, more intense. Some of you may need more help than others, depending on how those land mines are situated in your careers.

Here is a good road map to use as you go down life's highway, trying to avoid career land mines. Start new today. *Establish* a firm, *personal* relationship with our Lord Jesus Christ. *Pray continually*, seeking God's protection and guidance. *Study His Word daily* to learn how He wants you to live and work. *Seek support* from your Christian brothers and sisters in the company of Bible-study groups, accountability groups, prayer partners, and corporate worship services. *Flee from any evil* temptations. Use this compass at all times to keep you headed in the right direction at work, as well as at home.

You will face trials in your career, but how you respond to the "land mines" will make a difference. Do you serve confidently, diligently, and without complaining? When your job requires distasteful aspects, do you choose to do the task well, as for the Lord? When work relationships become strained, are you able to deal with conflicts with love, without a blaming spirit? Do you build others up rather than tearing them apart? When colleagues disappoint you, can you forgive and encourage one another? When you fail at something you attempt, can you learn from it, forget it, and move forward with confidence toward your next success? Here are a few of the many practical approaches I recommend to maximize your possibilities for career success:

- Stay focused.
- Serve others.
- Care for fellow employees.
- Give more than is expected.
- Work as you would for God.
- Keep your integrity intact.
- Learn from every mistake.
- Build relationships.
- Persevere through pain.
- Remain selfless.
- Look for ways to improve.
- Keep learning and growing.
- Remain fearless.
- Manage self; lead others.
- Know your purpose.
- Dream large.

Again, you have no guarantees against losing your job. So remember what the apostle Paul said, *For I have learned to be content whatever the circumstances. I know what it is to be in need, and I know what it is to have plenty. I have learned the secret of being content in any and every situation, whether well fed or hungry, whether living in plenty or want. I can do everything through him who gives me strength* (Phil. 4:11b-13).

Paul's wisdom shows that the circumstances you face do not determine your outcome; your attitude and response toward each circumstance may help you avoid the land mines along your path.

58

Into the Career HOV Lane

*How do you get into the HOV lane when
your career seems to be just limping along,
bumper-to-bumper, in rush-hour traffic?*

If you have been in the *slow lane* of your career while
others seem to continually pass you by year after year, you
can do something about it. It's simple but not easy. Bring
Jesus along, and together, the two of you can slide over into
the HOV lane of your career.

The HOV (High-Occupancy Vehicles) lane, sometimes
called the "carpool lane", allows drivers to zoom past those
other poor souls, bogged down in traffic during rush hour. In
most states, you need only one additional passenger with you
to qualify for admittance into the fast lane. Why not take Jesus
along? While He is with you, He is easily seen by anyone who
is watching you zoom along in your career.

Jesus can be seen because of your love for others
along the roadway, your joy in the journey, your peace in the
bumpy spots, your patience with delays, your kindness when
others need direction, your goodness when you let others
merge in front of you, your faithfulness in your obedience to
His road signs, your gentleness as you are cut off by those not
paying attention, and your self-control during road repairs

causing undesirable detours. A few will doubt you are riding with your Lord and Savior, who makes your trip wonderful, even through all the challenges along the way.

Once in the HOV lane, you can really get up to speed. First step on the gas and make that decision to move on out! *For we are God's workmanship, created in Christ Jesus to do good works, which God prepared in advance for us to do* (Eph. 2:10). Our Creator did not fashion you to schlep along in your career. He wants you to make a commitment to be your best for Him.

One of His greatest gifts is explained in this wonderful verse: *Whatever you do, work at it with all your heart, as working for the Lord, not for men* (Col. 3:23). God gave you something precious—the opportunity to commit yourself to a very important path.

Second, you may choose to get on with life, knowing that a new and improved career doesn't happen overnight. It is a lengthy journey but greatly enhanced by being in the HOV lane. Once you have found that next best job, work at it with all your heart, do well, and begin to create new successes.

If you have a history of job-hopping, work at this new position, focusing on erasing your past pattern. This is why selecting your next employer, your next position, and your next boss very carefully is vitally important. Keep our Lord next to you in the front seat at all times.

If you became discontented in earlier jobs, look around for the reason. Perhaps you selected the wrong employer. Was the job way over your head? Were you under-employed? Did you lose interest in the company? Did you have relationship problems with ex-bosses? Were you a victim of company restructuring or department cutbacks?

Accept responsibility for your choices right now. *Do not conform any longer to the pattern of this world, but be transformed by the renewing of your mind. Then you will be*

213

able to test and approve what God's will is—his good, pleasing and perfect will (Rom. 12:2). Find the job God wants you to have; then stick with it. Before long, you'll stay in the HOV lane.

Third, remember all jobs have some responsibilities, some duties, and some aspects that are displeasing. The grass seldom is greener on the other side of the road. Many times God uses challenges and hurdles in your work to help you grow in your faith. God desires to teach you one of life's most difficult lessons—perseverance. When you face great difficulties at work, you may be tempted to walk away. *But as for you, be strong and do not give up, for your work will be rewarded* (2 Chron. 15:7).

Next to maintaining career momentum, staying focused on the long-term destination is the most difficult aspect. Noah, Abraham, Moses, Samuel, David, the apostle Paul, and even Lois and Eunice—Timothy's grandmother and mother—are among the many whose *careers* were blessed over a long period. You have heard the expression—**stay the course**—so for emphasis I'll add **for the long haul**. If you truly dare to succeed as God desires, the next course of action is to adopt an attitude and a desire for personal growth. Employers value those who learn, grow, and become more valuable. Continue to raise your *value* through increased knowledge and capability.

Learn your job well. Do your best every day to improve your contribution. Give of yourself more than your employer expects. Go back to school, learn new skills, or ask to be given additional, on-the-job training when you are ready. Those who only *do enough to get by* seldom do for very long.

Along the way, guard how you speak to others and what words you use. Your words can either be a blessing or a curse. Can you recall the last kind words someone spoke to you? Have you ever forgotten harsh words spoken to you?

Few of us prefer the company of those whose words are poorly chosen. In fact, most of us choose to be around people whose words are encouraging, whose words are positive, helpful, and uplifting. Consciously choose to speak encouraging words so others will value your company, while your career moves into the fast lane.

Finally, treat everyone with love—even the unlovable. Beyond loving God, this is the most important command the Lord has given you. *A new command I give you: Love one another: As I have loved you, so you must love one another* (John 13:34). The workplace is a wonderful place for ministry; the Lord will be pleased as you extend His love to others at work through your kindness, peace, joy, longsuffering, and generosity.

Imagine for a moment, developing a *wonderful work life.* Think back to the classic movie, *It's A Wonderful Life,* in which actor Jimmy Stewart played an immortal character named George Bailey. Bailey shared his love with everyone in his community. He was an unforgettable example of what having a wonderful life meant because of what he gave to others.

What would be your wonderful work life? Make a plan as you start your new job. Find passion in your career success by following God's will. It is best summarized in this single verse, *For this very reason, make every effort to add to your faith goodness; and to goodness, knowledge, and to knowledge, self-control; and to self-control, perseverance; and to perseverance, godliness; and to godliness, brotherly kindness; and to brotherly kindness, love* (2 Pet. 1:5-7).

Most employers will value your living example of the above Scripture if you live it out in your place of work every day. They don't need you to quote it, but they will be delighted to see these behaviors in each task that you undertake. *Do you see a man skilled in his work? He will serve before kings; he will not serve before obscure men* (Prov. 22:29).

When you have the Lord Jesus along, riding beside you in the profession He helped you obtain, doing the work He chose for you, using the gifts He's given you, and working for Him, you will find yourself cruising along in the HOV lane of your career. The Lord will help you when you get lost. He will stay with you when you hit a stretch of bad road. He will provide the fuel needed when you run low. Our Lord and Savior will keep you from disaster and allow you to fully enjoy the sights of the wonderful trip called *your career*. He wants you to succeed because He loves you. Our Lord will ride along with you if you invite Him. It will be a joyous journey!

In the Rear-View Mirror

You who have read about the suggestions I have shared in theses pages are only halfway home. Now, apply them.

Those who have read about the Lord Jesus Christ in these pages and in the Bible are only halfway home. Jesus must be received in your heart to receive the fullness of life.

I hope you find the way to the career that our Lord wants for you. It has been established just for you. He loves you so much that He gave you the gifts with which you were born, the talents you have the developed, and the skills you have learned.

Just as I began this book with a prayer, I end it the same way, with a prayer for you:

Father in Heaven; hear this prayer for each one You have called. Lord God, forgive us for the many times we attempt to do things in our own power. Forgive each disobedient act. Forgive our offenses when we think we know better how to live our lives and careers.

Father, thanks for Your patience, for Your faithfulness, for Your boundless gifts of grace, full of mercy and love.

Father, we now ask that You show us how to apply these truths You have shared; show us the road ahead and the turns we are to make; show us each signpost along the way.

And Father, help us to receive the gifts You give, to serve Your purpose for our lives, and to be a blessing to others along the way. I ask these things in Jesus' mighty name, Amen.

End Notes

Chapter 1: O'Dooley, Patrick, *Flight Plan for Living* (New York: Mastermedia Limited, 1992), 104.

Chapter 3: Maxwell, John, *Failing Forward* (Nashville: Thomas Nelson Publishers, 2000). Resch, Philip, *Conversations on Leadership* (Sevierville, TN: Insight Publishing Co., 2004), 154.

Chapter 5: Tracy, Brian, *Focal Point* (New York: AMACOM, 2002), 12.

Chapter 6: Muchinsky, Paul M., *Psychology Applied to Work: An Introduction to Industrial and Organizational Psychology* (7th ed.) (Pacific Grove, CA: Wadsworth Thompson Learning, 2003), 375-378.

Chapter 11: Adams, Clint and Cotton, Steve, (2004), "Financial Freedom" Seminar, CAREERWORKSHOPS Inc.® access: *www.careerworkshops.org*

Chapter 13: Li, Charlene, "The Career Networks" (Boston: Forrester Research, February, 2000), 1.

Chapter 14: Sue, Marsha Petrie, *The CEO of YOU* (Scottsdale, AZ: Communicating Results Press, 2002), 123.

Chapter 16: Morley, Patrick, *The Man in the Mirror* (Nashville: Thomas Nelson Publishers, 1992), 271-289. Farrar, Steve. *Point Man: How a Man Can Lead His Family* (Sisters, OR: Multnomah Publishers, 1990), 150-152.

Chapter 17: Beatty, Richard, *Job Search Networking* (Holbrook, MA: Bob Adams, Inc., 1994), 15-18.

Chapter 19: Crabb, Larry, *Connecting* (Nashville: W Publishing Group, 1997), 6.

Chapter 20: Warren, Rick, *The Purpose Driven Life* (Grand Rapids: MI: Zondervan, 2003), 232. Ibid., 228. Ibid., 233.

Chapter 21: Richards, Mike, "Networking on Steroids" Seminar, CAREERWORKSHOPS Inc., 2003. access: *www.careerworkshops.org*

Chapter 41: The United States Equal Employment Opportunity Commission. *"Title VII of the Civil Rights Act 1964."* Access: *http://www.eeoc.gov/policy/vii/html*

Chapter 42: Anspaugh, David, film director, *Rudy* (Hollywood: Columbia-Tristar Pictures, 1993).

Chapter 46: Carey, Anne R., and Coddington, Ron. *USA Today Snapshots* (April 22, 2004) 1. access: *www.usatoday.com*

Chapter 53: Anderson, Hans Christian, with illustrator Eve Tharlet, *The Emperor's New Clothes* (New York: North South Books, Inc., 2000).

Chapter 55: Sewell, Carl, *Customers for Life* (New York: Currency Books, division of Random House, Inc., 1990). Thornton, Charles, *Headed Home* (Grapevine, TX: Self-published, 2003), 54.

Chapter 56: Hahn, Don, film producer, *The Lion King* (Burbank, CA: Walt Disney Pictures, 1994).

Chapter 58: Capra, Frank R., film director, *It's a Wonderful Life* (Hollywood: Liberty Pictures, 1947).

Sample Résumé

Fran G. Executive

245 Trail Way
Any Town, Texas 76028   *fge@email.com*   519-333-5555
519-447-3333

SPECIALTY RETAIL EXECUTIVE
CEOM, COO, President

Senior retail leader with extensive turnaround capabilities in three different retail industries (furniture, crafts, and office supplies). Customer service and sales oriented with extensive P&L management, analytical, and strategic-planning skills.

ACHIEVEMENTS

- Expanded Right-On Office Supplies from 17 to 35 stores in one year and increased net operating results from $1.3M loss to a $3.4M net profit.
- Increased Right-On's sales by 140 percent while holding expenses to a 74-percent increase and increasing the employee base by only 34 percent

EXPERIENCE

GRAND ART & FRAME, Commerce, CA
Division of Goodycrafts, Inc.
Consultant—Special Projects   2003-2004
- Sold $2.4 million excess frame and framed art inventory yielding 75 percent of cost
- Managed due diligence, disclosure documentation, and post-closing associated with the sale of Right-On Office Supplies, Crafty Leather & Cargo Furniture
- Coordinated Form 6 and Form 7 filings for Chapter 11

RIGHT-ON OFFICE SUPPLIES, Armadillo, Texas
Subsidiary of Goodycrafts Inc.
Regional discount office supply chain with 44 retail locations in 7 Western states
President & CEO   1999-2002

- Developed plan to reinvigorate sales following the entry of "Big Box" competitors resulting in full sales recovery in less than 12 months
- Established and implemented roll-out plan for "Copies Plus" as store-within-a-store concept generating incremental annual sales of $69K per store and adding $19K per store to the bottom line.
- Positioned company for sale to new owner. Sale completed in June 2002.

CRAFTY LEATHER COMPANY, Austin, Texas
Division of Goodycrafts, Inc.
Leading retailer of leather supplies with 201 stores and sales of $42 million.
President & CEO   1997-1999

- Directed the conversion of the company from a national retail chain to a direct marketing catalog business including Internet sales
- Implemented installation and training for first-ever POS system in stores dramatically reducing replenishment costs, improving product flow
- Developed business plans, strategies and managed $14M inventory liquidation saving $12M from the budgeted costs of closing the retail stores

EDUCATION

Bachelor of Science—Business Administration,
University of Miami

ASSOCIATIONS

University of Miami Alumni Association
Board of Directors, Casual Concepts Inc.
Former Director, Sales & Marketing Executives of Armadillo, TX

Sample Cover Letter

Susan Academia
55 McBride   home (817) 555-5656
Grapevine, TX 76137   cell (817) 555-5555

September 26, 2004

Ms. Michelle Jones
Superintendent of Schools
GC Independent School District
611 Circle Avenue
Chicago, IL 60000

Dear Ms. Jones:

I understand that a mutual friend and colleague submitted my résumé as a candidate for the assistant principal position at GCISD. Through my research into your district, I have discovered that much of the expertise and many of the talents that I possess will add tremendous value to your secondary schools.

GCISD's growth will be enhanced by my successful track record in transitioning schools through the uncertainty and change associated with integrating diverse cultures. I bring tremendous expertise in improving test scores and improving student motivation. I have successfully managed classroom projects, organized parent volunteer programs, and motivated students to accept the challenge of successful academic achievement.

One of GCISD's core values is "be the best." My ability to continually be the best resulted in my receiving the "Teacher of the Year" award in my last district. Both peers and parents have expressed appreciation for my accomplishments with secondary children.

You will find that my résumé reflects the detail to support my qualifications. I look forward to discussing how I can help you meet your goals and objectives. I will call you next Wednesday.

Enthusiastically,

Susan Academia

How to order additional copies of

Finding a Job God's Way

and obtain a free Hannibal Books catalog
FAX: 1-972-487-7960
Call: 1-800-747-0738 (in Texas, 1-972-487-5710)
Email: hannibalbooks@earthlink.net
Mail copy of form below to:
Hannibal Books
P.O. Box 461592
Garland, Texas 75046
Visit: www.hannibalbooks.com

Number of copies desired   _____
Multiply number of copies by $12.95   ___X___$12.95___
Cost of books: $_____

Please add $3 for postage and handling for first book and add 50-cents for each additional book in the order.
Shipping $_____
Texas residents add 8.25 % sales tax $_____

Total order $_____

Mark method of payment:
check enclosed   _____
Credit card# _____ exp. date_____
(Visa, MasterCard, Discover, American Express accepted)

Name _____

Address _____

City State, Zip _____

Phone _____ FAX _____

Email _____

About CAREERWORKSHOPS Inc.®

Our ministry was formed to help individuals find meaningful work and then succeed in their careers. We are a
501(c)(3) tax-exempt, non-profit corporation.

For more information about our workshops, seminars,
printed manuals, audio CD's, and opportunities to help
in your community, visit *www.careerworkshops.org*

Discover Christian-based programs available through
this valuable community ministry, helping people and
organizations God's way:

• Workshops and seminars for the unemployed,
unhappily employed, and under-employed

• Workbooks, audio CD's, and program manuals.

• Seminars for Church and Ministry leaders to improve
hiring and motivation of staff members

• Seminars for small business owners and managers
wanting the best and most from their team members

• Train-the-trainer for the job-seeker ministry, CAREER-
SOLUTIONS Workshop®, anywhere in the world, to
help you get started

Let us know:

Tell us your best "success story" concerning your own
career. David would like to hear what has worked well
for you. Attach a MS Word document to your email
directly to David.

Need a Speaker?

Contact internationally known speaker David Rawles
for information about speaking engagements, keynotes,
kick-offs and workshops:

David.Rawles@careerworkshops.org